P9-DVC-689

premier consulting firm *Market Unbound:*

- Explores and defines the dynamic impact the converging markets will have on every sector of society

- Examines how the foreign exchange and bond markets are integrating to the point where they are fundamentally acting as one

- Explains how to seek profit and avoid loss in the impending economic climate

- Reveals how a government's ability to exercise control over its own financial system is being undermined by the global capital market

As the global capital market continues to mature, those who adapt to new rules will find the opportunity for tremendous gain; those who don't face catastrophic loss. This invaluable book is must reading for every investor, economist, banker, policymaker, and international businessperson.

LOWELL BRYAN and **DIANA FARRELL** are senior consultants at McKinsey & Company, Inc. He is the author of three previous business books, and a leading authority on both financial and regulatory issues, and the global capital market. She led the research that is the foundation of this book.

Market Unbound

Market Unbound

Unleashing Global Capitalism

Lowell Bryan
and
Diana Farrell

JOHN WILEY & SONS, INC.
New York • Chichester • Brisbane • Toronto • Singapore

Copyright © 1996 by Lowell Bryan and Diana Farrell.
Published by John Wiley & Sons, Inc.

Library of Congress Cataloging-in-Publication Data:

Bryan, Lowell L.
     Market unbound : unleashing global capitalism / Lowell Bryan and
Diana Farrell.
        p.   cm.
     ISBN 0-471-14446-0 (cloth : alk. paper)
     1. Finance, International. 2. Capitalism. 3. International
economic relations. 4. Foreign exchange. 5. Free trade.
6. Investments. 7. Stocks. I. Farrell, Diana. II. Title.
HG3851.B79   1996
332'.042—dc20   95-50490

This book is dedicated to our families,
particularly to
Debbie Bryan and Scott Pearson.

Foreword

In the late 1980s, Lowell Bryan and I—and a number of our McKinsey colleagues—began to notice a disturbing trend in what we read, heard, and even thought about the workings of the global economy. Everything in the business world was changing. We saw this every day in our client work: new products, new markets, new modes of organizations, new technologies, and new competitive threats.

Yet for all this change in the business world, the conventional wisdom about the forces at work in the global economy seemed to be unchanged from the time that Lowell and I started our careers and our friendship at McKinsey some 20 years ago. Moreover, these assumptions were leading to conclusions that ran counter to our daily observations: A capital shortage was likely to constrain the growth of the world economy; Japan and Germany were thought to have a new model for sustaining high economic growth through higher savings rates; the United States was an out-of-date model with a capital market that hindered effective long-term investment. There were many things everybody seemed to accept as true, without any real evidence. Even worse, some of our work with clients and on our firm's strategy began to tell us that these "truths" might be entirely wrong. Our rhetoric and conventional wisdom had come to differ, in significant ways, from the economic realities of the world. It had to be brought back into line.

This book is part of an effort to do just that, to create a new fact-based "conventional wisdom" about the global economy. Lowell has personally been attacking the conventional wisdom in the U.S. banking industry for many years, notably through his previous books, *Breaking Up the Bank: Rethinking an Industry Under Siege,* and *Bankrupt: Restoring the Health and Profitability of Our Banking System.* This latest effort is different. It draws conclusions that have far-reaching implications across all parts of the global economy. It grew out of a research project that Lowell Bryan and Diana Farrell led as part of the research program at the McKinsey Global Institute.

The McKinsey Global Institute was established in 1990 as an independent research group within McKinsey & Company. Its primary purpose is to do original research and develop substantive points of view on the critical economic, social, and geopolitical issues facing our clients around the world. The Institute seeks to help business leaders understand the evolution of the global economy, thereby improving the performance and competitiveness of their companies. We have also tried to provide a fact base for sound public policy making at the national and international level. This is critical because our research has taught us that regulation and global competitiveness of companies are closely linked.

This book—as in all of the Global Institute's work—is unique hybrid of two distinct disciplines: economics and management. Economists have scant access to the real life problems facing senior managers, while managers often lack the time and incentive to look beyond their own situation at the larger issues in the global economy. Both suffer because of this. We strive to remedy this situation by combining the academic rigor and breadth of economics with the deep industry knowledge and management understanding we use in our work with clients every day. The result is something that neither economists nor senior managers could produce on their own, but is invaluable to both.

This book is based on a study of the global capital markets conducted in just this way. Lowell and Diana led a team of consultants assigned to the Global Institute that conducted a year-long effort to explore the evolving global capital markets. They were guided by a review panel chaired by Robert Glauber, formerly Assistant Secretary of the Treasury and now at Harvard's Kennedy School of Government, and made up of Francis Bator, Harvard University; Axel Börsch-Supan, the University of Mannheim; Martin Baily, formerly of the Brookings Institute, now with the President's Council of Economic Advisors; and Joe Grills, an independent investment consultant. I had the privilege of serving on the review panel. Diana, the immensely talented day-to-day leader of the project, contributed significantly through her considerable organizational skills and intellect. Co-sponsored by the McKinsey Financial Institutions practice, this team drew on the insights of many McKinsey practitioners around the world and built upon the previous work of the Institute through the ever-present guiding hand of the Global Institute's founding director, Bill Lewis. The effort resulted in a formal report published in November 1994 titled, *The Global Capital Market: Supply, Demand, Pricing and Allocation,* that was shared widely among our colleagues and clients. Our report received substantial recognition in the business press, including *The Economist,* the *Wall Street Journal,* and the *Financial Times.*

However, Diana and Lowell did not feel that the release of this formal report was sufficient. Despite the positive response of our clients, the press, and our colleagues, they were left with an uneasy feeling that this was not enough. The world is changing so significantly that competing in the near future will be very different than it has been in the recent past. Extraordinary changes are occurring in the financial markets and in the underlying real economy and this new emerging economic structure inevitably will change how companies compete in a very fundamental way. Yet, few managers seem to have come to grips with these realities in their daily lives. In this book, Lowell and Diana have taken on the formidable challenge of interpreting the findings of the Global Institute's work so that it is approachable and useful to senior managers from many different industries. In the process, they add their own speculation on how the global markets will evolve and paint compelling scenarios of how the future may unfold.

The result is a serious book. While its objective is to make the subject accessible to as large an audience of business leaders as possible, it is conceptually rigorous and is founded on a solid base of fact and analysis. It challenges implicit and explicit assumptions long held in business and academic circles.

The framework whose applicability this work challenges was developed during the Industrial Revolution, and it goes something like this: The world consists of a series of closed national economies, each with its own unique set of factors of production. These economies compete with each other on the basis of manufactured goods strapped to the decks of ships. What determines the standard of living of any one of them is the effectiveness with which it produces the goods that it exports. Savings are channeled within these national economies by a capital market that interacts with other countries only at the margin. National governments through their monetary and fiscal policies are the dominant force in influencing economic conditions.

Over time, this framework has spawned many ideas, such as the notion that nations compete head-to-head in a zero sum game and that domestic savings rates are the only significant source of investment funds to improve domestic economic performance. Most importantly, this framework has provided the foundation context upon which most business and government leaders begin their interpretation of the world around them. But there is a problem with this view of the world. It may have been applicable in 1860, and perhaps even in 1890. By 1910, however, it was beginning to break down. Today, it is increasingly irrelevant. Yet we remain captive to this intellectual framework and the interpretations it spawns despite overwhelming evidence that the core assumptions no longer apply.

The findings of our studies at the Global Institute have seriously challenged the closed national economy framework and its many corollaries. This book is no exception. Diana and Lowell confront head-on the inevitable integration of national capital markets into a single, powerful global market. Powered by a technological revolution that has resulted in the cost of communicating and computing effectively going to near zero, the capital markets are approaching at breakneck speed the single market conditions long ago predicted by economist Adam Smith. The enormous analytic power and richness of information available to capital market participants have finally made the theoretical techniques of isolating risk a reality. Technology has also enabled the transfer of capital market know-how to virtually every corner of the world. The result is a market that knows no master: A market that will integrate developed and developing countries alike, deploy the national savings of nations rich with baby boomers to new distant venues, and will defy the control of virtually every government in the world.

Energizing this process of global integration are largely productivity differences across the countries of the developed world and still larger differences between the developed and developing world. These differences have been well documented by the Global Institute. But, what has been less well understood is that the global capital market will enable companies of all shapes and sizes to viably pursue the closure of these gaps. Lowell and Diana argue persuasively that closing these productivity gaps is the single largest business opportunity in the world today. Managers developing strategies for their companies and policy makers seeking to improve the economic status of their citizens cannot ignore this way of thinking about their options and opportunities.

The sweeping transformation of the world's capital markets is one of the primary engines for the remarkable transformation of the world's collection of segregated national economies into a truly economic system. I know of no book that so clearly lays the intellectual foundation necessary to understand what has happened, what is happening, and what will happen.

TED W. HALL
Chairman, Advisory Board
McKinsey Global Institute

January 1996

Preface

Given the range of subjects touched on in a book about the global economy, we recognize that the potential readers of this book are an exceptionally diverse group (including public policy leaders, corporate executives, and capital market participants) from many nationalities and with many different interests. We recognize that not all readers will be equally interested in all parts of the book, though we believe all would find it worthwhile.

Therefore, we would like to use this note to orient the reader to the book, by providing a brief description of each chapter. Throughout the book, we have tried to keep the text intriguing to readers with strong financial backgrounds without losing readers lacking such a background. With this objective in mind, we have added some technical reading in boxed notes and chapter appendices for those with an interest. Readers who just want to understand the storyline can skip this material.

The first chapter, "The Global Capital Revolution," provides an overview of the main themes in the book.

Part One, titled The Market Unbound, comprises four chapters that describe how the global capital market came into existence and where it is headed. Chapter 2 gives a brief history of the evolution of the global capital market from the breakdown of the Bretton Woods system through today. Chapter 3 describes the barriers to the evolution of a global capital market and describes the forces at work that are leading to the erosion of those barriers. Chapter 4 projects forward our expectation of how large and powerful the market is likely to become. Chapter 5, which is perhaps the most difficult chapter in the book for readers without a financial or economic background, describes why and how the market is integrating into a single market and why national governments are losing their ability to control foreign exchange rates and interest rates. It also describes why the concept of full capital mobility, or the existence of a capital market that operates globally without regard to national borders, is rapidly becoming a reality rather than a theoretical concept.

Part Two is titled Unleashing Global Capitalism and draws out what are the implications of the enormous, integrating global capital market on the real economy for goods and services. Chapter 6 argues that depending on how governments react, we can either have global prosperity or economic devastation. Chapter 7 describes how capital mobility is transforming the way national economies work and how the market will force governments, like it or not, to open up their economies. Chapter 8 describes how we believe the role of governments must change if they want their nations to prosper in an open, global system.

Part Three, Capturing the Global Opportunity, takes the perspective of business leaders and investors. Chapter 9 provides a number of examples of how different companies are capturing the global opportunity. Chapter 10 provides some first thoughts on how corporations should respond to the challenges and opportunities posed by this global capital revolution. Chapter 11 describes what we believe are some of the investment implications of our work (we like equities). Nonetheless, we urge anyone who is reading this book with an eye on investing to read the entire book, not just this one chapter.

Finally, Chapter 12 provides some short summary thoughts.

This book is based upon extensive research by McKinsey & Company over many years, and in particular, on research undertaken by the McKinsey Global Institute. However, the opinions expressed in this book are those of the authors, and do not necessarily reflect the views of our colleagues.

LOWELL BRYAN
DIANA FARRELL

New York, New York
Washington, DC
February 1996

Acknowledgments

To complete this book, we drew upon many resources that we gratefully acknowledge.

First of all, we would like to acknowledge the broad institutional support we received from McKinsey & Company. Much of the research in the book is drawn from the results of a self-funded, year-plus-long effort by the Financial Institutions Group (FIG) of McKinsey & Company, Inc., and the McKinsey Global Institute (MGI), an effort that we both led. The results of that project were published in a publicly released report in November of 1994. As with any project of this scope and size, the output represents the work, directly and indirectly, of a large number of people both within McKinsey and outside of the firm. McKinsey colleagues in offices around the world contributed their insight, knowledge, and information to our effort. Important among them were Ted Hall, chairman of MGI, and Bill Lewis, director of MGI. Ted has written the foreword to this book.

In addition, the working team included Kevin Berner from the Cleveland office; Isobel Coleman from the New York office; Jeremy Dann previously from the Washington, DC, office; Yuko Kawamoto from the Tokyo office; and Scott Newman previously from the New York office.

The project's working team benefited from a committee of internal McKinsey counselors from the Financial Institutions Group and a formal advisory committee. Internal counselors included Joel Bleeke from the Chicago office, Dominic Casserley from the New York office, Heino Fasbender from the Frankfurt office, Philippe Giry-Deloison from the Montreal office, Juan Ocampo previously from the New York office, Robert Reibestein from the Amsterdam office, and Greg Wilson from the Washington, DC, office. Our internal counselors were part of the team and participated in the external advisory committee meetings, providing critical input and insight throughout the project.

The project's advisory committee included Martin Baily of The Brookings Institution and of the University of Maryland who was a Fellow at MGI; Francis Bator of Harvard University; Axel Börsch-Supan of the University of Mannheim; Robert Glauber of Harvard University; Joe Grills, an independent investment consultant; and Ted Hall from

McKinsey's San Francisco office. They contributed invaluable insight and knowledge of the various issues covered.

Since the release of the November 1994 report, we have discussed the work with literally hundreds of individuals, including bankers, investment bankers, lawyers, accountants, journalists, academics, researchers, regulatory officials, and politicians, in addition to members of McKinsey & Company. In these discussions, there has been a free flow of ideas. In the process, we have contributed to the thinking of others and have drawn on their thinking. The opinions expressed in this book, however, are our own.

We would also like to thank Stuart Flack and Bill Matassoni, from Communications at McKinsey, who worked with the publishers and us during the writing of the book. And we would like to provide a special thanks to Lore McKenna, who provided the administrative support to help us throughout the entire process of drafting and redrafting the book's manuscript.

Finally we would like to thank our families for their strong support and understanding during the entire process.

L.B.
D.F.

Contents

Market Unbound

—1—

Global Capital Revolution

We have all grown up in a world where the critical economic decisions for nations have been made by a small group of people at the center of each national government. Whether elected by voters or protected in office by the military, these national political elites have played the decision-making roles in setting interest rates and foreign exchange rates and in allocating capital within the nation. The power of these political elites to control the flow of capital within their nations has been directly derived from the historic province of the nation state to regulate, to print money, to tax, to subsidize, and to borrow money largely without constraint.

We are now witnessing the transfer of this power away from these small elite groups to a global capital market that is only now beginning to flex its muscles. Like an awkward adolescent, the global capital market is just now discovering its own strength and potential.

Increasingly, millions of global investors, operating out of their own economic self-interest, are determining interest rates, exchange rates, and the allocation of capital, irrespective of the wishes or political objectives of national political leaders.

We are moving toward a world where the capital markets constrain what governments can do—not the other way around. In this environment, government policy is influenced in real time by whether or not it makes economic sense. Bad policies will carry real penalties, and good policies will be quickly rewarded.

This shift in power has not gone unnoticed by political leaders. James Carville, President Clinton's political advisor, remarked: "I used to think, if there was reincarnation, I wanted to come back as the President or the pope or a .400 baseball hitter. But now I want to come back as the bond market. You can intimidate everyone."

1

Not all the political leaders of the world have reacted to this power shift with good humor. Fresh from losing a battle of wills, not to mention billions of dollars, to global market participants, the French finance Minister Michel Sapin said in a 1992 radio interview, "When you are faced with speculation, the only thing to do is to make them pay the price for their speculation. During the (French) Revolution, such people were known as *agiteurs* (political speculators) and they were beheaded."

We are in the midst of a global capital revolution and revolutions spark strong emotions. Just as the French Revolution led to a fundamental transfer of power and economic transformation, so will the global capital revolution. Is the coming of this revolution good news or bad news? The question remains open.

As the market becomes unbound from the constraints of national governments, it is creating the potential for a tidal wave of global capitalism that could drive rapid growth and highly beneficial integration of the world's real economy well into the next century. There is also a somewhat less probable, but nonetheless significant, chance that the power of this market could turn destructive and unleash financial instability and social turmoil such as the world has not seen since the 1920s and 1930s.

Whether we have the best of times or the worst of times will be determined by the way that national governments react to the growing power of the market. If they embrace the market and use its power in concert with the power of the state, national governments have every opportunity to ensure prosperity for their citizens. If they work in opposition to the market, using it, for example, to fund unsustainable fiscal deficits, they could push beyond the limits of their debt capacity with destructive consequences.

The danger is that we will let petty politics get in the way of pursuing rational policies and addressing serious challenges. Depending on your political viewpoint, the growing power of the global capital market relative to national governments may either be exhilarating or terrifying. Indeed, it is difficult to discuss these issues without becoming deeply entangled in a political discussion. However, it does not matter whether a national government or a political party likes or dislikes the development of such a powerful global market and the loss of direct control of its domestic economy any more than it matters whether a national government likes or dislikes nuclear weapons. The global market, like nuclear weapons, has become a reality that is too big to ignore, and national policy must reflect this reality.

And it is not just governments that will need to adapt. All of us must adapt. The global capital revolution underway is already transforming national economies and the industry structures and labor markets underlying them. Global capitalism is being unleashed with an intensity and scale we have not witnessed before in economic history, in a world where national governments are becoming progressively less able to protect businesses, investors, and individuals from rapidly evolving market forces. These changes will drive household decisions on jobs, saving, buying houses, and providing for comfortable retirement.

These changes will also shape the choices businesses must make to be successful. Successful corporations will need to adopt a global mind-set, and think about strategy as a portfolio of options and choices, not a portfolio of static businesses. Corporations will need to think like global principal investors, and they will depend on strong leadership. Finally, these changes will transform the landscape for investors. Investors seeking comfortable retirements will not necessarily find bonds and bank accounts attractive. Wise investors will more than likely tilt their portfolios strongly toward equities, particularly those of the United States. They will follow the U.S. market, and other market events, very carefully.

As this market matures, it will drive a fundamental change in the way the economy works and how the nation state's power is exercised. We can imagine some future economic historian making the following observations about this transformation:

The year 2000 serves as an approximate marking point for the emergence of a truly global economy. The increasing mobility of capital unleashed a wave of global capitalism that rapidly accelerated the globalization of the world's entire economy for goods, services, and labor. Not surprisingly, the years surrounding this transition were extraordinarily turbulent as national governments struggled with how to work in harmony with an overwhelmingly powerful global capital market, and faced the difficulties of curtailing popular entitlement programs. However, through the collective leadership of the major nations of the time, such as Germany, Japan, and the United States, working with international agencies, calamity was avoided, and the stage was set for several decades of economic growth unparalleled in human history.

And, at the center of this process was the global capitalist. Far from being the villain envisioned by Karl Marx in his famous book Das Kapital, *the global capitalist has been the hero of this fundamental economic transformation . . . .*

Opening comments by Professor Lau in her book *Emergence of the Global Economy,* first taped before a live student population at Adam Smith University in Shanghai, China (September 2030)

THE POWER OF THE MARKET

The engine behind this change is the growing power of the global capital market. Its power is coming from its overwhelming and increasing scale and ability to integrate and act as a single market. Individual national financial markets are losing their separate identities as they merge into a single, overpowering marketplace.

The global market for tradable financial assets, including the money supply, bonds, and equities has already attained considerable scale (well over $41 trillion in assets by year-end 1994) and is growing rapidly. The stock of liquid financial assets is expanding at about three times the rate of growth in the real economy. This is the case because of the rapid issuance of new securities, particularly government debt, the conversion of formerly illiquid financial assets, such as bank loans, into tradable assets, and the ever-expanding group of countries that are linked into the market. In 1992, the world's liquid financial stock was roughly twice the size of the $16 trillion a year nominal gross domestic product (GDP) of the Organization for Economic Cooperation and Development (OECD) nations. By the year 2000, projections suggest that it will be roughly three times the then $27 trillion nominal GDP of these nations. There is no natural limit preventing the liquid financial stock from continuing to grow more rapidly than the world's real economy for a long time.

Turbocharging the growth of the world's liquid financial stock over the next 15 to 20 years will be the savings generated by the aging population of the developed world. We estimate that just between 1992 and the year 2002, some $12 trillion of personal savings will be invested in the world's liquid financial stock. About $5 trillion of this increase represents extraordinary growth over the baseline growth for the previous 50 years and will come about because of the dramatic increase in the number of "savers" (those aged 40–64) in the developed world.

In addition to growing in size, the world's market in liquid financial assets is rapidly integrating into a single market. In particular, the foreign exchange money and bond markets in the developed world have integrated to a point where they are beginning to act as one market. As a result, the real interest rates on government debt (measured as the domestic long-term interest rates less the rate of inflation) for countries of equivalent risk have converged substantially. Governments in many smaller nations are losing their ability to significantly influence their exchange rates or interest rates, and larger countries are finding it more difficult to control those rates.

Among these nations, the United States, in particular, retains the largest degree of influence over exchange rates and interest rates, especially when it acts in concert with other central banks as it did in mid-1995. Nevertheless, the real interest rates of the major countries have begun to converge to a sufficiently narrow range that it is now meaningful to discuss a global risk-free rate of return.

In fact, the operations of the global capital market are enough like those of a single market for us to discuss full global capital mobility as an actual, rather than as a theoretical, principle determining the allocation of capital. The concept of full capital mobility assumes that capital will seek its highest returns, worldwide, without regard to national borders. Full global capital mobility has been discussed theoretically by academics for decades but there have long been a host of physical barriers to making capital fully mobile including inadequate information, inadequate skills, and the inability to uniformly price risks. There have also been government barriers, including foreign exchange controls, regulation of local banking systems, and government's ability to affect interest rates and exchange rates directly. Over the past two decades, these barriers have progressively been overcome, and we can now observe a true global capital market emerging for foreign exchange and bonds. While the world's equity markets are a long way from fully integrating, even in these markets, the globalization process is increasingly discernible.

Even though the integration of the market is still incomplete, its development is unleashing global capitalism in full force and is already spearheading world economic development and the globalization of the world's real economy.

This is change on a scale quite unlike anything we have seen before. In the future, the global capital market will match supply and demand for capital worldwide and in the process, integrate the economies not just of the developed world, but also the Latin American, Chinese, South Asian, Indian, and Russian economies. This market will be so huge, and its level of activity so extensive, that it will increasingly dictate capital movements and thus capital pricing and allocation. In the process, the world economy will work differently and the political systems of nations will be reshaped.

This revolution will be sufficiently powerful to change the traditional roles of governments. The world will move from closed nationally controlled systems toward one open, global system under no one's control. At the center of this open system, a global capital market will motivate businesses to become more productive and motivate governments to dismantle restrictive regulation, cut deficits, and pursue sound monetary policy.

GLOBAL CAPITALISM

The benefits from these developments could create staggering potential for real economic growth worldwide. This growth is possible partly because the global capital revolution enables the transfer throughout the world, and particularly to the emerging economies, of both excess savings of an aging developed world and state-of-the-art production techniques. The opportunities for these "productivity transfusions" are so vast that they could provide rapid worldwide growth for decades. Just maintaining the average growth rates of developing countries over the past decade, which included the developing country debt crises, would increase world GNP from $29 trillion (at today's purchasing power parity exchange rates) to $88 trillion by the year 2020. At the same time, the emerging markets' share of GNP would increase from 45 percent today to 69 percent. In all likelihood, we should expect these growth rates to accelerate above the rates of the past decade. The global capital revolution can also revitalize growth in developed world nations, particularly those in Europe, many of which are relatively stagnant today.

The source of this growth in both the developing and developed world will be the unprecedented transference of best-practice production techniques financed through global capital flows. Up until now, the global economy has been limited to the international trade of goods and services. In most nations, however, tradable goods and services make up less than 20 percent of GNP and in major nations less than 10 percent of GNP. Most goods and services are locally produced and consumed. And it is in these locally produced and consumed sectors, which are the least exposed to global competition, that nations tend to have lowest productivity levels.

As capital becomes fully mobile, the global capital market becomes a force that breaks down the barriers to the globalization of the economy and creates the conditions for the accelerated flow of capital and transfer of production techniques. This sets the stage for rapid globalization in nation after nation of the remaining 80 percent of the world's economy that is locally produced and consumed, including service sectors such as retailing, utilities, food processing, financial services, and health care. Since our work has shown that U.S. companies in many industries are at, or near, world-class levels of productivity, much of this opportunity will advantage them. The U. S. economy will be relatively less affected by the transplant of technology, but other developed nations, including Germany and Japan, will be significantly affected. Moreover, the growth and productivity impact on developing nations from best practice transplants can be enormous, as has already been demonstrated in countries ranging from Argentina to China.

Because investing capital in technologies with known productivity advantages can achieve high risk-adjusted returns, it will attract huge capital flows; and the combination of increased capital mobility and high risk-adjusted returns will drive a transformation in the production of goods and services worldwide. In particular, all companies with productivity advantages will seek to capitalize on them through foreign direct investment, alliances, licensing, franchising, and acquisitions. As the force of global capitalism accelerates, all participants will face new opportunities, threats, and risks. The underlying growth in the global real economy will multiply the opportunities created by the global capital revolution. This, then, is the unleashing of global capitalism to which we are referring.

The processes underlying this transformation have been at work for a long time. The mobility of capital and the scale of the global capital market have been developing since the early 1970s. Multinational corporations have been undertaking foreign direct investment since the late 1950s. Local corporations have been importing capital and production techniques from abroad for centuries. In particular, the infrastructure to globalize the world economy—from telecommunications, to information technology, to jumbo jets—has been evolving particularly rapidly in the last twenty years. Finally, the long slow process of educating enough people from various nations and cultures with the language capabilities and the skills to globalize the real economy has been underway since the end of World War II.

Now, however, the global capital revolution is serving as a catalyst to the rapid acceleration of all of these processes. Economies will now be superconductors of the vast flows of capital and transfer of techniques of production. What is different about the immediate future is that up until now, the changes have been evolutionary. The profit opportunities now available are so large and the level of capital seeking those opportunities is so high that their pursuit will no longer be evolutionary, but instead will be discontinuous.

POLITICS

It would be naive to believe that this revolution will be bloodless. National governments have long been the most powerful agents on the planet and are used to exercising control over most aspects of their local economy. In particular, they have controlled the local financial system and financial markets through bank regulation, directed lending, capital controls, subsidies, and direct intervention in the markets. They have also been the ultimate guarantors of the safety and soundness of the financial system, as well as, in developed countries, of minimum health and living standards for their populations.

However, the ability of a single national government to control its own financial system is being undermined by the growing power of the global capital market. And many governments can no longer guarantee the safety and soundness of their financial system because the governments themselves are becoming increasingly indebted.

One of the first effects of the globalization of the capital markets was to allow national governments to run budget deficits of unprecedented size for peacetime economies. Currently, almost every developed world government is incurring large fiscal deficits to finance consumption spending through various entitlement programs including pensions, health care, welfare, and unemployment. While the U.S. deficit has received the most global attention, many countries such as Italy, Canada, and Belgium have much greater debt levels outstanding relative to their gross national product.

Viewed from a certain perspective, the global capital market has provided a valuable service. In the absence of the global capital market, the large deficits incurred by some national governments (including the United States) could have sharply reduced the ability of the private sectors in these economies to fund investment in physical capital. On the other hand, by mitigating the adverse effects of economic deficits, the global capital market has allowed governments to continue running deficits much longer than they would have in years past. By running budget deficits, these countries are incurring debts that will have to be serviced or repaid in the future and are exacerbating the problem of rising social expenditures.

We believe the only participants who can cause real havoc in the global capital markets are the national governments themselves because they have the power to distort the market through their influence on capital flows. They can do so by guaranteeing risk, by regulation, by printing large amounts of money (and thereby causing inflation), and by borrowing extensively. While the likely costs of an orderly liquidation of a large financial institution are probably no more than 10 percent of its assets, the costs of any national government that were to default today would be absolutely enormous.

For example, if a nation with debt of 150 percent of GDP were to default on that debt, the loss of wealth in the affected nation would be staggering. Moreover, the default would also cause most of the financial institutions in the nation to become insolvent since the loss in value on their government's bonds would exceed the equity capital of many institutions. Finally, any government safety nets behind the banking system would be viewed by the market as worthless. Because the global financial stock has become integrated, the shock of such a failure would be felt throughout the world.

Anyone who has studied the history of capitalism has a healthy concern about the potentially destructive consequences of financial markets. Charles Kindleberger in his classic book, *Manias, Panics, and Crashes* (1978), provides a rich history of the capacity of financial markets to self-destruct and, in the process, to damage the real economy. Many people are still alive who remember the worldwide stock market crash of 1929 and the Great Depression that followed.

We do not need to flirt with such danger.

There is a real risk that the aging of the developed world's population, with its concurrent increases in entitlement spending is likely to cause many developed world governments to push to the limits of their debt capacity. Our work indicates that holding entitlements per person and taxes constant, nations such as Italy will be in an inescapable "debtor's trap" soon, if indeed, they are not trapped already as their populations age. Even nations like Germany will face major debt issues by early in the next century. Our work indicates that increases in taxes, or entitlement cuts, on the order of 25 to 30 percent, will be necessary simply to keep the debt-to-GDP ratio in these countries from deteriorating. Voluntary changes of this magnitude—unless forced by severe market crises—will be politically difficult in all these countries. Therefore, even if we avoid a worst-case scenario, some severe market crises are highly likely.

Despite the huge issuance of debt securities, the United States is less likely to face such a debt crisis. This is partly because it has less debt outstanding relative to the size of its economy than many other nations. It also has a younger population than most other developed world countries and thus has more time before it faces the full entitlement pressures on an aging population. Moreover, the United States is unique as the reserve currency nation in that it theoretically has the option of inflating its way out of a critical debt problem. Finally, the United States shows real signs that it is beginning to get its budget in balance anyway.

The more likely trigger point for debt crises will be the confrontation between the developed world nations with the highest debt levels (e.g., Sweden, Italy, Canada, Belgium), which may lack the political will to make the necessary entitlement cuts, and the global capital market, which will become increasingly unwilling to finance the resulting deficits. Our base case projection is for high market volatility—an expectation of severe market crises in these countries' currency and government debt markets, which will be necessary to create the political will to cut spending. The collective size of the national economies of these nations, the scale of their debt outstanding, and the importance of their banks as counterparties suggest that the resulting global market crises are likely to be far more serious than the Mexican crisis of 1995. The central challenge to the governments of the major stronger nations will be how to assist these nations to manage through these crises without doing structural damage to the world's economy and avoiding massive social unrest. Similarly, the challenge to market participants will be how to avoid falling victim to the unexpected defaults, sudden losses of liquidity, and extreme market volatility that are the likely results of government debt crises.

This is not to say that severe market crises due to government debt are completely unavoidable. Canada, for example, showed some signs of addressing its debt challenge in 1995. But, it will require extraordinary political leadership.

AN OPEN, GLOBAL SYSTEM

It is critically important for national governments to realize that the global capital market is now a powerful force of its own and that it will be progressively less possible for an individual government to pursue policies under the assumption that it can directly control its own domestic financial market. This will be true even of the largest nations, including the United States. This does not, however, mean that nations are powerless to influence their economies. This book will emphasize the power that governments have. But it does mean that governments will be less able to use the direct control of their domestic financial markets to achieve their objectives in the global capital market.

In this book, we will describe why a national government has no choice but to move forward to embrace the global capital revolution unless it wants to harm its own citizens, its economy, and its own purposes. We cannot go backward. What has been done cannot be undone without truly destructive consequences. No one designed this global market. It came into being as the result of billions of individual decisions made by investors seeking higher returns, funds raisers seeking more cost-effective funding, and intermediaries seeking profits, despite the physical risk and regulatory barriers that originally limited the market's existence.

This global capital market can serve us well provided national governments curtail their appetites for debt and shift their viewpoint from operating in a closed, national system to operating in an open, global system.

An analogy from design engineering will illustrate this issue. Design engineers often talk about "closed" and "open" systems. For a closed system, the designer tries to think through how everything should work in all circumstances, anticipating everything that could possibly go wrong, and devising solutions to each and every problem. Much of the design work, therefore, involves insulating the system from the outside environment. Engineering a nuclear power plant is a classic closed system design problem. This engineering approach is designed to thwart Murphy's Law that anything that can go wrong, will go wrong, at the worst time.

In contrast, for an open system, the designer tries to think through how everything should work in response to changing conditions. Open systems usually rely on individuals to respond to new information and make appropriate adjustments. Highway driving, for example, depends on drivers to use their steering wheels, brakes, gas pedals, windshield wipers, and lights to respond to changes in road conditions, weather, flow of traffic and so forth. Accidents will still happen, but the damage is limited to the involved individuals and not to the system as a whole.

For most of the post-World War II era, national governments used their domestic financial institutions and markets as tools to control their economies. This generally worked fine, as long as the national government was in complete control; the system could work because these tools were exercised in a relatively closed national economy. However, now that all nations are part of a much larger open system, it is no longer possible to exercise the same kind of control.

In designing for an open global system, the goal of government must be to make the market work better rather than to control its pricing or its allocation process. Governments should regulate to improve the effectiveness of competitive and economic forces as they operate in the global world.

To return to the highway driving analogy, open system government regulation should motivate safe and sound driver behavior through registration, emissions controls, speed limits, and strict law enforcement; it should not provide a government chauffeur to drive the car.

TRANSFER OF RISK

Moving from a closed, national system to an open global system changes who bears the risk. In a closed, national system, the nation state absorbs much of the risk. Market forces are tempered by regulation and by direct and indirect subsidies. In an open, global system, each participant bears the risk.

Risk absorption by governments has been more pronounced outside the United States. In the typical European country, product market restrictions have historically shielded businesses and labor from competition. Direct and indirect subsidies have helped individual companies compete in world markets despite having lower productivity than nonlocal competitors. Generous unemployment benefits have protected individuals from economic hardship when jobs are lost. However, because these same restrictions and subsidies have led to lower productivity and soaring government deficits, they are unsustainable, and European nations have begun to dismantle them under the increasing pressure from the marketplace.

This process will cause enormous disruption as governments cut entitlements, particularly pensions and health care, and as businesses dependent on government protection must restructure or perish. These changes, in turn, will lead to large job losses and enormous personal dislocation. There will be high levels of volatility in financial markets and uncertainty about the future.

Industry structures will be under constant siege, particularly in Europe and Japan, as nonlocal competitors enter local markets with state-of-the-art production techniques and as local competitors import nonlocal techniques. All participants will be increasingly competing against the best methods of production in the world. The collision between entrenched local players with "deep pockets" and nonlocal players with huge productivity advantages may lead to structurally depressed returns until new, stable, global industry structures emerge.

The resulting turmoil will be the greatest in Europe, Japan, and in the developing countries, but even in the United States, we should expect significant social unrest. This will increase the potential political risk in country after country as national governments struggle to deal with these change issues. Political risk will likely be greatest in the most heavily indebted nations. The greatest challenge facing individuals and businesses in a heavily indebted nation will be their own home country risk. Over the next 15 to 20 years, the U.S. government seems likely to be the most secure, even relative to Germany or Japan, since the United States stands to be a net beneficiary of many of these global trends.

CAPTURING THE OPPORTUNITY

Many of the forces driving the global capital revolution have been operating in a more muted form for nearly two decades. The financial press has been writing about "global capital markets" for some 20 years as if they already existed. The truth is that we are only at a midstage in the market integration process, and it is only now that we find the pace of change accelerating faster than we find comfortable.

This pace will continue to accelerate and we will all have to adapt. But, all of us have a real barrier to making the necessary changes. We are trapped in obsolete mental assumptions about how the world should work because we grew up in a world dominated by nations and their governments. Now, like it or not, we are becoming citizens of the world.

To take advantage of the global capital revolution, we must adopt a global mind-set, embrace the market changes, and adapt to them. This will require a fundamental rethinking of many of our assumptions about the world. It will require real heroes at the national political level and true leaders at the corporate level. For those who cannot make the shift in thinking, or who fail to adapt to the new market system, the consequences will be painful.

Understanding the global capital revolution now in progress is essential to taking control of your own destiny. Our objective in this book is to help you gain such an understanding.

Part One

Market Unbound

— 2 —

Market Unbound

Like Prometheus, the global capital market is unbound. The release has taken nearly 50 years, but the global capital market has just about thrown off its bonds.

Prometheus was chained to a rock at the command of Zeus for giving fire to humanity. The financial markets of the world were placed under the control of national governments using a blueprint designed at a 1944 conference in Bretton Woods, New Hampshire, by an American and British team that included, most notably, John Maynard Keynes, the English economist. This plan was developed to provide financial stability for rebuilding the world after the devastation of World War II. The goals of the conference were to design and put in place an economic framework that would facilitate reconstruction and promote world trade.

The central plank of the Bretton Woods platform was the maintenance of a fixed exchange rate (which was essentially an adjustable peg exchange rate against the U.S. dollar and against gold) and direct controls on capital flows. The Bretton Woods agreement also created the International Monetary Fund, the planned role of which was to work with central banks to manage this new international monetary order. A final element of the Bretton Woods design was the creation of the World Bank which was to provide loans to nations for rebuilding and development.

The "fixed rate" system designed and agreed on at Bretton Woods was put into force through the rules written into the Marshall Plan (for Europe) and the Dodge Plan (for Japan). Through these plans, the United States provided much of the capital to rebuild postwar Europe and Japan after the devastation of World War II. All in all, it was a remarkably well thought out and well-designed system that was imposed on the participating nations, like it or not, as a condition for receiving the capital they needed to rebuild. And, in the first 20 years after the war, it worked remarkably well and led to an era of economic growth and international trade.

THE BOUND MARKET

Under the Bretton Woods system, the inputs to production, including labor, capital, rent, technology, and product design, were primarily national. Therefore, the financial economies of the various nations of the world, for the most part, were connected only through traded goods and the capital flows required to finance them.

What made this adjustable peg exchange rate system workable was the willingness of the governments of the major nations of the world to submit to the system's rigid discipline. In particular, governments could run only modest government deficits or trade deficits without running out of money because the only sources of liquidity were the reserve balances held with the International Monetary Fund (IMF), and the Federal Reserve, which controlled the issuance of dollars. In this system, the Federal Reserve was almost the de facto central bank for the world since the dollar was the primary reserve currency for most nations. Individual governments had to maintain a relatively stable monetary policy or their currencies would become substantially under- or overvalued relative to the pegged exchange rate.

Under such an adjustable pegged rate system, there was no global financial marketplace; there were only national financial markets that were largely independent of one another. The international capital market that existed in the first two decades after World War II, primarily out of London and New York, was largely an interbank market. Local currency lending was provided to multinational corporations through local banks and the local branches of multinational banks. Only a small cross-border Eurodollar market created by banks in Europe offered dollar-denominated deposits.

During this period, all the major nations maintained strict regulations to limit competition among financial institutions in each nation. Since most of the flow of funds in each nation was through depository institutions, and since the regulations in place prevented competition, every nation maintained, in effect, a highly profitable, safe, and stable banking oligopoly. And in every major nation, banks were more than willing to be used as instruments of national policy because their respective governments were vital to the banks' success. As a result, the leading banks in most countries developed close, cooperative working relationships with their governments on such issues as implementing monetary policy, financing exports, or lending to developing nations to finance export of their country's goods. In fact, in countries such as France and Italy, the government actually owned the leading banks outright.

The combination of the Bretton Woods system and complete control of governments over their domestic financial institutions gave each national government relatively complete control over the country's supply of money, liquidity, and interest rates. Many governments also used their power over local financial institutions to control the allocation of capital within the nation, either through creation of specialized institutions (e.g., savings banks to invest in residential mortgages, export banks to help finance trade, development banks to channel investment into specific local industries), through incentives, or through directed allocation of credit to specific industries or classes of borrowers.

In Japan (in particular) and in Germany, the governments used control over their financial systems to encourage the development of exporting industries. In nations like Italy and France, the governments used their control over their financial systems to subsidize government-owned businesses. And most nations used their control to lower the cost of financing their own government debt.

Thus, in the Bretton Woods era, the world's financial marketplace was segmented into local national markets. Each local government had effective control over its own market and used that control to achieve policy objectives.

Not surprisingly, national financial systems and national financial markets evolved from country to country in dissimilar ways. Local laws and regulations and cultural diversity created financial institutions that behaved quite differently from one another. Since the instruments for raising money and for investment varied enormously from country to country (as did the related risks and returns), investor and borrower behavior also varied significantly, and any change in monetary or fiscal policy had a different impact from one country to another. Finally, divergent cultural attitudes among nationalities about borrowing and saving money influenced the local financial industries.

Under these closed national systems, the risks and returns to be earned on financial investments were largely determined by each country's particular conditions and circumstances. In most countries, the dominant force was the nation's central bank, which controlled both the supply of money and interest rates and was often also responsible for regulation of the financial system.

The localization of national capital markets also led to significant differences in how similar financial instruments were valued from one country to another—the tradeoffs between risk and return from investing in money, bonds, equities, and real estate were nationally determined. For example, in Germany during the postwar era, the stocks of companies have usually been valued at low multiples to earnings, about 6 to 10, whereas in Japan, the stocks of companies in the same industries have often been valued at 50 times or more.

Also, under the Bretton Woods system, international trade was of paramount importance because it was the primary method of integrating the various national economies. Maintaining a relative balance in trade was essential to maintaining independence from the discipline of the Bretton Woods system. If a nation wanted to be truly independent while simultaneously creating local jobs, and be a net creditor to the world rather than being a net debtor, then it had to maintain a trade surplus. Only the United States was largely free of the motivational disciplines of the Bretton Woods system (since it could print dollars pretty much whenever it wanted to); its commitment to the system was voluntary while everyone else's was obligatory. And, significantly, from the late 1950s onward, the United States began to run small, but persistent, trade deficits.

The key to making this system work was that the U.S. government was willing to run continual, modest fiscal and trade deficits that provided growth stimulus for the remaining developed nations of the world. Moreover, the United States served as the police officer for the entire international monetary system by controlling the monetary value of the dollar, the currency to which the values of all other currencies were linked.

Why dwell on the Bretton Woods system when that system broke down nearly 20 years ago?

It is simply because most of us still have a mind-set that was shaped by how the system operated at that time. We still tend to think about financial markets largely in national terms because, until recently, the instruments of investment, the prices, and the risks have varied so widely from country to country. We are conditioned to think about global integration in terms of trade flows even though, as we will explain later, the world's economy is increasingly being driven by capital flows. Most people in each nation believe that their respective national governments still have complete control over their own local financial economy. In fact, they have lost much of their ability to control exchange rates or interest rates, and they are gradually losing control over the financial institutions they regulate.

Most of us are conditioned to think about the world economy in national terms, except for the trade of goods. In the remainder of this book, we will explain why thinking in such terms is counterproductive and even dangerous.

UNLOOSENING OF THE BONDS

While Aeschylus, in his play *Prometheus Bound,* described how and why Prometheus was chained, we do not know how Prometheus became free since the second and third plays of the trilogy, *Prometheus Unbound* and *Prometheus the Fire Bearer,* did not survive to modern times.

However, we do know how the world's financial markets were released from the bonds of the Bretton Woods system. The markets freed themselves—with a little help from the U.S. government.

The adjustable peg exchange rate system broke down for a variety of reasons, including the actions of governments and the changes in technology that enabled greater capital mobility. Whereas the relative importance of these two reasons is debatable, both were evident. It is true that the United States did not maintain the fiscal and monetary discipline necessary to make the system work and that other nations, specifically Germany and Japan, pursued policies that led to persistent trade surpluses. In particular, the soaring budget deficits and the inflationary pressures built up by the rapid U.S. expansion in the 1960s and the Vietnam War caused a fundamental decline in the value of the U.S. dollar relative to the rate at which it was fixed. Without fiscal and monetary discipline, fixed rate commitments among multiple currencies are not likely to be credible, and therefore sustainable, in the long run.

Also, technological advances made possible massive speculation (by the standards of the day) against the dollar by private institutions, primarily corporations and banks, that held assets and liabilities in both U.S. dollars and other currencies. In effect, these were the international assets and liabilities that had been accumulated as a result of persistent trade surpluses by non-U.S. nations and persistent trade deficits by the United States. Essentially, in the early 1970s, everyone who could borrowed in dollars and invested in stronger currencies. For example, multinational companies used techniques such as "leading" and "lagging" trade receivables effectively to "borrow" dollars.

Finally, the pressure of the adjustable peg exchange rate system was too great and resulted first in devaluation of the dollar in 1971 and eventually to a complete abandonment of the system in 1973. This was the birth of the global capital market. From this point on, cross-border market forces began to take over.

The floating of exchange rates had many consequences. In particular, the floating rate system provided national governments with freedom from the disciplines of the fixed rate system. Later on, we will describe what impact this has had on government behavior.

For now, however, we will concentrate on an unintended consequence of the abandonment of fixed exchange rates—the birth of the global market for foreign exchange.

BIRTH OF THE GLOBAL FOREIGN EXCHANGE MARKET

Until foreign exchange controls were removed, there was a limited international foreign exchange market because international capital flows were largely permitted only to finance trade and to finance carefully controlled cross-border foreign direct investment. In other words, an international market for foreign exchange and money market instruments existed prior to the abandonment of exchange rate controls, but it was largely an interbank market to help finance the operations of multinational corporations and to pay for imports and exports.

At this point, it will be useful to distinguish between *international* and *global*. The way we will be using the words, "international" refers to cross-border activities between nations (usually bilateral) such as the trade of goods. "Global" refers to international activities that transcend national markets. A global market operates across national boundaries as if it were a single market. Prior to the breakdown of the Bretton Woods system, the foreign exchange markets were largely international, or bilateral, markets primarily between each national currency and the U.S. dollar.

Once foreign exchange rates were allowed to float, however, it became possible to refer to a single global market for foreign exchange. This market was an infant market because it was still operating under the constraints of foreign exchange controls in place in most nations, and under the constraints of the heavy local banking and securities market regulations. The large multinational banks already had foreign exchange trading rooms in place in most of the major nations. They were quick to spot opportunities to profit from floating rates especially since they could access (through interbank placings and takings) foreign currency borrowing and lending that would be free of foreign exchange controls. They discovered that they could borrow for a short period, (e.g., 90 days) in one currency at one rate, and lend in another currency at a higher rate, while protecting themselves from foreign exchange movements by drawing a forward foreign exchange contract with a local bank that would protect them from foreign exchange rate fluctuations. These contracts were available because they had been used during the Bretton Woods era primarily to protect exporters and importers from the occasional movement of the adjustable peg rate.

This trading practice of arbitraging differences between two different interest rates in two different currencies, which is called *covered interest arbitrage,* can be an effective way to make money. A wide variety of other arbitrage transactions have become possible and have been exploited by traders as more and more financial instruments have been traded, as foreign exchange controls have been lifted, and as the supporting infrastructure (e.g., computer assistance, telecommunications) has been developed.

If you can do thousands of these arbitrage transactions in a year, you can make more than enough profit to make the effort worthwhile, even with very small differences in rates. If the revenues from undertaking such transactions exceed the transaction costs, institutions will continuously arbitrage these cross-market differentials as long as they persist.

In the mid-1970s, most such arbitrage transactions were originally undertaken by investment bankers using slide rules, and then electronic calculators, with rates quoted to them by brokers over the telephone. It used to cost several thousand dollars to complete such a transaction. But at the time, the arbitrage spreads between the markets were more than large enough to support these costs. Today, traders use computers and the Reuters and Telerate global information systems to find arbitrage opportunities. Twenty years of technological innovation and regulatory change have eliminated most of the physical and regulatory barriers that used to preserve pricing anomalies across foreign exchange markets. However, arbitrage remains profitable for high-volume participants because telecommunication and computer systems have cut marginal transaction costs to single hundredths of a percent of the value traded. Many major participants continuously search for arbitrage opportunities through computerized, simultaneous analysis of data for multiple markets.

In today's gargantuan and highly efficient market, covered interest rate and other arbitrage opportunities in the foreign exchange market persist for only moments and then disappear; but because of the enormous trading volumes involved, the profits for the leading players—major commercial and investment banks—still are frequently large.

Arbitrage is just one of the ways financial institutions make money in the global foreign exchange markets. A simpler way to make (or lose) money is to take a position by betting on a price movement. For example, if you believe that the U.S. dollar is going to decline against the Japanese yen, you can simply borrow dollars and convert them into yen. If the yen appreciates as you expect, you simply sell the yen after it has risen in value, convert it back into dollars, pay off the U.S. dollar loan, and pocket the amount by which the dollar had depreciated relative to the yen less the interest on your borrowings. Or, if you didn't want to borrow money, you could simply buy a foreign

Covered Interest Arbitrage

One of the simplest, and most important, arbitrage techniques is covered interest arbitrage. Covered interest arbitrage involves taking advantage of interest rate differences between two different currencies. Arbitrage transactions of this type took off in the mid-1970s shortly after rates were floated.

To take an example, assume that at one time, the interest rate for borrowing U.S. dollars for 12 months was 8 percent, and, at the same time, the 12-month rate for lending Italian lira was 20 percent. By converting dollars into lira, an investor could earn 12 percent higher interest. Unfortunately, the investor would also be exposed to the risk that the lira would decline in value relative to the dollar, and this could more than wipe out any profit. However, if an investor could fix the future rate of exchange of lira back into dollars, it would provide protection from the exchange rate risk. A forward exchange contract, which is an agreement between two parties for exchanging a specific amount of currency at a specified future date at a specified rate, allows investors to do just that. Assume at the time of conversion, the rate between dollars and lira was 100 lira per dollar (the lira was worth 1 penny), and that through a forward contract, an investor could secure a price of 110 lira per dollar in 12 months' time. The investment is then a risk-free profit opportunity.

The investor enters into a forward contract at 110 lira per dollar for 12 months, and borrows $1 million at 8 percent in London. The dollars are converted into 100 million lira. The lira are lent out at the prevailing 20 percent rate. At the end of the 12 months, the investor reconverts the 120 million lira (100 million lira from the original foreign exchange transaction into lira, plus 20 million in interest) back into dollars at the guaranteed rate of 110 to 1 and receives $1,090,909. The original $1 million loan is paid off, plus the 8 percent ($80,000) interest owed, leaving a $10,909 profit, risk-free (except for counterparty risk).

Real transactions increasingly took place by arbitraging differences in interest rates between U.S. dollars, yen, marks, pounds, Swiss francs, French francs, Australian dollars, and so forth. An actual example of a mid-1980s covered interest arbitrage, illustrating the spreads available at that time is shown in Exhibit 2.1.

Exhibit 2.1.   Covered Interest Arbitrage

Foreign Exchange Market

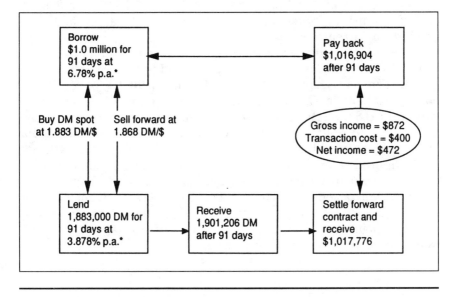

Source: Simple interest, 365 days/year; McKinsey analysis.

exchange derivative contract such as a foreign exchange option to buy yen at a given price for a given future time period or a forward foreign exchange contract that locks in a future price at which you can exchange dollars for yen. Of course, if you take a position either in the market itself, or through a derivative contract, and you are wrong about the price movement, you will lose money.

Another way that traders make money in the global foreign exchange market is through market making. A market maker is a trader who is willing to simultaneously offer to buy *or* sell a particular instrument between the "bid" and the "ask" spread. Often market makers also use the information they gain from market making to take positions.

All this activity has led to huge surges in foreign exchange trading volume. In 1973, at the end of the fixed exchange rate era, daily foreign exchange was probably no more than $10 to $20 billion a day. By 1986, when the foreign exchange markets were already significantly globalized, daily foreign exchange trading volume in London, New York, and Tokyo alone was roughly $200 billion a day, even despite residual foreign exchange controls in some major developed world countries such as France and Italy. Today, with foreign exchange controls eliminated in every major country, daily volume in these three cities alone is over $1 trillion a day (see Exhibit 2.2.) The foreign exchange and money markets are essentially fully globalized for developed world currencies.

It is easy to prove that the foreign exchange market for the freely convertible currencies of the developed world is fully globalized, and acts, indeed, as a single market. For example, using the prices shown on a typical day in *The Wall Street Journal,* (see Exhibit 2.3) the conversion of U.S. dollars to yen, yen to Deutsche marks, and Deutsche marks back to dollars, results in virtually the same price as would have been achieved by converting U.S. dollars to Deutsche marks directly. In other words, you would have to trade over a million dollars of foreign exchange value to make a $10 arbitrage profit. Actual trading activity is based on much more precise quotes. Such convergence is hardly surprising in a market that trades $1 trillion a day and where one basis point (one-hundredth of a percent) of arbitrage opportunity would be worth $100 million in revenues.

Exhibit 2.2.   FX Daily Trading Volume,* 1986–1995

U.S. $ Billions

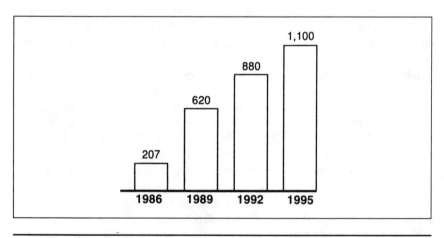

* Includes all volume traded as reported to the Bank of International Settlements; 1995 represents latest estimates..
Source: BIS.

Exhibit 2.3.   FX Arbitrage Opportunities

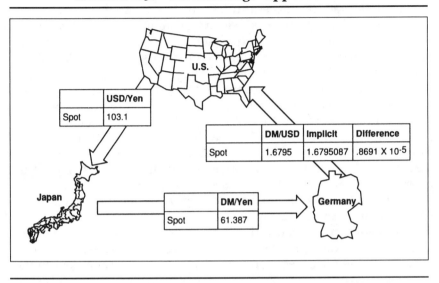

Source: The Wall Street Journal "Cross-currency listings," Tuesday, April 26, 1994; McKinsey analysis.

However, a global foreign exchange and money market is not yet a global capital market. A capital market includes bonds and equities in addition to money market instruments.

If you define a global capital market as a market in which money, bonds, and equities are fully globalized (they act as if they were a single market), then we do not yet have a global capital market. Nevertheless, the world's bond markets have been rapidly globalizing since the early 1980s, and the world's equity markets have been doing the same in the 1990s. We are clearly headed down the path of creating a single global capital market.

GLOBALIZATION OF BONDS

After the foreign exchange markets, the bond markets were next in line to globalize. The process of globalization, which began in the late 1970s and early 1980s, was first driven by the issuers of international corporate debt with the help of their investment bankers.

In particular, the internationalization of the bond market was driven by issuers of international bonds seeking cheaper or less restrictive financing across national borders. During the 1980s, the discrepancies in pricing and in the terms and conditions of the bonds were often quite large because of differences in each country's accounting standards, credit rating practices, access to information, regulatory constraints, tax system, financial services industry structures, cultural patterns, and investor preferences and expectations. These differences, in turn, created opportunities for corporate issuers to save money by raising money internationally versus domestically.

We will illustrate this process by giving a few examples involving U.S. issuers of international corporate bonds. While we are using examples from the viewpoint of U.S. corporate bond issuers, similar examples could be used for issuers from Japan, Germany, or other countries.

During the 1980s, U.S. corporate issuers working with their investment bankers found they could save money simply by issuing dollar-based bonds and selling them to Swiss banks for their private client portfolio. Enormous foreign investments have been built up in Switzerland, partly because tax evasion is not a criminal offense in Switzerland, and partly because that nation's tough privacy laws protect investors who evade their local national laws. These investors created a huge demand for unregistered instruments that do not identify the owner, known as bearer bonds. Eurodollar bonds by U.S. issuers are in "bearer" form, whereas corporate bonds and equities issued in the United States are registered. In the 1980s, U.S. issuers found that they could place their bonds with private banking clients of Swiss banks in the Eurobond market at lower rates than they could get in the United States because portfolio managers working for private investors in Switzerland often cared more about privacy for their client than obtaining the absolutely highest yield.

U.S. issuers of corporate debt also found that they could take advantage of the fact that Eurobonds were historically priced largely on the "name" recognition of the issuer. In contrast, U.S. investors have historically been more sensitive to the nuances of credit risk than European investors. While European investors have now begun to use credit ratings extensively, they were less sensitive to credit rating differences in the early to mid-1980s. Therefore, in the 1980s, a well-known, single-A company was often able to raise money in the Eurobond market at rates more typical of a AA or even AAA company, thus saving ¼ to ½ percent on its dollar borrowings.

Both of these examples involve corporate issuers. However, by far the largest U.S. issuer to draw on the international bond markets was the U.S. government, which used this source to finance its large fiscal and trade deficits. Total foreign purchases and sales of all U.S. bonds increased from less than $50 billion in 1983 to over $500 billion in 1993. The only inducement the United States used to attract investors was yield. For example, to Japanese investors, such as the large life insurance companies, U.S. Treasury bonds with a real yield (the yield on the bond after adjusting for inflation) of 6 to 8 percent in the mid-1980s looked attractive relative to the 4 to 5 percent real yields in Japan. Unfortunately, for unhedged Japanese investors, the weakness of the dollar relative to the yen over most of the last half of the 1980s caused them to suffer currency losses of such magnitude that they wound up losing, rather than gaining, from investing in "safe" U.S. government bonds at a higher rate.

American investors, even sophisticated investors, have also suffered losses in international bonds denominated in other currencies. For example, U.S. investors in late 1993 and early 1994 lost significantly from investing in apparently high-yielding government bonds from such nations as Canada and Sweden.

Over time, European, Japanese, and American investors have become smarter about international investment in bonds. Europeans, for example, have become more sensitive to credit risk ratings, and Japanese investors have become more sensitive to assessing the yield on bonds net of the cost of hedging the relevant currency risks.

At this point, remember the distinction between "international" and "global" we made earlier. A market is not global until it operates as if it were a single market without regard to national borders. While the development of an international bond market for bonds was driven by issuers, the real globalization of the bond market has been driven by traders and investors, particularly in the late 1980s and early 1990s. Although the volume of new issues, or the primary market, is still important, it is increasingly the aftermarket for bonds, or the secondary market, that is driving the globalization process.

Bonds, of course, remain outstanding until they are redeemed, are called, or default. With maturities on the notes and bonds ranging from 2 years to 20 years or more, the only way for an investor to get the principal back is to sell it in the secondary market. When the international bond market was just beginning to develop, the supply of newly issued bonds played a big role in determining prices. Over time, however, the stock of existing bonds is growing in relationship to the annual supply of newly issued bonds. Since an investor in a new bond is always trading off the price of a new bond against the price of an existing bond, over time, the existing stock of old bonds is becoming more important than the volume of new issues in the pricing of all bonds.

And, it is in this international secondary market for bonds where the real globalization of the world's bond markets is occurring.

Traders are continually looking across the various national markets to buy bonds that are undervalued and to sell bonds that are over-valued. Trading practices in this market that are equivalent to cov-ered interest rate arbitrage now use bonds and currency swaps, rather than money and foreign exchange market instruments, to ar-bitrage interest rates in bonds with maturities of up to 10 years. Moreover, investment banks, global commercial banks, and a class of highly skilled global investors called "hedge funds" have become particularly adept at using their investment skill to profit from dif-ferences in the risk and reward relationships between the yields of bonds denominated in different currencies. These investors are al-ways trading off the risks and returns of short-term money market in-struments with medium- and long-term corporate and government bonds across national bond markets. They are also trading off the different credit, liquidity, and prepayment risks of different bonds against the differences in yield.

Investors and traders in the secondary market are also undertak-ing "structured transactions" to increase the return on their invest-ments, just as bond issuers use "structured transactions" to lower borrowing costs. For example, they use a technique called an "asset swap" to enhance the all-in-yield of an investment. They purchase a bond in the secondary market denominated in another currency and use currency and interest rate swaps to increase the yield relative to the returns earned on investing in a bond denominated in their own currency.

As the differences in information access, in risk assessment, and in investment practice between investors in different countries disap-pear, the bond market is globalizing. Investors in bonds worldwide are increasingly beginning to make similar tradeoffs between risk and re-ward, using similar information and investment techniques. Over time, as the bond market continues to globalize, issuers will find fewer op-portunities to benefit by raising international bonds instead of issuing bonds domestically, and investors will be less likely to increase their yields by investing internationally. Paradoxically, the more global the bond market becomes, the less advantage there is from issuing or in-vesting in international debt because the prices of bonds, with the same risk, will be similarly priced.

There is real evidence that such convergence in bond pricing across national markets is occurring as the globalization of the bond markets continues to take place. Starting in 1993 and continuing in 1994 and 1995, the pricing of the world's bond markets, and particu-larly the government bond markets, has become more and more tightly linked.

GLOBALIZATION OF EQUITIES

The equity markets have been slower to globalize than the foreign exchange or bond markets. Price linkages still remain weak across equity markets. Significant differences in valuation of equities still exist across different national equity markets even for comparable companies in identical industries.

Equity markets have been difficult and slow to globalize for many reasons. Unlike foreign exchange and government bonds, equities are not pure commodities. The valuation of the equity of a company is unique to the particular circumstances of that company, and the total amount of market value being traded can also be relatively small. As a result, these markets are less liquid and the full transaction costs, such as equities research or commissions, are higher than in the money and bond markets.

While the total daily volume of the global foreign exchange markets is now well over $1 trillion a day, and the total daily trading volume of government bonds is on the order of $200 billion a day, the total daily volume of all the world's stock exchanges is only around $25 billion a day.

In addition, there have been many barriers to making cross-border investments in international equities. Investors have lacked access to consistent and comparable information needed to make investment decisions. Many national equity markets are insider markets with few of the protections provided in the United States by government regulation. The infrastructure to facilitate global equities trading, such as settlement and custodial services has only recently been put in place. Furthermore, in many countries investors such as pension funds have been restricted by regulation in the amount they could invest offshore, and equity ownership of these same companies by foreigners has also been restricted.

One of the greatest limitations to the globalization of the equity markets has been the lack of any powerful agent to drive the process. The illiquidity and volatility of individual equity prices makes it prohibitively risky for the highly leveraged, multinational commercial banks to hold equities in volume for even a short period. As a result, multinational banks have historically been reluctant to try to make money (even where permitted by regulation) by trading or investing in international equities and, therefore, have not driven the globalization of equities. Moreover, securities firms specializing in equities traditionally have been almost exclusively focused on domestic markets.

In general, major institutional investors in the largest countries, including those in the United States, Germany, and Japan, have invested primarily in domestic equities and concentrated their international investments in bonds, particularly government bonds. Recently, however, new, powerful agents have been leading the globalization of equities. Increasingly, the institutions that have historically managed the domestic investment of equities in their local countries have been looking offshore to increase their returns.

In effect, two things are happening. The amount of money being invested by institutional investors is growing rapidly, and institutional investors are rapidly increasing the share of international equities in their portfolio. We will examine these trends separately.

In almost all nations of the developed world, the share of total household assets being invested by institutions, such as life insurance companies, pension funds, and mutual funds, has been increasing at a fast rate (see Exhibit 2.4). Since household assets themselves have been growing rapidly, the combination has led to an explosive growth of investment money in the hands of institutions. There are multiple reasons for the institutionalization of funds. First, the aging of the developed world's population is reflected in the increased need for pension funds. Second, institutions have greater bargaining power

Exhibit 2.4.   U.S. Mutual Funds Outstanding

U.S. $ Billions

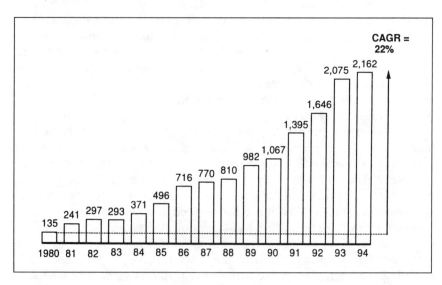

Source: ICI.

advantages in negotiating commissions and custodial services than do private investors and can pass these savings along. Third, a combination of deregulation of the banking systems and increased access has accelerated growth of mutual funds. As the investment markets have become more complex and more global, individual investors have felt less confident about their ability to invest for their own account. And finally, these institutional investors benefited from the buoyant markets of the 1980s and early 1990s and, as a result, have grown by increasing the value of the funds they are investing.

Institutional investors have also become more international. Most institutional investors began by investing in international government bonds as described earlier. In the past few years, however, they have begun to invest in international equities in large volumes.

In some cases, diversification has contributed to enhanced performance. Modern portfolio theory is based on the concept that a broadly diversified portfolio of assets has less risk than a concentrated portfolio because the risks of loss on the individual assets are less correlated. Many investment managers have been applying this notion in making their decisions. Thus, investors who want to lower the risks from investing in high-return, but risky, assets like equities should invest in a more broadly diversified portfolio of risky assets. Investing in a diversified portfolio of equities in a single country is less risky than investing in a single stock. However, many of the risks of a portfolio of equities from a particular country are highly correlated, including the health of the domestic economy, the rate of inflation, the value of the nation's currency, and the domestic interest rate structure. Thus, an institutional investor who wants to invest in equities, but also wants to diversify the risks, would be wise to increase the percentage of international equities in their portfolio since those risks will be less correlated than would be a portfolio of domestic equities.

It is no coincidence that the institutions that first began to invest internationally in equities were from nations such as Switzerland, the Netherlands and the United Kingdom, which either had only limited opportunities to invest locally or which did not find many attractive local companies in which they could invest. Many of these investors were particularly attracted to the efficiency of the U.S. market, its scope and breadth, the greater protection afforded the investor by the Securities and Exchange Commission (SEC) regulation, and the lower institutional equity commissions charged (which were deregulated in 1975).

Over time, more and more institutional investors in more and more countries have started focusing on international equities. And they have begun to develop the collective muscle to gain the removal of some of the barriers that have inhibited the globalization of equities. Companies in many countries have begun to disclose more information at the same time that quality equity research in many countries has become available. Settlement costs have gone down: Domestic custody fees dropped from close to 20 basis points in 1980 to less than 7 in 1992. Global custodians now exist that can hold securities for investors in multiple countries commissions on trading equities have also gone down. Many countries have liberalized their local ownership roles. Stock exchanges have modernized their facilities and established procedures that make them more fair and much less insider markets.

By the early 1990s, institutional investors in equities began to go global in earnest. Large amounts of funds began to be raised in mutual funds, particularly in the United States, to invest in international equities. Many institutional investors have built up strong capabilities in

Exhibit 2.5.   Gross Cross-Border Equity Transactions in the U.S., 1980–1994

U.S. $ Billions

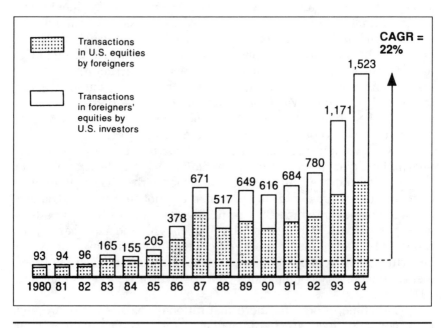

Source: U.S. Treasury Department; McKinsey analysis.

foreign markets. Moreover, they have learned to use derivative instruments to neutralize risks they do not want to take, including foreign exchange risk, and interest rate risk. To meet their needs, the use of equity derivatives has also proliferated. As a result of this activity, the world's equity markets are now becoming far more international.

Cross-border equity flows have increased dramatically. Gross cross-border equity transactions, including all foreign purchases and sales of corporate securities in the United States, increased from under $93 billion in 1980 to over $1.5 trillion in 1994 (see Exhibit 2.5).

The internationalization of the equity markets, however, represents only the early stages of globalizing equities. The world's domestic equity markets are a long way from acting as if they were a single market. Although the foreign exchange markets for the developed world currencies are fully global and the markets for government bonds in developed world currencies are largely global, the globalization of the world's equity markets is just beginning.

In summary, the foreign exchange and money markets are now almost fully global. The bond markets are rapidly globalizing. Together, these markets account for nearly 70 percent of all the financial assets in the world. The globalization of the world's equity markets has started, and the direction is clear. We are headed down the path toward a single, truly global capital market. While the process is not yet complete, the global capital market has been unbound.

In the rest of this book we will explore where this global capital market is headed now that it has been released from its bonds, and how this market will affect us all as it begins to mature.

—3—

Hunting for Woolly Mammoths

Economists, financial journalists, politicians, and traders have been talking about "global capital markets" for some 20 years as if they already existed. You would think, that after 20 years, the globalization process would have been nearly complete. The truth is that if a truly global market operates as a single market without regard to national boundaries, the globalization process is not yet close to completion. The reason it is taking so much time is that for a truly global capital market to exist, so much must change.

There are many barriers to globalization. A truly global capital market that operates without regard to national boundaries implies the following characteristics:

- All issuers, all investors, and all financial institutions in the market have relatively equal access to the same information.

- Each of these participants has relatively equivalent skills and uses equivalent valuation techniques.

- Risks, which require subjective judgment, are assessed worldwide using similar techniques, and those risks, once assessed, can be uniformly priced.

- The infrastructure needed for the market's operation (e.g., telecommunications, computers, etc.) is in place in every national market.

- All the participants view the world globally, as opposed to internationally, and they have a global rather than a national mind-set.

- There are no financial regulations restricting the market's operation in a meaningful way.

- No national participants, including governments, are able to control pricing in the market.

These conditions clearly have not been met.

The global capital market is unbound, but the movement to a world where the capital market operates entirely without regard to national boundaries is still in process. As described in Chapter 2, while the markets for money and bonds are now significantly global in the developed world, the globalization of equities and of the financial markets in the developing countries has just begun.

Although many participants have equal access to information and use similar valuation techniques, others do not; nor do all participants have the equivalent required skills. Many of the risks in the global market are now being uniformly priced but others are not. Much of the needed infrastructure is still being put into place. And whereas many participants have a global mind-set, others are still locally focused.

And much of this national focus is warranted. National financial markets are still significantly local primarily due to continuing the influence of national governments who still control many aspects of their local financial markets. In particular, national governments exercise this influence through their regulation of their local banking systems and through their ability to influence market pricing.

This influence is not surprising given the starting point. Countries emerged from the aftermath of the Depression and World War II with almost complete control of their local banking systems. Much of this regulation was put in place to help countries meet the strict requirements of the Bretton Woods system. Despite some considerable liberalization, much of this regulation remains in place.

In fact, in all the major developed nations of the world—including the United States, Japan, Germany, France, United Kingdom, Canada, and Italy—national governments still have regulatory control over their local banks, which have historically held the vast bulk of the national financial stock.

Local control of financial systems is even more pronounced in most of the emerging economies in the world, where, in addition to controlling their banking systems through regulation, many national governments still maintain significant capital controls.

But, as important as regulatory barriers have been, perhaps the greatest barrier to the full globalization of the capital markets has been the ability of governments to influence their financial markets directly through their control over monetary policy and their ability to intervene directly in the foreign exchange and interest rate markets through central bank action. National governments, particularly large nations, have long had the ability to control prices or support an over- or undervalued currency, or to maintain a particular interest rate for extended periods.

As long as local governments maintain significant control over local market pricing either through their control of the banking system or through direct intervention, then the world's financial markets will maintain country-specific traits that prevent it from fully acting as a single global market.

The question, then, is not, Why has it taken over 20 years for the market to reach its current style of globalization? Physical barriers to globalization, including the lack of access to adequate information, or the lack of supporting infrastructure; mental barriers such as the lack of equivalent knowledge, skills, and mind-sets; risk barriers; local regulatory barriers; local bank-dominated stocks of financial assets; exchange rate and interest rate barriers raised by national governments—all these factors help maintain local, national financial markets. The real question is, With all these barriers to the globalization of the capital markets, what are the forces that are driving it to become a single market so quickly?

The answer is straightforward. The market is becoming global because it is so profitable for the participants in the market to take actions that severely undermine the barriers.

THE SEARCH FOR WOOLLY MAMMOTHS

The fundamental drive behind globalization is the rich set of opportunities available to fund-raisers, financial intermediaries, and investors from participation in the market. An analogy from early human history on the American continent can help demonstrate the dynamics behind the transformation now occurring in the world's capital markets.

According to theories advanced by American geoscientists such as Vance Haynes and Paul Martin, early Americans helped cause the mass extinction of most of the large mammals on the North and South American continents within a short time after the arrival of human beings from Asia. Shortly after their arrival (toward the end of the last ice age at least some 12,000 years ago), all the woolly mammoths were gone. Also gone were the 3-ton giant ground sloths, the 4,500-pound armadillolike glyptodons, and the quarter-ton beavers. And all the camels were gone, as well as the saber-toothed cats, lions, cheetahs, and a wide variety of other beasts.

Early Americans (known as the Clovis people) came bearing new technologies: a two-faced, stone spearhead with a longitudinal groove that had been chipped out to make it easier to bind the point to the shaft; and the "atlatl," a prehistoric throwing stick that increased the force and speed of spears to more than 10 times the force and triple the velocity at impact of a spear thrown by hand. With these tools, they could hunt and kill the large land mammals they found on arrival. So there was a new technology, an abundance of targets of opportunity, and ambitious, hard-working people. What happened? Within a few thousand years, there were roughly 10 million people living in North and South America all the way down to Tierra del Fuego. There were no mammoths, or giant ground sloths, or lions, cheetahs, or camels. The combination of new technology, opportunity, and human initiative can have awesome effects.

The European immigrants to the United States demonstrated similar power in the 18th and 19th centuries—victimizing the Native Americans as their ancestors had victimized the mammoths. Early settlers brought new technology and found unlimited opportunity. Over a 250-year period, they civilized a vast wilderness. In fact, less than 40 years elapsed between Horace Greeley's advice, "Go West!," and the closing of the American frontier—with barbed wire dividing up previously open prairie, the American Indians killed off or placed on reservations, and railroads, telegraph, and roads binding the nation together.

We are in the midst of a similar transformation in the global capital markets. Only instead of hunting for woolly mammoths, fund-raisers, financial intermediaries, and investors are looking for opportunities to profit from "anomalies" in the market.

For a fund-raiser, a market anomaly occurs whenever money can be raised at a lower rate or with better terms and conditions than raising funds domestically. For an investor, an anomaly occurs whenever the returns for investing internationally are generous for the risks taken, relative to domestic investment alternatives. For a trader, an anomaly occurs whenever an instrument can be bought in the international market and immediately sold at a higher price, providing an opportunity for "risk-free" arbitrage.

Sometimes people make mistakes and the "anomalies" in the market then represent mistakes in judgment. When a mammoth hunter made a mistake, the penalty was injury or death. A market participant who makes a mistake simply loses money.

For the most part, fund-raisers, investors, and financial intermediaries have found an ample supply of market anomalies to pursue. Only instead of using two-faced stone spearheads, market participants are using technologies such as computers, telecommunications, and financial innovations, including derivatives and structuring techniques, to convert market anomalies into profit.

TECHNOLOGY

At every stage in the globalization process, participants have used the technologies available to them at the time to search for easy profit opportunities. In particular, the rapid advances in computer technology and communications have been, and will continue to be, a critical force in the development of the global capital market. As we have moved from slide rules to electronic calculators to PC-based spreadsheets to laptops with processing power exceeding that of mainframes in the early 1980s, more and more analytic power has become available for capturing opportunities. As we have moved from closely controlled information available only to "country insiders," to knowledge-based research using local conventions for calculating returns, to printed professional publications geared to the global market, to today's vast electronic databases provided by global vendors (e.g., Reuters, Telerate, Bloomberg), we have acquired more and more information and ever-increasing analytic power to understand it. As we have gone from telexes, to private phone systems, to high-quality facsimiles, to video conferencing, to interactive cable, it has become easier and easier to transfer knowledge, ideas, and techniques.

A few examples will illustrate the vital role of technology in globalization. The covered arbitrage example described in the box in Chapter 2, would have been a very expensive, tedious, and highly time-consuming transaction as recently as the mid-1970s. This changed rapidly over the next 20 years, first, with the use of calculators, then computer spreadsheets. Now, high-speed computer programs with 24-hour worldwide minute-by-minute price tracking make it possible to transact billions of dollars in covered interest arbitrage transactions. And, as transaction costs decrease, smaller and smaller differences in prices can be arbitraged profitability.

Processing capacity has also been important in driving volume and globalization. Program trading, made possible by highly reliable computers, is becoming widespread through electronic trading alternatives such as Instinet and Posit. The sophistication and processing power of computers have also made possible the instantaneous calculations necessary to structure and price sophisticated arbitrage transactions by simultaneously comparing the returns that can be earned from different instruments in different currencies.

Technological change will continue to be an important force. Advances in computer programming such as object-oriented programming now allow investment bankers to use cut-and-paste computer programming code that easily and quickly tailors software to new instruments and new markets. Further developments in computing and programming are continuously underway. New technologies, such as the various multimedia technologies, are also likely to facilitate numerous, additional opportunities for global transactions. The transfer of existing technology to developing countries will accelerate their participation in the global capital market.

Importantly, many of these technological advances are almost immediately transferable across product markets and countries. A large institution in New York can set up a world-class trading operation in Tokyo, Buenos Aires, or Moscow in a matter of months, assuming regulations do not prevent it from doing so. Rapid transferability will continue as new technologies become more flexible and more easily tailored to diverse situations.

The profit opportunities have made it economic to spend massively on technology to operate in this market. For example, from 1980 to 1995, annual operating expenses other than compensation, largely technology expenses, grew at a compounded rate of 16 percent for the 10 largest U.S. investment banks, from $2 billion in 1980 to $17 billion in 1994. These 10 banks are only a fraction of the institutions making technological investments. In addition, there has been massive spending by commercial banks and non-U.S. investment banks worldwide. It is not surprising that the technological base to convert market opportunities has been put in place in a relatively short time. As a result, there are no longer many technological or infrastructure barriers to globalization (in the developed world).

DERIVATIVES AND STRUCTURING TECHNIQUES

Derivative instruments are probably the single most important tool being used to exploit new market anomalies because derivatives allow the uniform pricing of risks. But before discussing this use, some background on derivatives will provide perspective on the subject.

Derivatives are bilateral contracts that are used for the exchange of the risks and returns of holding assets. They are called "derivatives" because the value of a derivative contract varies with the fluctuations in the value of the underlying asset. That is, the value of the contract is "derived" from the value of the underlying asset. For example, if you have an option to buy a particular equity at a particular price, the value of that option rises or falls with the value of the underlying price of the equity.

Many of the instruments now being lumped together under the umbrella category of derivatives have been around for a long time. Some historians have traced the use of derivatives back to Babylonian times, when the prices for corn and wheat were guaranteed by some purchasers. Certainly, they have been widely used for agricultural commodities such as corn, wheat, barley, pork bellies, or oranges for much of the past century. In equity markets, "puts," the option to sell a certain stock at a certain price over a defined time period and "calls," the option to buy a certain stock at a certain price over a defined time period, have been an integral part of the equities markets for many years. And in the foreign exchange markets, banks have long used forward exchange contracts to fix the future price of exchanging currencies.

However, over the past 20 years, and in particular, over the past 5 years, the use of derivatives in the global financial markets has exploded. More and more new types of derivatives are being created every day. The stock of derivatives outstanding (the notional principal) has grown enormously, 25 to 40 percent compounded year after year, as has the volume of derivatives traded.

Participants in the global capital market have used derivatives to lower their funding costs, to enhance yields, to manage their exposure to changes in interest rates or exchange rates, and to pursue arbitrage opportunities. Derivatives have also been used for proprietary trading, to speculate on the movements in the prices of the underlying assets. While the vast majority of participants have profited enormously from using derivatives, some participants have incurred substantial losses, particularly through making bad speculative bets, or buying complex contracts the risks of which they simply did not understand. Perhaps the most spectacular example of such a loss was the bankruptcy of Orange County, California, after an estimated $1.7 billion loss from investments in derivative-based securities. In this case, an estimated $7.6 billion in deposits with the County Treasury (made by 34 cities, 32 school districts, 5 community colleges, and 53 special district accounts) were leveraged to over $20.6 billion to take advantage of an expected decline in interest rates. When instead, numerous increases in short-term rates took place throughout 1994, Orange County experienced huge losses.

Because of the soaring volume, the well-publicized losses, and the bewildering jargon used to describe derivatives, significant anxiety in the press and among regulators has developed over the continued explosion in the use of derivatives particularly by commercial banks and by large dealers. The use of derivatives for speculation has attracted the most concern.

To date, most fears about the use of derivatives have been unfounded. For example, all the major dealers have earned profits from derivatives at multiples of their losses; indeed, some have never incurred losses from derivatives large enough to wipe out even a single month's earnings. In comparison, the U.S. commercial banking industry alone incurred credit losses of over $100 billion from 1988 through 1992.

There are many derivatives, and new types are being created all the time. However, we want to focus on the use of derivatives in the world's currency and money markets, in the bond markets, and in the

---

Using Derivatives for Proprietary Trading

Another common use of derivatives is for proprietary trading, including some "speculation," as central bankers tend to describe it. Derivatives are highly attractive for participants holding a view on which direction the market will move. For example, an option has far more upside per dollar of investment than does taking a position in the cash markets, while the downside is limited to the premium paid to buy the option. Or, a creditworthy investor or one with collateral to pledge can use a forward or futures contract to lock up the gain (or loss) from any future movement in the price of the underlying asset without putting up any money immediately. At the end of the day, the investor merely settles the gains or losses. Derivatives allow proprietary traders and investors to make highly leveraged bets on the future of markets. This use, in particular, has attracted the most criticism in the press and from regulators. In particular, central bankers who have wanted to intervene in the foreign exchange markets have been quick to criticize speculators using derivatives. So far, however, the evidence is that the losses from proprietary trading through derivatives by sophisticated traders, including global commercial banks, global securities firms, and hedge funds, have been much less than their gains, which is why such proprietary trading continues to increase. In contrast, large sums of money have been lost, collectively, by unsophisticated speculators and investors and by central banks trying to intervene in the markets.

equity markets since these derivatives are at the heart of the global-ization process.

First, let's consider the development of currency derivatives. As we described in Chapter 2, currency derivatives called forward for-eign exchange contracts predated the breakdown of the adjustable peg currency system in the early 1970s. Since then, the foreign ex-change derivatives markets have grown to include foreign exchange options ("calls") to buy currencies at a particular price at a particular time in the future and "puts" to sell currencies at a particular price at a particular time in the future. Now, a large market has developed in currency swaps. A currency swap can be thought of as a long-dated, multiple-year forward foreign exchange contract; it fixes the price for exchanging two currencies at regular intervals over a specified pe-riod, such as five years.

Why did these new kinds of currency derivatives develop? Simply put, the issuers, investors, and intermediaries across the world found major opportunities to increase their returns or to lower their risks. One of the major reasons participants use currency derivatives is to hedge currency risks. For example, if a participant who is "long," or exposed to an underlying currency risk can, through the market, find a participant who is long to the offsetting risk, they can exchange the risks though a swap contract and effectively hedge each other's risks.

For example, a German manufacturer with an investment in a U.S. subsidiary is exposed to the decline in the value of the dollar rel-ative to the Deutsche mark; and a U.S. manufacturer, who has an in-vestment in a subsidiary in Germany, is exposed to the decline in value of the Deutsche mark relative to the dollar. If the market can link these risks and offset them against one another through a currency swap, then the risks of both parties can be hedged. In this case, the dealer, who put the parties together, or "made the market," would profit from the "bid" and "ask" spread. To illustrate how far this mar-ket has evolved, when this market first started in the early 1980s, the bid and ask spread was nearly 1 percent of the contract value. Such a "plain vanilla" currency swap today has bid and ask spreads of only a few basis points, or hundredths of a percent.

Similar instruments have been created in the interest rate mar-kets. Interest rate swaps are a particularly important example of an interest rate derivative. Around 1980, interest rate swaps were in-vented to convert interest returns from floating rates to fixed rates. For example, a party with a three-year, fixed rate U.S. dollar Treasury note can buy a three-year interest rate swap from a dealer that effec-tively converts the returns on that note to a floating rate return for the duration of the asset. Interest rate swaps have proved to be very

A Structured Interest Rate Swap

The simple structured transaction in this example was common in the mid-1980s. Assume there was an industrial company with a single A rating that wanted to raise $100 million in 10-year, fixed-rate funds to finance the acquisition of another company. With its credit rating and recent issuance of fixed-rate debt, the company could borrow 10-year funds in the U.S. dollar market at 10 percent, or 150 basis points over the 10-year U.S. Treasury bond. The company could obtain variable-rate bonds at 75 basis points over the London Interbank Offered Rate (LIBOR). Assume, at the same time, another industrial company with an AAA rating wanted to take advantage of favorable market conditions and raise variable-rate funds to build a new plant. This company could raise variable debt directly in the market at LIBOR plus 25 basis points. Having very little fixed-rate debt and such a high rating, it could have also obtained the funds in the U.S. dollar bond market for 50 basis points over the U.S. Treasury. This means that the borrowing spread between the two companies in the fixed-rate market was 100 basis points and, therefore, that there was an arbitrage opportunity of 50 points. If the arbitrage opportunity is captured, one or both firms can lower their funding costs. While the AAA firm has an absolute advantage in both markets, it has a relative advantage in the fixed-rate market, where it can borrow at 100 basis points less than the A company. The A company has a relative advantage in the variable-rate market, where the borrowing spread is only 50 basis points. If each company issues in the market where it can borrow at its lowest cost, and if they then exchange payments through an interest rate swap, both borrowers can lower their funding costs. The exchange would typically have been arranged by an investment bank.

More commonly, today, in such "structured" transactions the investment bank would be a dealer and would simply write the derivatives contract with whichever of these parties was its client and would lay off the risk with another dealer, if it could not find an immediate match itself. Also, more commonly today, many such structured transactions would also involve the use of currency swaps and other derivatives.

popular. The notional amount of U.S. dollar-based interest rate swaps outstanding is now over $1 trillion. This is quite spectacular growth for instruments that have been in existence for less than 15 years. In addition to swaps, a wide variety of other interest rate derivatives, including "options," "puts," and forward rate agreements, have been created.

After corporate issuers exhausted the advantages of simply raising debt in their own currency and selling that debt to international investors, the next step was to take advantage of the differences in the interest rate structures between different countries. For example, by the mid-1980s, U.S. corporate issuers working with their investment bankers found they could lower their financing costs by issuing bonds in non-dollar currencies and using currency and interest rate swaps to convert the borrowings back into dollars at a lower "all-in cost." These structured transactions have soared in volume and, in fact, now account for a large proportion of all corporate debt raised in developed world currencies. Today, issuers routinely benchmark the costs of raising debt in their own country against the all-in costs, net of the cost of swaps and transaction fees of raising money internationally. If the all-in cost is lower, they raise the money internationally, otherwise, they raise the money domestically.

The various national interest rate swap markets and the global currency swap markets are coming together to form a gigantic integrated global marketplace for interest-bearing instruments. Through this market, a participant can convert a floating or fixed rate asset from any one major currency to a floating or fixed-rate asset in any other major currency. For example, an investor can take a floating rate, dollar-based asset and convert the returns from it into the returns from holding a fixed-rate, yen-based asset through a currency swap and an interest rate swap, without the purchase of any new underlying asset.

While the global currency and interest rate markets have been evolving rapidly for the past 15 years or more, equity derivatives have gained importance only recently. In particular, equity swaps are now being used to provide investors in one country with equity investment opportunities in another country at a lower all-in cost than if they made the investment directly. While equity options have long been written in many individual countries (and, in particular, in the United States), equity swaps are only now becoming widespread. In an equity swap, an investor who owns an equity can swap the total returns from owning the equity to another investor for a price. These equity swaps are being underwritten on a cross-border basis with greater frequency. As the equity markets have begun to globalize, international investors who are not insiders in local markets have begun to hire agents, who are insiders, to buy and hold equities in an arrangement in which the agent passes on all the gains or losses to the international investor for a fee. This approach gives the international investor access to the market without having to pay extraordinary local execution costs or being a victim of local insider trading practices. Moreover, such an approach disguises the identity of the international investor from the other local participants.

Derivatives are at the heart of the evolution of the global capital market because they enable participants to manage many of the risks of participation, to take the risks they want to take, and to shed the risks they do not want to take for a known price. In the global capital markets, many risks are aggregated. That is, an investor who wants to take an equity position in a foreign oil producer would need to take not only the operating risk of the company's performance, but also take currency risks, petroleum price risk, and liquidity risk. A sophisticated investor can use derivatives such as currency swaps, petroleum futures, and equity swaps to disaggregate the risks and thereby reduce or eliminate all the risks he or she does not want to take.

Large proprietary traders are heavy users of derivatives to hedge their risks. If the market begins to move against them, they can use derivatives to neutralize their exposure, thus locking in losses and preventing further declines. If their exposure to loss is through a derivative instrument, they can hedge by purchasing another derivative. For example, you can purchase another call to neutralize a "call" exposure.

But people argue the risk does not go away, that someone has to take the risk, that the whole process is a "zero sum game," that for every winner there has to be a loser.

In fact, risk is often in the eye of the beholder. Different participants are exposed to different risks, have different risk/reward preferences, have different skills in assessing risks and have different capabilities to absorb losses. A global capital market for derivatives allows these different participants to take risks, for a known price, that are compatible with their preferences and competitive advantages. This creates an efficient global exchange of risks and rewards.

For example, consider the risks of participation in the global capital market by large, global commercial banks. These banks are already conglomerates of risk. They are exposed to credit risk, interest rate risk, and currency risk, among other risks, through their day-to-day operations. The derivatives market allows sophisticated global banks not only to neutralize their risks, but actually to profit from reducing them. For example, a commercial bank with a large, natural exposure to floating interest rates due to a large depositor base, can offset that risk by writing interest rate swaps. In this case, the commercial bank, as the "dealer," is simply earning a bid and ask spread where one of the customers is the bank's own balance sheet. Since so much of their original business was simply to offset the natural risks of being a large commercial bank, these banks have come to dominate the market for interest rate and currency swaps.

Derivative volumes are growing (see Exhibit 3.1) because they are valuable to users. More types of users are participating in the markets at the same time that the underlying product bases are expanding. Initially, only traders and institutional investors participated in the derivatives markets. Now, many large corporates and some small corporates are participating. Also, sophisticated investors and retail investors will increasingly have access to derivative products through instruments such as hedge funds. Similarly, the underlying product

Exhibit 3.1.   Total Interest Rate and Currency Swaps

Nominal Amounts Outstanding, 1980, 1990–1994

U.S. $ Billions

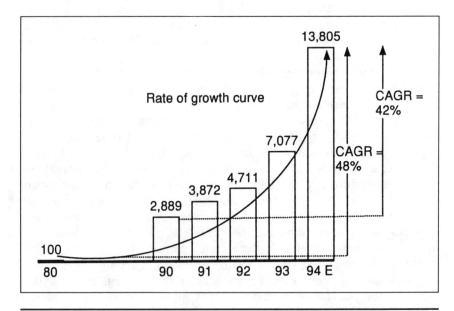

Source: ISDA; BIS.

base was once limited to financial asset prices or rates. Other types of underlying products, such as natural commodities (oil) or manufactured commodities (pulp, electricity) are now becoming the references in derivatives contracts. Finally, the derivative markets are increasingly moving to new countries including non-OECD nations.

As a result, a powerful "shadow" global market for derivatives has been created and continues to mature. This enables more players to participate in the underlying cash global capital market, and allows this market to undertake its fundamental task of allocating capital where it can be best employed. Simultaneously, as these linkages deepen, the world's national capital markets are becoming more tightly integrated and are behaving as a single market.

Derivatives are not a panacea. They can be used badly and are particularly dangerous to those with inadequate skill in using them. Moreover, derivatives introduce a potentially great risk of counterparty default. On balance, however, derivatives enable far more efficient and effective means of managing risks and rewards than have been available in the past.

In addition to derivatives, participants may use tools called "structuring techniques" often in combination with derivatives, to exploit anomalies in the market. Investment bankers, working with clients to raise money, use structuring techniques to convert one set of risk/return relationships into a different set of risk/return relationships often involving the issuance of new securities. By decomposing risks and returns into component parts, they can then repackage those risks and returns to make them more appealing to different segments of the investor market. In the process, they use the resulting savings to lower the costs of raising money to the issuer and to increase their own returns. Investment bankers also use structuring techniques with investors to increase the returns on their assets without increasing their risks.

Structuring techniques involve the use not only of derivatives but also of such techniques as "credit enhancement," which uses credit guarantees to relieve an investor from the risk of default, special purpose vehicles (to segregate the cash flows of the new transaction from other risks and returns) and "tranching," the repackaging of cash flows to segregate low-risk/low-return cash flows, from high-risk/high-return cash flows.

In the process, the activity in derivatives and structuring techniques are creating an efficient market that prices risks consistently around the world. By providing more uniform pricing and isolation of risks, derivatives and structuring techniques have improved clarity and efficiency in the global capital market.

THE HUNTERS

Technology, derivatives, and structuring techniques have transformed the search for market anomalies from an ad hoc process driven by individual investment bankers searching for opportunities for their issuing clients and individual traders looking for "quick kills" into a highly organized and institutionalized process.

The most important participants driving the globalization process are the leading global investment banks and the global commercial banks who developed much of their skill in the global capital market trying to find better solutions for their corporate finance clients. Competition for this business became so intense that they became the most skilled hunters in the marketplace. There are well over 50 institutions with both the scale and the skill to aspire to global leadership roles in the capital markets. Some of these institutions are specialists in the institutional markets, including Goldman Sachs, or J.P. Morgan, whereas others are "universal banks" with retail customers as well, such as Union Bank of Switzerland, Deutschbank, or Citicorp. Although many of the best players are headquartered in the United States, there are major players in the United Kingdom, Switzerland, Germany, Japan, France, Canada, and Holland. A host of other countries have at least one or two institutions that specialize in linking their country's clients, and their country's capital markets, to the global capital market.

These same institutions have all discovered that they can use the skill they developed to serve their clients for better management of their own financial assets. Most of these players, have found investing and trading for their own account is an important source of revenue. Because of their skill in the global capital markets, many of these leading players are also among the most prominent participants in the investment management businesses, particularly in the management of pension funds.

In addition to these large institutions, there are thousands of commercial banks, savings institutions, and insurance companies who serve primarily retail customers but, nonetheless, are investing in the global capital markets primarily for their own account. Because of the scale of the assets involved—the 500 largest commercial banks in the world have over $22 trillion of assets by themselves—even modest improvements in returns from their investment portfolios can have huge benefits. Therefore, in the late 1980s and early 1990s, most of these institutions began to make serious commitments to improving their skills in the global capital market.

Many of these same institutions serve as advisors for pension funds and mutual funds. There are also a large and growing number of independent investment advisors, particularly in the mutual fund industry. And, finally, there are a growing number of "hedge funds" that simultaneously invest for their own account, and the accounts of others, by comingling their own money with the money of contributing investors. Over the past few years, these hedge funds have become more and more important in the globalization process.

A large number of very smart people are now engaged in the global financial markets. If we consider the 10 largest U.S. investment banks alone, head count has increased from under 17,000 people in 1980 to nearly 41,000 in 1994 (see Exhibit 3.2). A rough estimate would place the global number of full-time investment bankers, traders, salesmen, and portfolio managers at well over 500,000 people (over 250,000 in the United States alone) representing hundreds of thousands of independent decision points, all trying to outperform each

Exhibit 3.2.   Headcount

10 Largest U.S. Investment Banks

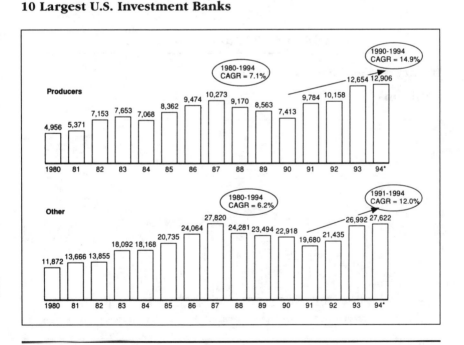

* 1994 forecast = 1993 Q3 actual.

Note: Classification into producers and other done by the 10 largest U.S. investment banks.

Source: SIA.

other. Many of these people are involved in delivering services to clients. The reason the pay in this industry is so extraordinary is that the ability of these people to find and exploit market anomalies both for their clients and for themselves is enormous. The total compensation expense for the top 10 U.S. banks has increased aggressively, at 15 percent annually on a comprehended annual growth basis (see Exhibit 3.3).

Now, the average annual compensation for each employee in these 10 largest investment banks in the United States is over $150,000. Since at least half the employees in these firms are lower paid support staff, the average professional pay was well above this figure. Many individuals earn over a million dollars each year. And, the averages are misleading because the top people within these firms, the "stars," often earn multiple millions of dollars. They receive this compensation simply because they are the best at finding and exploiting market anomalies.

Exhibit 3.3.   Total Compensation

10 Largest U.S. Investment Banks

$ Millions

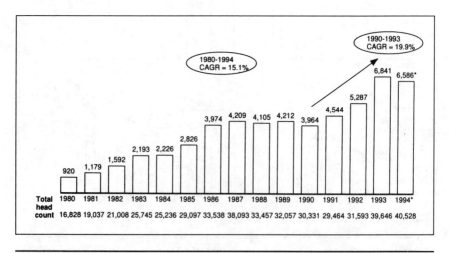

* Conservative estimate: 1994 forecast = 1994 YTD actual results through Q3 + Q3 and 1994 Q3 actual for head count.
Source: SIA.

It is not surprising that these firms have been able to attract some of the smartest, hardest working people in the world. The opportunities have been extraordinary.

HUNTING FOR MARKET ANOMALIES

The development of most of the advanced techniques for capturing market anomalies grew out of investment bankers and other participants looking to save money for issuers.

For example, currency swaps and interest rate swaps grew out of the search to hedge clients' exposure to risks. Then, they became a weapon to win bond mandates by offering clients lower all-in financing costs relative to domestic sources through the use of structuring techniques. Now, structured transactions have become routine. Global investment bankers, all using similar techniques, compete with each other, rather than against domestic financing alternatives, to offer the best combination of derivatives to deliver the best all-in cost of financing to the clients. As this has taken place, the relative size of the differences in financing costs have shrunk so that pricing differences are tiny (the issuers are capturing most of the value of any market anomalies rather than their investment bankers).

For this reason, as the use of structured transactions to benefit issuers has become commoditized, much of the action has shifted to serving "buy" side (investing) clients, rather than "sell" side (issuing clients).

For example, "asset swaps" are increasingly being used to increase returns. An asset swap is a structured transaction providing a risk-free increase in yield to an investor. In addition, investors have been more inclined to undertake structured transactions where notes have been issued, in combination with derivatives, for the sole purpose of capturing specific market anomalies.

But, perhaps the biggest change of all has been the tendency of players in the 1990s to pursue market anomalies for their own account. Global commercial banks, investment banks, and hedge funds have used derivatives, structuring techniques, and great amounts of leverage (high ratios of debt to equity) to increase returns for their own account.

Most of this activity has been focused on anomalies that involve linking interest rate markets in different currencies. What is particularly significant about this surge in proprietary trading activity is the sheer volume of funds that have been committed to pursuing cross-currency interest rate anomalies. As we will discuss in subsequent chapters, this activity is beginning to have significant influence over how national interest rates are being set.

ERODING REGULATORY BARRIERS

Not all the barriers to the full globalization of the capital markets are natural barriers like information barriers or risk barriers. Some of the most important barriers—the local regulation of national markets—are made by governments. However, these legal and regulatory barriers are also being overcome for essentially the same reasons that the natural barriers have been overcome: It has been profitable for participants to do so.

Regulatory barriers create market anomalies just like natural barriers. Many of the regulatory barriers were put in place to ensure the safety and soundness of local banks and one of the chief means of accomplishing this in almost all countries was to restrict competition. In turn, this led to the creation of highly profitable local banking and securities cartels worldwide. And, herein is a critical flaw that led to the breakdown of government regulated, bank dominated financial systems worldwide. Cartels, by their very nature, are founded on being able to exploit some customers by denying them the benefit of competition or access to markets. Customers who are being overcharged because of regulation will move their business if they find an opportunity to earn higher revenues or to get the same service at a substantially lower price. Moreover, some smart competitors, particularly participants that are not part of the cartel, are always willing to use financial innovation and new technology to get around regulation.

Consider how market and competitive forces undermined the regulation of deposit pricing, which was the central feature of the government-sponsored banking oligopoly that existed in the United States until the late 1970s. The combination of price controls and other regulations essentially forced customers to keep all their liquid funds in the banks and thrifts. This deposit monopoly made the banking and thrift franchises very profitable during the postwar era through the late 1970s. Borrowers had no place else to go to borrow money at reasonable rates, and depositors had no place else to go to invest their liquidity. However, the creation of money market mutual funds by nonbanks began undermining this liquidity monopoly during the late 1970s. When inflation soared in the late 1970s and money market rates also soared, depositors found the deposit price ceilings absurdly low (5 percent relative to the 15 percent plus interest rates available in money market funds) and went to the (then) recently created money market funds in droves. Eventually, the growth of these funds became so phenomenal that banks and thrifts in the United States got together, for one of the first times in their histories, to urge the elimination of interest rate ceilings on deposits. The resulting changes in law in 1982, the Garn-St. Germain Depository Institutions Act, enabled banks and thrifts to compete for deposits on price.

Similarly, investors being denied market opportunities because of local cartels, local capital controls, or excessive local taxation will also use international financial markets and new technology, if not outright evasion, to get around laws or business practices they view as unfair. For example, the investors who first provided the money to bond issuers in the Eurobond market, as described in Chapter 2, were largely private clients seeking higher returns than were available to them in the cartelized, bank-dominated, high-tax markets that prevailed in most Continental nations in the 1970s and 1980s. Italian investors, for example, have long been faced with restrictive controls on foreign capital investment and thereby have had few legitimate options other than depositing their money in a cartel-dominated, state-owned banking system, which paid depositors rates below the domestic inflation rate (and, in turn, invested these funds in national government bonds). It is not surprising that enormous flows of cash found their way into the Lugano branches of Swiss banks right across the border. Huge flows of private capital have left such countries as France, Italy, Spain, and Belgium to evade capital controls and/or taxation, to be placed in banks in Switzerland, Austria, or Luxembourg. In turn, these funds were invested in the global capital markets.

Such flows are called "flight capital." They can also be thought of as investors seeking higher returns through pursuing market anomalies (getting paid higher risk-adjusted rates by going abroad). Only, rather than using derivatives and structuring techniques, these investors are using airplanes and numbered accounts to increase their returns. The results are the same; taking action to increase returns speeds the globalization process.

The end result of such evasion is eventually to undermine regulation. The successful evasion of capital controls was one of the major reasons that capital controls were finally eliminated in Europe. Over time, this sequence has been repeated throughout the world as regulation after regulation, and law after law, has fallen victim to economic forces. The pattern is generally the same. Regulation designed to forestall competition or to deny access to markets creates profit opportunities for those who devise ways around the barriers. Resourceful participants use financial innovation and new technology (or outright evasion) to capture these profit opportunities. Eventually, the regulation or law becomes unworkable and is changed.

It is misleading to use the word *deregulation* to describe the changes in banking and securities laws and regulation that have taken place. Deregulation implies there is a proactive intent to liberate market forces. A better description of what has been taking place worldwide is that law and regulation are changing in reaction to market and economic forces. The liberation of financial markets is the result, not the intent.

In truth, governments in most of the nations in the developed world have been engaged in rearguard actions to insulate their national banking industries and their national financial economies from market forces. As we will describe later, only in some developing countries are governments genuinely embracing market liberalization as a proactive policy. Throughout the developed world, regulators and legislators have tried to moderate the effects of fundamental economic forces on their national banking and securities industries by maintaining existing regulation as long as possible. When these regulations eventually become unworkable, the then inevitable revision of regulation and law causes explosive change. In many countries, particularly in Europe, this period of rapid restructuring is just now gathering momentum. While some countries are still lagging, it appears inevitable that there will be fundamental, continuing liberalization of the laws and regulations governing financial institutions and securities markets in almost all nations of the world throughout the next several years.

Over time, the process feeds on itself. The more markets are liberalized, the more opportunities are available for participants and the more market, economic, and competitive forces are unleashed. And once unleashed, more pressure is placed on the remaining regulations and laws. As these are changed, still more opportunities become available for resourceful intermediaries, issuers, and investors.

Liberalization in law and regulation is therefore one of the most important forces at work in the globalization of capital markets simply because the heavy national regulation of banks and markets since World War II has been the chief determinant of how the financial system of each nation has worked. And as liberalization has proceeded, it has simultaneously helped accelerate the securitization of the flow of funds in nation after nation.

No one set out to create a global capital market any more than did the early mammoth hunters set out to populate the Americas with 10 million people in less than 1,000 years. The mammoth hunters wanted food, and they had the tools and techniques to get that food. The result was the extinction of most of the large mammal population of the Western Hemisphere. But, it was not the hunters' original intent.

Similarly, fund-raisers, investment bankers, and investors did not set out to create a global capital market. They were simply seeking profits. In the process, for better or worse, a global market has developed spontaneously from thousands and thousands of participants seeking, out of self-interest, market anomalies, using available technology and tools such as derivatives and structuring techniques.

RAPID GROWTH PHASE

We believe the globalization process has now entered into a critical transition period. With the exception of government's power to influence market pricing through monetary policy and direct market intervention, there remain no fundamental barriers to the continued globalization of the market that either have not been overcome or which will not soon fall. Other barriers such as language and culture, while significant, have time and time again been overcome by profit seekers. However, for now, we will save our views on the role of markets versus governments in influencing market pricing until later chapters.

A sufficient technological infrastructure is now being put in place to make it relatively easy to obtain the information necessary to be a global participant. The tools of the trade, such as derivatives and structuring techniques, are now becoming widely accessible; and more and more issuers, intermediaries, and investors are adapting a global mind-set. Regulation after regulation, in country after country, is being liberalized.

We are in the midst of a fundamental transition in how the market will work. We have, in fact, entered into the rapid growth phase of that transition. There are still abundant market anomalies to exploit. As described in Chapter 2, the process of globalization is still in the very early stages in the equity markets. In the emerging markets, even the currency and money markets are not yet fully global. Liberalization of regulation is on the drawing boards in most countries but much of the actual changes in regulation lie in the future.

In the foreign exchange and bond markets in the developed world, where the globalization process is the furthest advanced, participants are rapidly increasing their volumes as they try to make the same amount of money from ever smaller market anomalies.

Therefore, we believe the globalization process, while well advanced, is not yet reaching any natural limits.

We believe the process will continue until there are no market anomalies worth pursuing.

Until the last woolly mammoth is dead.

Until we have a single, overwhelming, fully integrated, global capital market.

—4—

Trees Don't Grow to the Sky

How far will the globalization process proceed before it slows down?

There is an old Wall Street adage, attributed to the former Soviet premier Nikita Khrushchev, that "Trees don't grow to the sky." This expression just confirms that any growth process, at some point, runs into limits. Just as the size of trees has limits based on how far the root system can go to reach nutrients, how much capillary pressure can be created to push those nutrients to the highest leaves on the tree, and how strong the trunk must be to support the branches, there are natural limits to any growth process. Redwoods can grow to be 360 feet, or 110 meters, in height; however, there can never be a mile-high redwood because the physics simply do not work.

The process of globalization, however, does not seem to be reaching any real limits in the near term. It will continue until there is a single, fully integrated global capital market.

What will first distinguish this market will be its size. This market is growing rapidly because of the issuance of new securities, particularly government debt, the conversion of formerly illiquid assets, such as bank loans, into tradable assets, and the ever-expanding group of countries that are linked into the market. Its financing capacity will eventually dwarf any national capital market because it will be intermediating the savings and investments of most of the world's citizens—not just for the developed world but also for the Russians, the Chinese, the Indians, South Asians, and Latin Americans.

What will also distinguish this market will be its ability to integrate—to act as a single market. Because of some unique aspects of financial markets relative to markets for goods and services, financial markets will probably integrate tightly on a truly global basis, while goods and services markets will integrate more loosely.

In turn, the combination of the scale of the financial market and its ability to integrate will give it real power. Indeed, what will truly distinguish this market, relative to any previous market, will be its power relative to the power of any single sovereign nation.

This is not to say that the role of governments relative to this market is not a vital concern. In fact, we will argue later in the book that the policies pursued by each government relative to this market will be a critical determinant of the long-term welfare of its own citizens. What makes the global capital market unique in history is that it operates largely free of the control of any one nation's politics and that it has real power. This is already true today and will be even more true in the future.

LARGE NUMBERS

Millions of dollars. Billions of dollars. Trillions of dollars.

After a while, the very words lose their meaning. To most people, a million dollars is a lot of money. As is a billion dollars. As is a trillion dollars.

But, in reality, the words mean vastly different amounts of money. A million dollars is equal to a stack of thousand-dollar bills that is some eight inches high.

A billion dollars is equal to a stack of thousand-dollar bills that is over 600 feet high—taller than the Washington monument. A trillion dollars is equal to a stack of thousand-dollar bills that is over 120 miles high—a height equal to a low-orbiting satellite or some 20 times higher than Mount Everest.

A trillion dollars is a truly impressive amount of money. And, when you are discussing the size of the global capital market, you wind up using trillions as the unit of measure.

The world's liquid financial stock has grown to be of considerable size. By liquid financial stock, we mean money and any financial asset that can be readily convertible into money through sale in a market, such as a tradable security. At the end of 1994, the world's stock of liquid financial assets, including all money, bonds, and equities, represented over $41 trillion (see Exhibit 4.1).

This liquid financial stock has been growing explosively. In 1980, some 7 years after the adjustable peg exchange rate system had broken down, the world's liquid financial stock was less than $11 trillion. Thus, the world's liquid financial stock grew by over $30 trillion in 14 years. This represents a compounded nominal growth rate of 10 percent, or a real rate of 5 percent (half of this growth was simply inflation). However, 5 percent real compounded annual growth is still very rapid.

Exhibit 4.1.   Growth in Developed World Financial Stock, 1980 and 1994

U.S. $ Billions

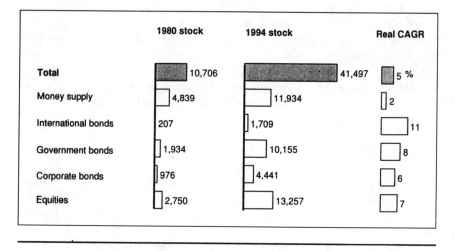

	1980 stock	1994 stock	Real CAGR
Total	10,706	41,497	5 %
Money supply	4,839	11,934	2
International bonds	207	1,709	11
Government bonds	1,934	10,155	8
Corporate bonds	976	4,441	6
Equities	2,750	13,257	7

Source: IMF; Salomon Brothers; IFC; BVIM; Baring Brothers; ISDA; McKinsey analysis.

What is behind this real sustained growth?

This is an essential question for us to answer because we are going to try, later in this chapter, to project how big the global capital marketplace will become so that we can understand its potential power. And to do that, we need to understand the dynamics behind its historic growth so that we can make reasonable projections about the future.

The rapid growth rate of the real liquid financial stock is at first rather puzzling since overall, the growth in the world's real liquid financial stock has significantly exceeded growth in other real economic measures both in terms of total stocks and annual flows. For example, a good measure of tangible private stock in the economy is gross fixed private capital formation. From 1980 to 1994, real gross fixed capital formation in the developed (OECD) countries grew at about 2 percent per year. In contrast, real growth in the stock of liquid financial assets in the developed world was over 5 percent over the same period, or two and one-half times faster.

So this leaves us with an apparent mystery. How does this happen since financial instruments are nothing more than claims on this real economy?

Said differently, we know that all this growth in the liquid financial stock did not come from real savings. We know from economics that savings must equal investment. So if real investment in physical capital grew at about 2 percent compounded, then real savings used to acquire financial assets that were invested in physical capital also grew at about 2 percent a year. But where did the rest of the growth in the liquid financial stock come from if it did not come from real savings that was used to acquire financial assets to invest in physical capital?

To help us understand where this growth came from, we need to look at the different components of the liquid financial stock. We need to look at the growth in the stock of equities, of bonds, and of money.

The value of traded equities outstanding grew rapidly from 1980 to 1994. During this period, the value of traded equities increased from less than $3 trillion to over $13 trillion, which represents a nominal compound growth rate of 12 percent or 7 percent real, for the time period.

Only a fraction of the stock is new equity issuance, less than 3 percent of the total stock, in any given year. Therefore, most of the growth reflected an increased valuation of existing equities. That is, the value of equities is a function of both current and future income in the real economy and does not necessarily reflect new flows of funds. Rather, it reflects what the market believes the equities to be worth. And over the period analyzed, the value of equities rose significantly.

However, of the some $30 trillion nominal increase in the liquid financial stock from 1980 to 1994, only $10 trillion came from equities. Where did the rest of the growth come from?

The answer is that the lion's share of the rest of the growth came from the issuance of debt securities.

DIRECT ISSUANCE OF DEBT SECURITIES

The direct issuance of new debt securities has been a significant growth driver in the size of the liquid financial stock.

The development of an international capital market freed governments and corporations from the debt constraints imposed on them by local, national bank-dominated financial markets. Governments found that once the constraints of the Bretton-Woods system were removed, that they could raise large amounts of debt securities from international investors. Corporations found that they could raise debt with less cost and fewer constraints than raising money from banks.

When governments finance consumption with taxes, there is no increase to the global financial stock, but when consumption spending is financed with the direct issuance of government debt, there is an increase in the financial stock. As we will describe in later chapters, governments throughout the world have found it easier to issue bonds rather than increase taxes or cut consumption spending. As a result, all major governments have increased their debt levels in the past 10 years. From 1980 to 1994, the stock of government debt outstanding grew at a compounded real annual rate of 8 percent during the period (or 13 percent nominal), from approximately $2 trillion in outstanding stock in 1980 to over $10 trillion in 1994. In absolute terms, increase in government bonds outstanding was by far the largest source of growth in the world's liquid financial stock.

Corporate bonds outstanding also grew dramatically throughout the same period. National corporate bonds, bonds issued by companies domestically, grew at about 11 percent compounded rate (6 percent real) for the same time period from a 1980 stock of about $500 billion to a 1994 stock of $2.2 trillion. The outstanding stock of bonds issued by banks also grew by about the same amount from $500 billion to $2.2 trillion, over the same time period. Much of this growth was from the issuance of debt securities by banks such as Japanese long term credit banks and other intermediaries which passed the proceeds directly through to corporate borrowers. International bonds which were issued by both corporations and governments grew even more spectacularly as the stock outstanding grew at a 16 percent compounded rate (11 percent real) from 1980 to 1994 from a 1980 stock of about $200 billion to a 1994 stock of about $1.7 trillion.

There was also very rapid growth over the last several years in many countries of short term corporate debt securities, such as commercial paper. Except in the United States, it is hard to go back before 1986 because so little of this paper was issued in other nations. In the United States alone, in just 6 years, the volume of this paper doubled from $300 billion in 1986 to nearly $600 billion in 1992 while volumes outstanding in such countries as Spain, Canada, Sweden, and Japan more than tripled from much lower bases.

Beyond this growth in need for funds, much of this growth in corporate debt was the replacement of bank loans with securities. This process called disintermediation started in the early 1970s in the United States and has spread now throughout most of the developed world. Corporations issue debt securities rather than borrow from banks because it is cheaper and/or because they get better terms and conditions. In fact, as we described in the preceding chapters, corporations often issue international corporate bonds to capture the anomaly of being able to raise money more cheaply with better terms and conditions than they can from domestic sources (most often a bank). Anomalies can also be captured domestically simply through replacing bank borrowings with domestically issued securities, including either bonds or commercial paper.

Therefore, because of an increase in debt to finance government consumption and because of an increased use of corporate debt securities rather than bank loans, the liquid financial stock represented by notes and bonds increased by some $13 trillion from 1980 to 1994.

With some $23 trillion accounted for of the approximately $30 trillion growth in the liquid financial stock from 1980 to 1992, this leaves some $7 trillion, which represents the growth in the money supply over this time period.

SLOW GROWTH IN MONEY

In sharp contrast to the growth in the stock of equities and bonds, the world's money supplies did not increase very rapidly. The 1980 money supply, overwhelmingly domestic bank deposits, was about $5 trillion or close to half of all the world's liquid financial assets in that year. Some 14 years later, the domestic money supply of the developed world nations was only a little under $12 trillion which represented less than one-third of the world's liquid financial stock in 1994. That is, the developed world's money supply grew by about 7 percent nominal, which was a real rate of only 2 percent over that entire time period.

This loss of share is the other side of disintermediation. As banks are disintermediated, money and bank deposits become a smaller share of the world's liquid financial stock.

And this gets us to a fundamental point. What is going on is not just the creation of a global capital market. We are shifting how the world intermediates funds away from banks and toward the market.

Going back in history, there have always been two means of matching funds providers with funds users in an economy. One approach has been to bring parties together through banks. The other approach has been to use markets—through the exchange of securities. Until very recently, intermediation through banks has been the dominant form throughout the world, with the securities system being used primarily for high-grade government and corporate bonds or equities.

The banking intermediation system is straightforward. The core functions of a bank are to accept deposits and to make loans while earning a sufficient spread between what is paid depositors and what is charged borrowers to cover the costs of operating plus a profit.

Making a profit is critical to making this system work since the intermediary itself, the bank, is absorbing all the risks of operating. Banks guarantee depositors both liquidity and interest and absorb all the risks of lending, the risks of premature withdrawal by depositors, and the risks to returns caused by changing interest rates. The essential historical value added by a bank is the reliance on large volumes to provide liquidity to depositors by satisfying differing depositors' preferences for maturity. Banks take deposits that are government-backed through deposit insurance and other safety nets to provide illiquid loans to a diversified portfolio of borrowers. In some cases, banks also provide an agency function through enforcing the covenants of intervention. In return for safety and liquidity, depositors accept lower returns from the bank than they could make from higher return, but riskier investments. The banks earn their returns by skillfully extending credit, at higher rates, and getting the loans actually repaid when due.

Historically, almost all banks that get in trouble do so through making bad loan decisions. Unlike stocks and bonds, loans have been remarkably illiquid. The only way most loans can be converted back to cash is through repayment by the borrower. Since banks usually have only $5 of equity for $100 of assets, a bank that makes many loans to borrowers who default will eliminate its equity rapidly and its depositors quickly will lose faith in the bank. Therefore, for this system to work, banks have to be very skilled at taking credit risks.

In the securities market, the value added is different: Securities firms typically work with both issuers and investors to find terms and conditions that are mutually satisfactory. Unlike a bank, a securities firm does not want to hold an asset. While it may offer liquidity to investors after they have bought a security, a securities firm does so only at a profit. That is, a securities firm will maintain a spread between what it will bid for buying a security and what it will ask for selling a security. A securities firm therefore takes mostly market, rather than credit risks. The credit risks in the securities are taken by the investors.

Historically, only governments and large corporations had sufficient credibility with investors for them to be willing to take on the inherent credit risks. This meant that all other borrowers had no choice but to borrow from banks rather than in the securities markets.

The situation has now changed. We are now in the midst of a profound change that is increasing the share of intermediation by the market and decreasing the share of classic bank intermediation.

Financial participants have developed a term for this process. It is called securitization.

SECURITIZATION

Securities have many advantages over bank loans. Very importantly, to the holder of the asset, securities are liquid and tradable, while loans have historically been illiquid. With a security, if your conditions change, or you get new information, or you see a more attractive investment, or if you need your money back, you simply sell your current security holdings at the market price. You can quickly receive cash for an asset even if the asset itself has a long maturity, such as a 30-year bond or no maturity at all, such as common equity. In contrast, the only source of liquidity from a borrower, historically, has been from repayment. Moreover, at any given point in time, the owner of a loan does not know what the asset is really worth. While the value of a debt security is determined every day by the market, the value of a loan is based on subjective valuation. What, for instance, is the economic value of an equipment lease, at a 14 percent effective interest rate, on a computer to a company that has just undergone a leverage buyout—80 percent of its face value; 120 percent of its face value? Who knows?

Securities are also attractive to investors because they can select a portfolio of securities that are tailored to their own particular appetites while a bank's loan portfolio is shaped by the needs of the customers it is serving.

Probably the most important advantage to securitization is that it will always be cost-effective to securitize an asset rather than place it on a bank balance sheet. Putting loans on a bank's balance sheet is expensive partly because of the way banks are regulated and partly because of the economic model they use. In terms of regulated costs, for every $100 loaned by a typical U.S. bank in 1994, it had to kick in roughly 20 cents for required reserves, 30 cents for insured deposit premiums, and another $1.20 pretax profit to support its regulatory equity requirements. In addition, banks are expensive to operate. It takes at least 80 cents per $100 of loans in noninterest expenses (even for loans to midsize and large corporations) which means that the minimum spread a bank must earn between the interest it charges to borrowers and the interest it pays to depositors is 2.5 percent. In fact, the average spread a U.S. bank needs is roughly $4.50 of income for every $100 put on its balance sheet because most of its loans and deposits come from retail customers who are more expensive to serve than large corporations and institutions.

With these advantages, it is not surprising that any asset which can be securitized, will be securitized.

We have already described how governments and corporations have been active in the direct issuance of debt securities, rather than bank loans to borrow money. They have simply been pursuing a market anomaly. By directly issuing securities, they have been able to raise money at lower cost, and with better terms and conditions, than by borrowing from banks. And, direct issuance of securities has been a fundamental driver behind the increasing securitization of the flow of funds.

Another form of securitization that will become increasingly important in the future actually takes loans off the balance sheet of a bank and converts them into securities. This process is often called loan or asset securitization.

LOAN SECURITIZATION

Securities firms, particularly in the United States, have found they can actually securitize loans through the use of special purpose vehicles and advanced structuring techniques.

Mortgage loans were the easiest to securitize in the United States because federally sponsored enterprises, most notably "Fannie Mae" and "Freddie Mac," guarantee residential mortgages and cause all mortgages they guarantee to conform to set standards. This uniformity makes it relatively easy to package them into securities. In the mid 1970s, firms such as First Boston and Salomon Brothers pooled large numbers of these mortgages together into special purpose trusts and passed the interest and principal repayments from them on to investors who bought the securities. As the years passed, Wall Street used structuring techniques to find even better ways of repackaging these loans to provide investors with even more predictable returns. These mortgage-backed securities have eliminated much of the value of holding an unsecuritized mortgage loan on the books of a financial institution. A player such as a mortgage bank, that simply originated mortgages and got them off the books by securitizing them, could outcompete banks and thrifts that held these loans on their books. Given equal costs for originating the mortgage, a mortgage bank could avoid the cost of reserves, deposit insurance premiums, and capital that a bank or thrift would have to pay to keep the asset on its books.

By the mid-1980s, investment banks in the United States had found means of securitizing not just mortgages, but also automobile loans, credit card receivables, and other assets with high credit quality and predictable cash flows. Unlike mortgages, however, there are no government-sponsored enterprises that guarantee the credit of some of the other assets. The additional guarantee came from what is known in the industry as "credit enhancement." For fees and interest, a financial institution agrees to guarantee the cash flows that underlie the new security. These guarantees have come largely from the institution that made the loans in the first place, although in many cases, a foreign bank or an insurance company has reinsured the credit. This means that the bulk of the value added from securitizing these kinds of assets has remained with the institution that originally made the loan. Securitization has therefore not eliminated the value of distribution and credit underwriting made by the institution originating the assets although it has eliminated much of the value of holding the assets.

More recently, banks have been at the forefront of securitizing commercial real estate loans, high-yield loans, developing-country debt, and medium-term syndicated debt by making markets and trading these assets as whole loans. Even small business loans will become easier to securitize in the United States under pending legislation.

As long as the value of securitizing a loan exceeds the incremental costs, more and more loans will be securitized. As structuring techniques continue to advance, and as securitization costs decline, more and more loans will be securitized. This will be particularly true outside the United States as more and more non-U.S. banks begin to embrace the benefits of securitization and as regulation continues to be liberalized permitting the use of some of the securitization techniques that have been pioneered in the United States.

Going forward, loan securitization will be more important to the absolute growth of the world's liquid financial stock than it was over the past decade. In 1980, the base year for our analysis, the financial stock of securitized loans was tiny relative to the world's financial stock. It represented under $100 million or about a hundredth of one percent of the total stock, and therefore we did not include it in our base for analysis. By 1992, in just the United States, the stock of securitized mortgages, loans, and asset-backed commercial paper stood at $1 trillion and had been growing at a compound growth rate of 34 percent for the previous 4 years.

LIQUIFYING THE FINANCIAL STOCK

Securitization is extremely important to globalization because it is a fundamental underlying process driving the creation of more and more financial assets whose value is determined by the financial markets. Once an asset is traded in any national market, it becomes liquid and then gets linked into the entire global capital market as investors trade off investing in those new assets against other existing assets.

The growing importance of securitization of the flow of funds does not mean that banks are going to disappear. Banks remain vitally important because the world needs their skills in credit structuring and credit underwriting and in providing a wide range of important services including, in particular, deposit and payment services. However, the force of securitization means that banks need to embrace securitization, rather than resist it, so that banks can capture their share of the advantages securities have over the traditional system. And indeed, banks are taking actions to embrace the benefits of securitization—particularly in the United States but increasingly elsewhere.

In addition to securitizing loans they originate, banks are becoming much more active managers of their portfolio of assets and liabilities. Banks in all nations have some assets and liabilities that are illiquid and not tradable. Historically, for example, the investment portfolio of banks is generally made up of tradable assets while the loan portfolios and most of the local currency deposits, including demand deposits, and savings accounts from retail customers and small businesses are not tradable. However, as securitization has proceeded, and as banks have discovered the advantages of being active traders rather than "buy and hold" investors, a larger proportion of bank balance sheets have become tradable assets. The linkages to the global capital market take place even if the assets, once securitized, are acquired by a bank because the bank now treats the asset as an investment to be managed as part of a portfolio rather than as an illiquid loan to a customer. And, if a bank is only able to keep deposits by paying full money market rates for that money, then these deposits also become part of the global money market. As securitization proceeds, more and more of each bank's assets and liabilities have become linked into the global capital market. This is particularly true of the large commercial banks.

CAPITALIZING ON MARKET ANOMALIES

There is one other significant driver of growth of the world's liquid financial stock. This is the creation of new financial instruments solely for the purpose of capitalizing on market anomalies. For example, to accomplish short-term covered interest arbitrage transactions, banks undertake interbank placings and takings with each other, or they make loans to each other that, in effect, inflate both bank balance sheets. Financial institutions, particularly in the 1990s, have also used medium-term notes to capture long-term arbitrage transactions. The major source of these transactions are the global commercial banks, but investment banks, investment managers, and hedge funds are becoming more important. These transactions are completely uncon-nected to the real economy since their sole purpose is to capture prof-its from anomalies in the global capital market.

The stock of assets and liabilities arising from these transactions are quite large. For example, over 20 percent of the assets of the largest 500 banks in the world are funded by nondeposit liabilities that exceed $4 trillion as of year-end 1994. These nondeposit liabilities have been growing steadily over the past 5 years.

None of these funds were included in our estimate of the world's $41 trillion stock of liquid financial assets (in 1994) described earlier. They already have a very real influence on the emerging power of the market and will have an increasing role in the future.

FUTURE GROWTH OF LIQUID FINANCIAL STOCK

The question is then, how much will the stock of financial assets grow in the future? The qualitative answer is that we expect the global financial stock to grow rapidly far into the future.

To develop a quantitative answer, we extrapolated from recent trends to the size of the world's financial stock into the future. We started with the recent rates of growth in the stock of money, bonds, and equities, interviewed fund managers and other participants, and moderated future assumptions somewhat to be conservative. In nomi-nal terms, assuming recent inflation levels, the stock of financial as-sets would grow from about $41 trillion in 1994 to nearly $83 trillion in 2000, or $53 trillion in real 1992 dollars. In other words, the global fi-nancial market, which is already very large, is going to get even larger (see Exhibit 4.2). And the share that is liquid and tradable, versus illiq-uid and largely under the control of governments (the money supply), will be greater and greater (see Exhibit 4.3).

Importantly, these numbers exclude the probable impact of loan securitization, which could easily add another $6 trillion of liquid fi-nancial stock. They also exclude growth in the stock of interbank placings and takings, medium-term notes, and other instruments used to convert market anomalies. In other words, we are likely to be sig-nificantly understating the actual size of the liquid financial stock by the year 2000. That is, our sizing of the global capital market in 2000 at $83 trillion ($53 trillion in 1992 dollars) is a conservative estimate.

In addition to the growth in financial stock in the developed world, as we will describe in later chapters, more countries in the de-veloping markets will begin to join the global capital market. At about $2 trillion in 1994 (up from $800 billion in 1992), the stock of financial assets in the developing world is still small relative to the developed

Exhibit 4.2.   Stock of Financial Assets, 1992–2000

U.S. $ Billions

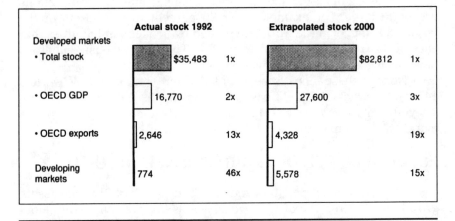

Source: OECD; McKinsey analysis.

Exhibit 4.3.   Distribution of Financial Stock Outstanding,*
1980–2000

U.S. $ Billions, Percent of Total

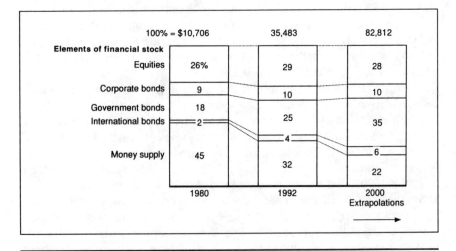

* Developed world only.
Source: IMF; Salomon Brothers; IFC; BVIM; Baring Brothers; ISDA; McKinsey analysis.

world. Even at growth rates that are moderate relative to recent history, these countries could contribute some $6 trillion additionally to the world's liquid financial stock by 2000.

Comparisons to the real economy help put these numbers into perspective. In 1992, the stock of financial assets was roughly twice the size of the $16 trillion a year (nominal) gross domestic product of the OECD nations. By the year 2000, even with our conservative estimate, it will be roughly three times the projected $27 trillion (nominal) GDP of these nations. In 1992, the stock of financial assets was roughly 13 times OECD exports. By the year 2000, it is projected to be roughly 19 times exports. In 1992, the financial stock of developing countries represented only about 2 percent of the world's total financial stock. However, reflecting their expected rapid growth rates, the liquid financial stock of developing countries is projected to equal nearly 7 percent of the total by the year 2000.

Moreover, the year 2000 is a somewhat artificial stopping point since the driving forces are unlikely to hit their limits until well into the next century. There is no reason the stock of financial assets could not be at even higher multiples of GDP. Even if the process reaches its limits in the OECD nations, the application of the driving forces to the growth of the liquid financial stock in the developing countries should continue for a very long time. As this takes place, the developing countries will become an increasingly important force in the global capital market. The financial stock of developing countries could reach close to 20 percent of the global financial stock by the year 2010.

As you continue to project forward in time you get truly mind-numbing numbers. For example, if the world's real economy grows at the pace it did over the past decade, it would reach a level of about $90 trillion (in 1992 dollars) by 2020. If the financial stock was then four times the size of world output, it would be some $360 trillion in size.

That's equal to a stack of thousand-dollar bills 43,200 miles high.

INTEGRATION

Until now in this chapter, we have been describing the size of the world's liquid financial stock rather than referring to it as a market. This is because the liquid financial stock is composed of many markets. It is through integration that the world's multiple financial markets become a single global capital market.

An economist's definition of an integrated capital market is a market in which any arbitrage opportunities are quickly traded away, and in which there is a free flow of saving to investment without geographic boundaries. Another way to state this is to rely on a version of the "law of one price" most notably advanced by Adam Smith as the equilibrium condition of aggregate, efficient markets (and subsequently used as the foundation for many equilibrium condition theorems). An integrated capital market is a market over which the impediments to exchange are sufficiently low that equivalent capital assets, or financial instruments sell at the same price, allowing for transactions costs. Or, more simply, the law of one price says that the same item in the same market must sell for the same price throughout the market.

The 50 state capital markets in the United States are integrated into a single national capital market, and we can draw examples of integration from it. For example, when mortgage-backed securities were first issued in the late 1960s, there were significant pricing differentials across states. These did not last long, however, as arbitrageurs quickly captured the profit opportunities from anomalies and thereby rationalized those markets.

A wealth of economic literature on the subject of capital market integration has been produced over the past decades. In particular, efficient market economists have been asserting the capital market's efficiency for decades. In spite of such predictions, the full integration of the global capital markets has been slower to develop than many expected. While the predictions were directionally correct, they underestimated the barriers to full market integration we outlined in

---

Ahead of Their Time

Efficient market economists including among others Frenkel and Levich, Jensen, Fama, and Roll, have been asserting capital market efficiency for decades. More recently, others have been predicting capital market integration and testing its existence, including Frankel, Feldstein and Horioka, Bayoumi and Rose, and Sinn. In a widely quoted article in *The American Economic Review*, Frankel spells out various measures of integration in the capital markets that synthesize much of the thinking on the subject.

Despite such predictions, however, capital market integration has been to date primarily a theoretical construct, not an empirical one. Only very recently, as the multitude of barriers have begun to break down is real global capital market integration becoming evident.

Chapter 3 and the technological innovation and investment required to overcome them.

Nevertheless, the global capital market is integrating and has far greater potential to integrate than do markets for goods and services.

One of the reasons it is possible to integrate financial markets more fully than markets for goods and services is that they have the potential to be more efficient. Financial markets quickly and cost-effectively reflect all available information through changes in market prices. For example, financial market reaction to releases of statistical information about the real economy is almost completely integrated into prices of all financial instruments within hours of the release of the information. In contrast, excepting commodities, most markets for goods and, in particular, services are relatively inefficient. It can take hours of work, even by a knowledgeable businessperson, to compare the relative prices of one law firm against another, even if they operate in the same city. Even then, considerable judgment is required to determine whether the services being priced are truly comparable.

This continuing search for the best risk-adjusted returns drives the continuing, explosive growth in trading volume. For example, the volume of traded equities grew at a compounded rate of 17.7 percent from 1980 to 1992, which was seven times faster than the 2.5 per year growth in the OECD economies. Global trading volume of foreign exchange, bonds, and derivatives grew at even higher rates.

Increasingly, then, the vast stock of liquid financial assets outstanding are beginning to act as if they were part of a single, integrated market that links together the foreign exchange, money markets, bond markets, and equity markets of all of the nations that have removed their foreign exchange controls. And, over time, this global capital market will become more and more integrated.

LINKAGES TO THE REAL ECONOMY

Why should any of this growth in size and integration of the financial stock matter? After all, unlike an increase in real savings, which allows a real increase in investment, is not all this growth in financial stock relative to the real economy merely the shuffling around of financial claims among financial participants, with little impact on the real economy?

We think it makes a great deal of difference to the real economy. For one, as we will describe later in the book, this global capital market activity helps the effective cross-border allocation of capital. But, the linkages of the global capital market to the real economy go beyond allocation. We believe that the developments in the global capital markets are going to have an escalating impact on the purely domestic real economy of individual nations including, in particular, on government policies.

Despite the differences between how financial markets operate and how markets for goods and services operate, the financial and real economies are inextricably linked. Although the financial economy is directly impacted by developments in the real economy, the reverse is also true: Developments in the financial economy directly impact the real economy. As the global financial marketplace grows and matures, and as it becomes more integrated, the influence of the financial economy on the global real economy will become more and more significant.

The fundamental linkage between the real and the financial economies starts with money. Money is the medium of exchange for both the real and the financial economies. It also serves as a yardstick to measure value in both the real and financial economies, including the price of a car, or the price of a corporate bond. Therefore, money (or anything readily convertible into money) can be used to buy anything in either the real or financial economies.

Since money is the medium of exchange in both the real and the financial economies, the value of money, or its purchasing power, is vital to both economies. Changes in the value of money therefore impact both the real and financial economies directly.

Because money inextricably links the two economies, the pricing of money (and instruments easily convertible into money) provides the principal feedback from the real economy to the financial economy and vice versa. The two principal prices of money are exchange rates (the price for exchanging one nation's currency for another) and interest rates (the price of renting money for a specific period of time).

Exchange rates and interest rates are by far the most powerful drivers of the pricing linkages that connect all prices for financial instruments in the entire global capital marketplace. If global market participants suddenly desire to hold more of their investments in Japanese yen than in U.S. dollars, the value of the dollar relative to the yen decreases and, through the global capital market, the prices of all dollar- and yen-based instruments (and to some degree all the other instruments in all other currencies) adjust as they are traded until a new equilibrium is attained or until a new shock affects the system. Or, if a major change in long-term bond interest rates takes place in one country, the prices of all other instruments of value in that country's currency, including money market investments or equities, adjust, as does the value of that country's currency relative to all others.

Naturally, the changes in the supply, demand, and pricing for an important asset category, such as German government bonds, or the exchange value of the dollar in closely linked markets will carry far more weight than changes in the supply and demand for minor instruments, in minor currencies, in loosely linked markets. A major change in the demand for Australian equity derivatives would have no noticeable impact on global markets, whereas major movements in the value of U.S. Treasury bonds can have a powerful impact on the entire global financial market.

POWER SHIFT

Exchange rates and interest rates are affected by changes in demand and supply in both real markets and financial markets. However, governments have long been used to being able to significantly influence supply and demand in local financial markets and thereby control domestic interest rates and, at least in the short term, exchange rates.

As we will explore in Chapter 5, a major theme of this book is that governments are increasingly losing control of exchange rates and domestic interest rates to the global financial markets. As the global financial market grows in size relative to the real economy, and as the linkages between the global financial instruments traded in the global financial marketplace get tighter and tighter, changes in supply and demand in the global financial market overwhelm attempts by local governments to control domestic interest rates and exchange rates directly. Similarly, changes in supply and demand for funds in the domestic real economy will become less important in establishing interest rates. The global capital market will increasingly drive interest rates and exchange rates and that, in turn, will strengthen its role in driving the real economy in each nation, as well as globally.

Governments can, and will, continue to intervene to try to influence foreign exchange rates and bond prices. But all they will be doing is creating anomalies from which participants in the market can profit. By definition, government intervention is an attempt to cause the market to establish a different price than the forces of supply and demand would otherwise dictate. When the stock of liquid financial assets was small and the market was far less integrated, government action (particularly when coordinated on a multilateral basis) could overwhelm the relatively weak market.

Now that has changed. A $41 trillion and growing global liquid financial stock that decides to move a price can overwhelm the firepower that central banks can bring to bear. For example, in 1983 the combined central bank reserves (which we use as a proxy for central bank intervention muscle) of the United States, United Kingdom, Japan, Germany, and Switzerland were about $140 billion, which was more than 3½ times the daily turnover in the foreign exchange markets in New York, London, and Tokyo of only about $40 billion. By 1992, these same central banks had $280 billion in reserves but this amount represented less than half the daily foreign exchange turnover of $620 billion in these three cities. The relative power of the central banks to intervene in 1992 had diminished to about one-seventh of what it had been in 1983. By 1995, daily foreign exchange turnover was well over $1 trillion a day.

Historically, central banks also have had an impact on domestic interest rates by controlling the quantity of money in their countries through monetary policy. This power is also being eroded as the size of the financial stock grows relative to the quantity that can be affected by central bank action.

Our colleague, Ted Hall, has used an analogy from the gold and oil markets to illustrate what has changed. In the past, when government controls over the flow of money in their country was large relative to the local unintegrated, domestic stock of liquid financial assets, then government monetary policy had a huge impact on domestic interest rates. It was like the oil markets in the 1970s when OPEC curtailed oil production. The stock of oil (primarily in tankers and at refiners), representing only a six- or eight-month supply, was small relative to the flow of oil production and therefore curtailment of supply by OPEC had a huge impact on price.

However, today (and to an even greater extent, in the future) in the vast, increasingly integrated, global capital market, the control by a central bank of the growth in any one nation's monetary base is dwarfed by the size of the global financial stock. The current situation is more like the global market for gold where you have a very large stock of gold that has been built up over thousands of years and a relatively tiny amount (in comparison to the stock) of new gold being produced. Restricting the supply of newly mined gold would have only a limited impact on world gold prices.

Likewise, the monetary policy of individual central banks is going to have less and less impact on the real interest rates of financial instruments in their own currency. The major nations, particularly the United States, still have some power to control interest rates. But, even in these nations, this influence will decline. Chapter 5 will offer empirical evidence that this inability of central banks to control interest rates is already beginning to happen. Governments are also losing power relative to the global capital markets because of their growing dependency on the market to finance fiscal deficits.

Later in this book, we will explore more fully the relationship of this global capital market to the world's governments. In particular, we will examine both the capacity of the market to enable nations to finance government spending and the potential power of the global capital market to discipline that spending.

So far, with the potential exception of Japan, most governments have been inclined to use the freedom provided by the global capital market to increase their reliance on deficit spending. Left to their own devices, many democratic nations find it easier to spend money than to raise taxes and they plug the gap with debt. This tendency has become more pronounced recently.

Over the past couple of years, every major developed nation in the world, including even Japan, has been running a significant budget deficit. Collectively, the governments of the major nations of the world spent more than their tax receipts. At the end of 1993, the total net public debt of these countries amounted to some 37 percent of their gross domestic product; as a point of comparison, the net public debt of these countries was about 21 percent of gross domestic product in 1980.

Averages, of course, can be misleading. The degree of dependency on deficit spending has differed from country to country. Japan, for example, has actually decreased its ratio of net public debt to its gross domestic product from 17 percent in 1980 to about 4 percent by the end of 1993. The United States increased its indebtedness from 19 percent of GDP in 1980 to 38 percent by year-end in 1994. Canada increased its net federal government indebtedness from only 13 percent of GDP in 1980 to some 64 percent in 1994. At the extreme, Italy went from 53 percent of its GDP in 1980 to over 121 percent in 1994.

The growth of government deficit spending has attracted great press attention in many countries, particularly in the United States, where it has been the focal point of much of the political debate of the nation over the past several years. But, the real issues of public debt lie ahead, and we will have much to say about them later in the book.

At this point, we want to limit our observation to the shift in power occurring as nations become more and more dependent on the global capital market to finance fiscal deficits. In any debtor/creditor relationship, as debt levels rise, the creditor begins to have real power to dictate the prices, the terms, and the conditions of continuing to lend money. Thus, some nations are beginning to face the prospect of real market discipline by this overwhelming, overpowering global capital market.

—5—

Approaching Absolute Zero

Some 70 years ago, Albert Einstein developed a theory, later modified and amplified by the Indian physicist Satyendra Bose, that if an element were to be cooled to absolute zero a new state of matter would be formed. Absolute zero (approximately minus 460 degrees Fahrenheit) is the temperature at which atomic activity ceases. At absolute zero, the Einstein-Bose theory maintained that individual atoms would lose their separate identity and would condense into a state of matter with properties quite distinct from the same element in solid, liquid, or gaseous form.

For years, there was no evidence to prove that the theory was true or false because of the difficulty in cooling a substance to absolute zero. Then, in 1995, a team led by Dr. Eric Cornell and Dr. Carl Wieman working in Colorado announced that they had been able to cool atoms of the element rubidium to a temperature within a few billionths of a degree of absolute zero using a magnetic trap and a process called evaporative cooling. Just as the theory had predicted, at that temperature the element formed a new state of matter with fundamentally different properties. The individual atoms of rubidium lost their identities, condensing and merging together to create a new unified state of matter.

We believe that eventually the world's financial markets also will be transformed into a unified "new state of matter." Just as the dramatic lowering of temperature to absolute zero through evaporative cooling provided the conditions for creating a new state of matter, the continued pursuit of "market anomalies" until they disappear provides the conditions for creating a global capital market that truly operates as a single market.

When this integrated capital market fully comes into being, it likely will have fundamentally different properties from the individual national financial markets it is integrating. Just as atoms lost their separate identities when the new state of matter was formed so eventually will the individual national financial markets lose their identity.

But where is the evidence that we are headed in this direction? If we are trending toward a single global market, we should find evidence in how the market sets prices. As stated in Chapter 4, the law of one price stipulates that the same item must sell for the same price throughout the market. If the law of one price is beginning to operate—as it must for there to be a single global marketplace—we should be able to see it in operation, particularly in the establishment of foreign exchange and interest rates.

However, until recently, there has been little hard evidence to support a view that the global market, as opposed to national markets and central banks, is the main agent in establishing foreign exchange rates and interest rates. This is not because of the lack of theories or the lack of research.

Even since before the breakdown of the Bretton-Woods system, economists have offered an abundance of alternative economic theories about global capital markets, about global capital mobility, and about how foreign exchange rates and interest rates would be set by the market. The problem that the various economists have had is that there has only been inconclusive evidence, or even contradictory evidence, to support their theories.

We think the reason for this lack of evidence is straightforward: Most economists doing the work have assumed that we already have an integrated global capital market when in fact, the process of integration is ongoing and far from complete. Just as you can cool an element for a very long time before its fundamental properties change, market forces can work to eliminate anomalies for a very long time before the market itself changes sufficiently to behave differently.

As described in earlier chapters, there have been ample barriers to the creation of a fully integrated global capital market, and the dynamic process of overcoming those barriers will take decades before it is fully complete. It may take several decades or more before all the woolly mammoths are gone and we have a fully integrated global market. As new techniques are discovered, as more participants bring more funds to bear to exploit market anomalies, the pricing relationships in the market will continue to evolve.

In fact, we are still a long way from a fully integrated global capital market. We are not yet approaching absolute zero, where national financial markets would lose their individual identities. Just as an element, when cooled, must first go from a gas to a liquid and then from a liquid to a solid before it can be transformed into the new state of matter that exists only at absolute zero, the global capital market must go through several changes in state before it becomes fully integrated.

At the moment, we are witnessing such a change in the state of the market. It is more like the shift from a liquid to a solid (national markets, like individual atoms, are still individually distinct) than to a new state (completely merged markets). We are moving on a path to a fully integrated, global capital market but we are not yet there. We are still a long way from absolute zero.

The market has gone through two distinct transitions. The first, which we described in detail in previous chapters, was the transition from the pegged rate system to a floating rate system. The system has more recently begun a second state-of-matter transition from a "liquid" to a "solid." Under each of these transformations, foreign exchange rates and interest rates are set quite differently. Before explaining the theory of why these transitions have occurred, we will describe the empirical evidence.

CHANGES IN THE STATE OF MATTER

The first transition, from a pegged rate system to a floating rate system largely involved the integration of the global foreign exchange market. As the various currencies of the developed world became free from foreign exchange controls, the pricing of spot foreign exchange rates integrated almost immediately because of the ease of directly arbitraging differences in spot exchange rates. As described earlier, this means that converting, for example, dollars to yen and then to Deutsche marks at the prevailing spot foreign exchange rates yields virtually the same result as converting dollars to Deutsche marks directly. In other words, from the early days of globalization, the spot rate for converting one freely convertible currency to any other freely convertible currency, at any moment in time had virtually the same price, worldwide.

However, while foreign exchange rates immediately integrated, interest rates did not. For the most part, interest rates in different countries were relatively independent. The interest rate yield curves between different countries had very different slopes, and the absolute real interest rates (the nominal rate adjusted for inflation) between different countries were also independent of each other.

As described in Chapter 2, the market accomplished arbitrage between different interest rates in different currencies during this period through covered interest arbitrage. Covered rate parity, the result of this arbitrage process, refers to the condition in which interest rates across countries are equal when they are contracted in the same currency; it is a market condition where there are virtually no risk-free interest rate arbitrage opportunities. This condition was also established during the early stages of globalization. In practice, an investor could obtain the same return from a 3-month, U.S. dollar-denominated instrument or a 3-month, Deutsche mark-denominated instrument with a forward exchange rate contract to purchase dollars at the maturity date.

Covered rate parity holds under the following conditions: where there is sufficient financial stock, where there is sufficient liquidity in the market, where there are sound counterparties, and where transaction costs are low. These conditions hold for most major currencies today and thus covered rate parity holds for those currencies. It does not hold for most of the currencies of the still-developing nations.

Covered rate parity has been holding for longer periods. In the early 1980s, covered interest parity began to extend beyond the 1-year range of normal foreign exchange contract to longer periods, through the use of cross-currency swaps. As in the previous example, an investor would obtain the same return from a 5-year dollar bond or from a 5-year yen bond with a 5-year yen/dollar cross-currency swap. By the early 1990s, covered rate parity had extended beyond the short term to the long term (now as far as 10 years) through the continued use of longer and longer dated swaps.

Thus, for nearly 20 years after the Bretton-Woods system broke down, foreign exchange rates had the same price worldwide, national interest rates were relatively independent, and the covered interest parity held for longer and longer periods. Under these conditions, how were the various foreign exchange rates themselves being set by the market during this 20-year time span?

During this period, foreign exchange rates were often traded with little regard to the relative purchasing power of the various currencies in the real economy of each nation. For example, in 1980 the dollar was valued at 195 percent of its PPP rate versus the Deutsche mark (DM). In 1985, the dollar was valued at 241 percent of its PPP rate versus the Deutsche mark. By 1990, it was down to 101 percent of its PPP rate versus the DM. Relative trade between the two nations did not change dramatically over the time period. Appendix 5A describes in more detail the relationship between exchange rates and purchasing power parity.

In part, this happened because the trade of goods and services is not the only market activity that drives exchange rates. It cannot be, given that trading in foreign exchange volume is now about 50 times greater than trade in goods and services, and dramatic swings in exchange rate prices take place absent any significant changes in international trade. In fact, the vast bulk of foreign exchange trading is undertaken for financial market purposes such as proprietary trading, market making, arbitrage, or risk coverage. Rather than purchasing power, it appears that differences in real interest rates between nations, combined with central bank action, drove exchange rates during this period.

Probably the clearest example of this was the movement of the U.S. dollar, the world's reserve currency, against other currencies. In 1980, the United States began to shift from being in fiscal balance to operating with a significant fiscal deficit. As a result, its real interest rates began to rise. The relative increase in the real interest rates in the United States was transmitted to the value of the dollar in other currencies, or to the dollar exchange rates. In fact, there was a relatively strong correlation between the U.S. dollar's value and to the real yield on its government bonds. As the government bond rate rose and fell, so did the value of the U.S. dollar relative to other currencies, regardless of the purchasing power relationship to other currencies (see Exhibit 5.1). The "Plaza Accord" of 1985, which involved both the lowering of real U.S. interest rates and coordinated intervention by the world's central banks to lower the value of the dollar, is a good example of successful intervention.

Central banks, however, are becoming less and less able to use interest rate increases or decreases of any kind to influence the value of their currency. This is probably because interest rates and exchange

Exhibit 5.1. Value of U.S. Dollars versus Real Government Yield, 1980–1990

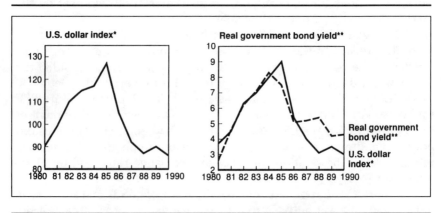

* Trade weighted index value of U.S. dollar against basket of 15 currencies, year-end data.
** Real current yields on 10-year government bonds, year-end data.
Source: J. P. Morgan; *The Wall Street Journal;* Bloomberg; McKinsey analysis.

rates are increasingly a pricing equilibrium established by the large relative stocks of financial assets held by nongovernment participants.

Probably the most spectacular recent example of the loss of power of central banks and governments to control rates was the breakdown of the European Rate Mechanism (ERM) in September of 1992. In that month, the Bank of England, the Bank of France, the German Bundesbank, the Bank of Italy, and most of the other central banks in Europe, lost a battle of wills, not to mention tens of billions of dollars, to participants in the global capital market. The governments of these nations had taken solemn vows together at the Maastrict summit of December, 1991 to move in the direction of a single common European current. As an essential first step in moving toward monetary union, the ERM was designed to limit currency fluctuations through coordinated central bank action. Many hopes and dreams were vested in the Maastrict plan. However, on September 19, known later as Black Wednesday, Britain and Italy were forced out of the ERM and the orderly plans of the Maastrict were thrown in disarray.

The ERM breakdown in September of 1992 was a watershed in the development of the global capital market. From that moment onward, market participants realized that they could win even against the combined resources of central banks.

Since then, the global capital market has had ample opportunities to demonstrate its power. A year later, in August of 1993, the market again demonstrated its power versus the European nations remaining in the ERM. The result was to force the central banks to widen the exchange rate fluctuation bands to 15 percent, a bank so wide that it is almost meaningless.

FROM A LIQUID TO A SOLID

The sudden visible breakdown in 1992 of the ability of central banks to control spot foreign exchange rates seems to have triggered a second state-of-matter transition in how both foreign exchange rates and interest rates are now being set by the market.

Since the ERM breakdown, real evidence has been building to support the theory that the world's interest rates are integrating. In particular, for the past 2 years, the real, inflation-adjusted, yield curves for holding period risk are becoming aligned across countries and the real interest rates for countries with different risks are tending to reflect the risk differentials between the countries.

Let's start with the evidence that real, risk-adjusted yield curves are aligning.

Without adjusting for differentials in inflation rates, the pattern is much less clear. However, by simply deducting the current inflation rate from the nominal interest rate in each country to obtain approximate real rates, it becomes quite easy to observe the alignment of real interest rates across currencies.

This evidence is strongest since early 1994, after the fallout from the end of the 1993 global bull market in bonds. It is also strongest in currencies with the most liquid markets and the deepest forward currency cover, including U.S. dollars, yen, and Deutsche marks. This alignment started with the breakdown of the ERM. The ERM breakdown signaled to the market that not only European central banks, but also the Federal Reserve and the Bank of Japan, were relatively powerless to control foreign exchange rates if the market wanted to move them. There was a sharp break in the holding period premium relationships between interest-bearing instruments denominated in U.S. dollars, Deutsche marks, and yen at the time of the ERM breakdown that started the convergence of real yield curves. Then, after the Federal Reserve raised interest rates in early 1994, real yield curves in these currencies aligned very quickly.

Exhibit 5.2 illustrates these shifts in alignment. As recently as 1992, the real yield curves of the United States, Japan, and Germany

Exhibit 5.2.   Real Yield* Curves in the United States, Japan, and Germany, 1992, 1994, 1995

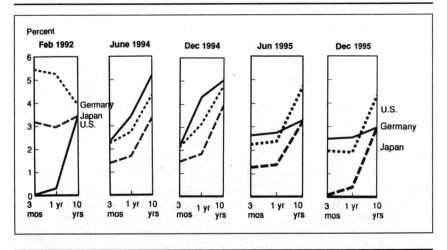

* Nominal government bond yields less change in previous year's CPI.
Source: Bloomberg; DRI; McKinsey analysis.

held no resemblance to one another. Since early 1994, the yield curves of the United States, Japan, and Germany have been remarkably close for a sustained period. In fact, the holding period premiums across all major countries has remained within a relatively small band compared to history for well over 18 months (Exhibit 5.3).

Skeptics have argued, however, that this alignment is so recent it could simply be a coincidence, reflecting a temporary situation such as one seen previously in the holding period premium (e.g., during 9 months in 1989). They also could note that the alignment of the holding period premium was less close in late 1995 than in 1994 and early 1995. We could argue that this change in alignment simply demonstrates that central banks still have considerable ability to impact rates. Whereas the intervention of central banks, particularly when coordinated among major nations, due to other major shocks, will still have a destabilizing impact, this impact will be diminished and likely of short duration. Even as central banks become more adept at intervening, either

Exhibit 5.3.   Holding Period Premiums,* United States, Japan, and Germany, 1983–1995

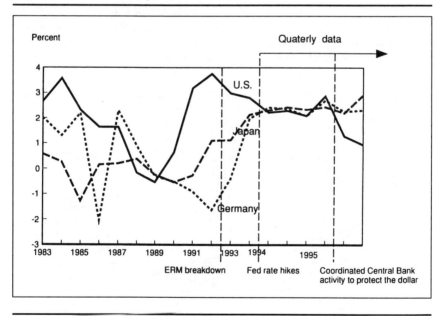

* Difference between the 10-year yield and 3-month yield; annual data from 1983 to 1994, quarterly data for 1994 and 1995.
Source: The Economist; McKinsey analysis.

by activity at different maturities, or through greater coordination, their adeptness will be matched by that of the market so long as the intervention is counter to the market direction. When intervention favors the market direction, it will be effective and help drive integration. Short-term (and even medium-term) aberrations may still take place, but over time, the periods of tight integration will last longer and longer as hunters become more powerful and more resourceful at hunting down anomalies (woolly mammoths) caused by central bank action.

To achieve any significant impact, central banks must now coordinate and bring their combined resources to bear. This was the case in 1995 when the combined coordination of the major central banks to protect the dollar flattened the U.S. dollar yield curve relative, in particular, to the Japanese yen yield curve and did help cause the dollar to strengthen relative to the yen. However, as the global capital market continues to grow and integrate, we believe even the coordinated actions of central banks are likely to have a diminishing impact.

The pattern is even stronger when you look across all the major currencies. Over the last several years, the consistency of yield curves (i.e., holding period premiums) across countries is considerable. As recently as 1992, the holding period premium across countries showed no consistent pattern. Some countries, such as Germany and Spain, had inverted yield curves while other countries, such as the United States had steep positive yield curves. Now, the yield curves

Exhibit 5.4.   Holding Period Premium—1993, 1994, 1995

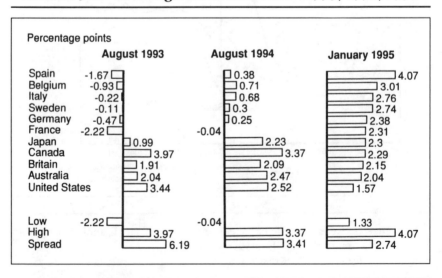

Percentage points	August 1993	August 1994	January 1995
Spain	-1.67	0.38	4.07
Belgium	-0.93	0.71	3.01
Italy	-0.22	0.68	2.76
Sweden	-0.11	0.3	2.74
Germany	-0.47	0.25	2.38
France	-2.22	-0.04	2.31
Japan	0.99	2.23	2.3
Canada	3.97	3.37	2.29
Britain	1.91	2.09	2.15
Australia	2.04	2.47	2.04
United States	3.44	2.52	1.57
Low	-2.22	-0.04	1.33
High	3.97	3.37	4.07
Spread	6.19	3.41	2.74

are positively sloped across all major countries and the holding period premium is within a relatively narrow range (see Exhibit 5.4). Again, this situation has been maintained for some time.

In addition, to the alignment of yield curves, there has been a second major change in how the market sets interest rates since late 1993. The market has developed the tendency to raise the differential between the real interest rates paid by the governments of highly indebted, "high-risk" nations, relative to the rates paid by the major, less indebted, "low risk," nations. High-risk nations are, in effect, paying a clear risk premium on their debt. In particular, the market appears to be acquiring greater sensitivity to the maturity-related risks of the relatively heavily indebted nations and of their prospects for adding to deficits going forward.

Exhibit 5.5 shows the real 10-year bond yields paid by Sweden, Italy, and Canada relative to the real 10-year bond yields paid by the

Exhibit 5.5.   Real Yields* on Long-Term Government Bonds, 1984–1995

Percentage points

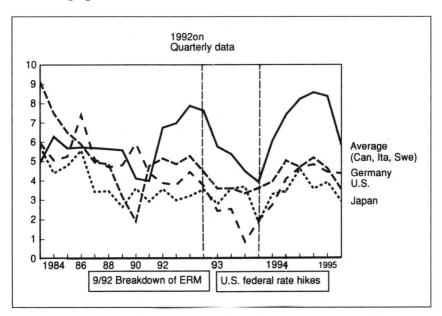

* Assumes the previous year's inflation level remains constant until the bonds' maturity.
Source: The Economist; McKinsey analysis.

Country Risk Premiums

Over the long run, investors, rather than those global market participants engaged primarily in financial arbitrage, will determine the real yields paid by each nation. Global investors are converging in their access to information, their valuation techniques, their analytic tools, and their use of derivatives. Over time, they will tend toward similar assessments of the interest-bearing instruments that have the best risk-adjusted returns (after the cost of hedging currency and other risks they want to avoid). Going forward, they will buy the interest-bearing instruments with the best risk-adjusted returns and will sell those with the worst. As a result, the yield curves will have further pressure to reflect fully differences in risk while causing the rates of instruments with similar risks to converge.

In fact, we believe that countries that are apparently viewed as risky are already beginning to pay significant, real country risk premiums relative to countries perceived as less risky. Once again, this is a disaggregation of risk, isolating the current inflation risk from future inflation and other risks in each currency. The kinds of future risks that investors may be including in these country risk premiums could be inflation risk, liquidity risk, political risk, credit (default) risk, or relative economic competitiveness. As the exhibit shows, again using very accessible data (e.g., bond rates and CPI), there is apparently a relationship between higher risk countries and higher country premiums. As also shown in the exhibit, there are nonetheless some anomalies. For example, Australia seems to be an anomaly in having to pay too much given its net debt to GDP and economic condition, whereas Belgium seems to pay too little given its very high debt to GDP ratio.

It is easy to see why investors are particularly concerned about Canada, Italy, and Sweden (Exhibit 5.6). Canada has high debt levels (particularly when provincial debt and national debt are added together) and has the added political risk of the possible secession of Quebec. Italy has one of the highest net debt to GDP levels in the world (117 percent). Finally, Sweden has a rapidly growing debt balance with an annual deficit of 13 percent annual deficit as a percentage of GDP, and a structural deficit of about 10 percent of GDP per year going forward despite a relatively low current net debt to GDP ratio. Of course, net debt is not the only indicator that concerns the market. Many other considerations are taken into account, including the rate of debt accumulation, the level of external to domestic debt, and the government policies toward businesses.

Exhibit 5.6.   Real 10-Year Yields and Estimated Country Premiums, 1995

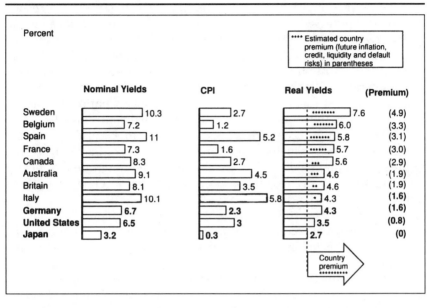

* Premium above inflation, greater than benchmark yields (Japan yield used for computing estimates); August 15, 1995 rate.
Source: Bloomberg, *The Economist;* McKinsey analysis.

United States, Germany, and Japan. During 1994 and persisting into 1995, the weighted average of the real yields paid on the 10-year government bonds in these three nations was well over 3 percent higher than the real yields paid on the weighted average of the government bonds of the United States, Germany, and Japan. In fact, the risk premiums being paid for the 10-year bonds by most nations is now generally aligned with the relative indebtedness of the nation and its perceived riskiness.

If these patterns continue, these highly indebted nations will be paying severe penalties to the market for absorbing the high risk of large debt levels, structured deficits, political instability, or inflation. And, of course, the high real rates make the debt itself difficult to service. Finally, the high real interest costs also are a large drag on the real economy of these nations.

THE PUZZLE

While the empirical evidence just provided is strong, the results are counterintuitive to most people and indeed to the theories that had been advanced prior to emergence of this evidence. Economists and market participants had long assumed that the equilibrium assumptions of the law of one price would continue to be satisfied by foreign exchange rate adjustments and the covered interest parity conditions and that interest rates would continue to be set by national financial markets and by the monetary policies of national central banks.

The central puzzle to most people is why in a world of multiple currencies is the pricing of real interest rates integrating? Why should interest rates align globally? After all, we had floating rates for nearly 20 years without any real integration of national interest rates. Why now?

To help answer this question, let's think for a moment about the alternative ways an economic or political shock to a particular nation can be reflected in the prices of financial instruments traded in the market.

To keep this from becoming overly complex, we will use a simplified example involving only two countries with one interest-bearing instrument each: Country A with a perpetual annuity bond yielding 10 percent and Country B with a perpetual annuity bond also yielding 10 percent. Both bonds are traded in the global capital market and one unit of Country A's currency can be exchanged for two units of Country B's currency. A major political shock takes place in Country B because the government increases spending and cuts taxes. This disturbs the existing equilibrium between the two countries' exchange rates and interest rates by 20 percent. Bonds in Country A now need to adjust in value by 20 percent to be once again equal in value to bonds in Country B. How does this shock get transmitted to exchange rates between the currencies in countries A and B, or to the value of their bonds? How do exchange rates and interest rates adjust to maintain parity across the two countries?

The answer is that the adjustment can take place in the exchange rate, in the interest rate in Country A, in the interest rate in Country B, or in a combination of changes in the exchange rate and interest rate in both currencies. If the interest rate in country A absorbed the total shock of the changes, interest rates must increase in Country A by 20 percent, causing the value of its bonds to fall in value by 20 percent. If the interest rate in Country B absorbed the total shock of the changes, the interest rate would have to fall by 20 percent. Alternatively, if the exchange rate fell from 2 to 1.6, the value of the bonds would be the same. Or, there is an infinite set of combinations of interest rate and exchange rate changes that would achieve the same effect. In reality, the global capital market clears prices for millions of bonds (which are not perpetual annuities) against an entire yield curve of interest rates across multiple currencies.

However, for most of the 20 years since the Bretton-Woods system broke down, most of the price adjustment for these kinds of shocks took place in foreign exchange rates rather than in interest rates. This was largely because central banks had significant control over domestic interest rates both through controlling the quantity of money in their economies, and through their regulatory authority over banks or other domestic financial institutions. Any one nation's control over exchange rates was more limited because the market for foreign exchange became global very quickly. Much of the control individual nations had over their own foreign exchange rates, other than through direct intervention, was through being able to raise domestic interest rates when they wanted their currency to appreciate or to lower interest rates when they wanted it to depreciate.

What then, happened to change these conditions of the marketplace? Why did the market change to a new state of matter?

We believe it was because the real interest differentials between nations combined with the increasing availability of forward foreign exchange cover (through forward foreign exchange contracts and currency swaps) across all major currencies for periods of up to 10 years created an abundance of large market anomalies to exploit. This foreign exchange cover created the opportunity to uniformly price foreign exchange risk and thereby exposed numerous market anomalies. And by the early 1990s, the number of participants engaged in pursuing these anomalies expanded both in number and effort. The hunters came out in droves to hunt for woolly mammoths.

In Chapter 3, we described how fund-raisers and investors used derivatives for either lowering their funding costs or increasing their returns to arbitrage real interest differentials. In the early 1990s, these differentials in interest rates between nations were very large. Within Europe, nations were trying to align their currencies through the European Rate Mechanism (ERM) as a step toward moving to a common currency. Interest rates in the lead currency of Europe, the Deutsche mark, were at very high levels, as the German Bundesbank was determined to fight the inflationary pressures of the reunification of East Germany. Meanwhile, in the United States, the Federal Reserve lowered rates dramatically to help combat the recession in the United

States and to help the U.S. commercial banking system recover after experiencing a massive credit crisis in 1988 to 1991.

This created unusual opportunities for market participants. For example, in 1992, it was possible to earn large returns by borrowing medium-term (e.g., 3 years) money in U.S. dollars at low interest rates, converting, those borrowing to Deutsche marks and then lending that money, short term, (e.g., 3 months) in Deutsche marks to German banks or to the German government itself through the purchase of notes. A forward foreign currency contract would then be used to cover the exchange risk for the short term Deutsche mark loan. This is an example of a trading practice we call cross-currency yield curve arbitrage. It involves borrowing in whichever currency has the lowest risk-adjusted interest rates, and lending in whichever currency has the highest risk-adjusted interest rates, net of forward foreign exchange cover. While this transaction has no foreign exchange risk, it does have interest rate risk. That is, this trading practice differs from covered interest arbitrage in that it does not cover interest rate risk—rather, it seeks out opportunities to take interest rate risk where the differentials in real interest rates are sufficiently attractive, relative to the risks.

These kinds of trading practices set the stage for the breakdown in the European Rate Mechanism in 1992.

The classic historic response central banks make to protect the value of their currency, when speculators are trying to devalue it, is to raise interest rates. Direct foreign exchange speculators that are expecting a currency to depreciate, borrow in that currency so they can convert it into a stronger currency they think will increase in value relative to the currency they are borrowing. Then, if the currency depreciates as expected, they convert back to the original currency and pay off their borrowings. This leaves them with a profit equal to the change in the relative value of the currencies less the difference between the interest they paid to borrow in the weaker currency and the interest they earned in the stronger currency while the transaction was outstanding.

Raising interest rates makes borrowing more expensive for speculators and signals that the central bank is prepared to defend the currency aggressively. It also increases the relative attractiveness of holding the currency for other market participants and raises the prospect that the currency will appreciate rather than depreciate. This prospect causes the speculators to worry that not only will they lose the extra interest they are paying on their borrowings but that the exchange rates will move against them thereby creating large losses.

However, unlike in the past, much of the speculation in 1992 was through the use of cross-currency yield arbitrage rather than through direct foreign exchange speculation. This was partly because the derivatives markets had matured to the point that forward cover in almost all currencies was relatively deep and partly because of the spreading knowledge of the technique. By 1992, central banks raising rates just increased interest rate yield curve differentials between currencies, which made cross-currency yield arbitrage more profitable. The more European central banks used short-term interest differentials to try to protect their currencies, the more profit opportunities they created for market participants.

By 1992, speculators practicing cross-currency yield arbitrage could simply borrow cheap money in another currency such as U.S. dollars, protect their exposure to foreign exchange risk through a forward foreign exchange contract, convert their borrowings to the local currency, and reap the high returns from the artificially high short-term rates being maintained by the central banks.

While the conversion of the borrowed dollars to local currency due to this trading practice would temporarily help strengthen the currency the central bank was supporting, the expiration of the forward foreign contracts at the completion of the transaction periods would then cause the currency to be sold again putting renewed pressure on the currency.

In 1992, for month after month, the German Bundesbank maintained its high rates. Since the Deutsche mark was the strongest currency in the ERM, this caused the central banks in nations such as the United Kingdom, France, Italy, and Sweden to maintain even higher rates to keep their currencies within the ERM band.

The continuing high short-term rates began to put more and more pressure on the domestic economies in these countries while making market participants undertaking cross-currency yield arbitrage richer and richer. As the stress on the system accelerated, direct currency speculators began to appear in volume. In direct currency speculation, participants seeking to profit from a devaluation of currency simply borrow at the prevailing high short-term rates and then sell the currency being attacked, without forward exchange cover, hoping that they will be able to make short-term gains that exceed their costs of borrowing. Speculators particularly attacked such currencies as the pound, krone, peseta, and lira. By late August 1992, the market was essentially market participants on one side and the central banks on the other. Finally, the losses to the various central banks became overwhelming, and the pressure on their domestic economies became politically intolerable; they threw in the towel in September 1992 and let the various European currencies float outside the ERM band.

Cross-Country Yield Arbitrage

As long as real yield curves in the currencies of countries perceived to have very similar risk profiles are different, there will be cross-country, yield curve interest rate arbitrage opportunities. As part of doing business, many banks and securities firms routinely take interest rate risk in their own currency (borrowing at a short-term rate and lending it out at fixed rates at longer maturities). For example, if an investor borrows at the 3-month rate at 4 percent and lends at the 5-year rate of 7 percent in a high credit quality instrument (a government instrument) the investor would earn a 3 percent yield, less the risk that interest rates will change, causing the fixed rate instrument to fall in value and increasing the cost of borrowing short. And, if that investor is willing to take interest rate risk in one currency, then he or she can enhance the real yield by lending it out at fixed rates in financial instruments of comparative credit risk and maturity in whichever currency has the highest real yield net of the cost of forward currency coverage. An investor could enhance real yields even further by borrowing in the currency with the lowest short-term real cost (net of the costs of forward currency cover).

In effect, the separation of the time-based interest rate risk versus the transaction-specific currency risk allows participants to engage in the cross-maturity, risk management activities they typically engage in, only now they can do so across currencies. As we saw in other cases, arbitrage will eventually result in the elimination of anomalies across real yield curves.

In fact, starting with the breakdown of the ERM, many global markets participants (global commercial banks, investment banks, and hedge funds) stepped up their cross-country, yield curve arbitrage activities. The more participants who engage in this type of cross-country yield arbitrage, the more anomalies will be eliminated and the higher the pressure for real, risk-adjusted yield curves to converge.

No one in the private sector knows how much money was lost by the European central banks but it has been estimated to have been in the tens of billions of dollars. The breakdown of the ERM in September 1992 was a watershed. Going forward, both the market and the central banks knew that in a contest of wills, the market was always going to win. While the European central banks tested the market again in June 1993, it was not a real contest as the markets won easily. By the fall of 1993, the central banks widened the ERM bands so much that they became essentially meaningless.

AFTER THE WATERSHED

The first breakdown of the ERM signaled the start of a great 1993 global bull market in bonds. As the European central banks quit using short-term interest rates to defend their currencies, their attention shifted to the recessions in their domestic economies, which had been largely caused by the high rates and they steadily lowered their short-term rates. Meanwhile, the U.S. Federal Reserve continued to lower short-term dollar rates. Bond prices, worldwide, were buoyant and global bond traders made extraordinary amounts of money.

As yields began to fall worldwide, there was a global scramble for yield. Market participants lacking opportunity in the major currencies, began to look for high returns in the bonds of more highly indebted nations and of emerging markets. Some market participants simply speculated in the bonds of these currencies directly. Others practiced cross-currency yield arbitrage, borrowed in dollars or yen, bought forward foreign exchange coverage, and then bought the debt issues of such highly indebted nations as Canada, Italy, or Sweden or the bonds of emerging nations. The result was a significant convergence of bond yields of these nations with the bond yields of Germany, Japan, and the United States.

Then, in September 1993, the Federal Reserve raised short-term interest rates. Everyone took it as a signal that the global bond bull market was over and simultaneously sought to cover their interest rate risks. Over the next several months, there was a bloodbath in the global bond markets. The Federal Reserve's actions exposed many participants who were taking more risks than they thought. In fact, two elements of risk were involved in cross-country yield arbitrage, the interest rate risk across currencies and additional risks associated with individual countries (future inflation, relative economic competitiveness, political upset, and default).

In other words, some participants who thought they were simply arbitraging yield curves with equivalent risks found out that they were arbitraging yield curves with different risks. In fact, many participants practicing cross-border yield arbitrage simultaneously went to cover their interest rate risks by, for example, selling their most liquid, long-term fixed rate instruments, such as 10-year U.S. treasuries, or 10-year Japanese government bonds, to shorten the duration of their interest rate mismatches. As they did this at the same time, bond prices plummeted worldwide, yields went up, and participants moved from higher risk, less liquid, long-term instruments to lower risk, more liquid, short-term instruments. By the time this trading frenzy was completed, the markets had begun to act differently and the empirical evidence cited earlier showing the alignment of yield curves and the emergence of significant risk premiums for highly indebted nations began to appear. By early 1994, the market had gone through a state-of-matter change. It was no longer a liquid. It was a solid. Yield curves worldwide were moving into alignment and country premiums between less risky and more risky nations became clearly visible.

THE GLOBAL FINANCIAL LAW OF ONE PRICE

Can we now unlock the puzzle of why in a world of multiple currencies real interest rates are integrating? Can we offer a theory that can explain the empirical evidence we see?

We believe so.

Prior to 1992, central banks, by using their control of short-term interest rates, could cause investors to hold or sell the nation's currency and thus get the currency to appreciate or depreciate, or they could use direct intervention (often in coordination with other central banks) as buyers or sellers in the spot exchange market to achieve the same effect. In doing so, they caused changes in the exchange rate that were subsequently reflected in the structure of interest rates in that currency. At times, direct central bank intervention in the currency markets was sufficient to cause spot exchange rates to adjust, which then caused interest rates in the currency to adjust in order to return to a pricing equilibrium. At other times, central bank intervention in the interest rate markets was sufficient to cause adjustment of spot exchange rates that reestablished a pricing equilibrium. In either case, the central bank achieved the short-term control of the spot exchange rate it sought. In the process, interest rates in that currency would reflect, as a risk premium, any expected future central bank activity that would affect exchange rates.

Foreign exchange risk and interest rate risk were, thus, significantly comingled in shaping the yield curve of any given country and in driving the movement of spot exchange rates. Thus, while individual traders, investors, and other market participants were able to use derivatives to capture market anomalies, the market as a whole was still aggregating the foreign exchange risks and interest rate risks together.

However, the continuing diminishment of the ability of central banks to control spot exchange rates and interest rates is a catalyst in allowing the full disaggregation of foreign exchange and interest rate risks.

As this breakdown into components occurs, the market can more and more precisely separate the various foreign exchange risks and interest rate risks from each other and price them more uniformly. Aggregated risks cannot be arbitraged. Disaggregated, uniformly priced risks can be arbitraged. Once the risks are isolated and uniformly priced, then arbitrage takes over. The volume of arbitrage grows to whatever volume it takes to cause the market pricing to adjust. This is what we believe has been happening in 1994 and 1995 in the world's interest rate markets. While this process is still incomplete, there are no real obstacles to the full integration of the developed world's interest rate markets.

We are now ready to propose a variant theory to the law of one price that will begin to hold true more extensively going forward. We can define the "global financial law of one price" as follows:

- In the absence of impediments to exchange and to the uniform pricing of risk, all tradable financial instruments and currencies with equivalent risk must sell at the same price everywhere, allowing for transactions costs.

- The relationship between the prices of tradable instruments with equivalent risk is brought about through financial arbitrage.

- In the short and long run, the financial arbitrage of tradable instruments causes all financial instruments and currencies to trade at their relative financial risk/return parity to each other.

For government bonds in a single national market, the yield curve captures the one market price for each risk level, in this case the maturity of bonds with equivalent credit risk. A country's yield curve, then, is a schematic expression of the financial law of one price for government bonds, which represents prices for interest-bearing instruments with equivalent credit risk but with a different maturity in a given market. A risk/return curve is also a schematic expression that extends beyond the traditional yield curve to include instruments with higher risk than government bonds, such as equities and even real estate. A single country's risk/return curve is typically upward sloping, with lower risk instruments yielding lower returns, and higher risk instruments yielding higher returns.

Placing the risk/return curves of multiple countries in one market would result in multiple, possibly differently shaped, risk/return curves because the global capital market is not yet fully integrated. However, the constant pressure of investors looking for the highest possible risk-adjusted yields, issuers seeking opportunities to raise funds more cheaply, and intermediaries arbitraging and taking positions wherever they find market anomalies (returns too high for the risks taken), will continue driving alignment toward a more uniform global risk/return relationship. Since financial instruments must be denominated in a specific currency, there is always a currency-specific risk component to all financial instruments. Thus, we would expect the markets to converge in the long run to a single global risk/return relationship when currency-specific and all other risks are explicitly and consistently priced.

As described earlier, a critical barrier to integration, and thus to the operation of the law of one price, is risk. So long as equivalent risk across countries or markets is obscure, pricing across markets remains susceptible to highly subjective assessments of risk by all the market participants. As information barriers have come down, and risk management techniques such as derivatives have developed, risks have been more clearly isolated, more transparent, and more explicitly priced. Importantly, this isolation and clarification of risk makes pricing more consistent and uniform across markets, and allows for further application of the global financial law of one price. The application of the global financial law of one price is, in effect, the creation of "perfect markets" through the continuous isolation and pricing of all types of current and future risks, including currency, interest rate, inflation, and even default. In Appendix 5B, we describe the importance of covered rate parity and forward currency rates in the application of the global financial law of one price.

Investors are increasingly linking together the valuations of all the financial instruments being traded in the global marketplace. While, in the markets for goods and services, there is little linkage between, for example, the price of a haircut in Tokyo and the price of a haircut in Houston, in the financial economy the prices of all financial instruments are more often being linked together as, for example, the yield on a U.S. government dollar bond is being compared with the yield on a Japanese yen bond.

These linkages in the financial economy are a result of investors in the global marketplace seeking the highest risk-adjusted returns from their investments. As they seek to earn the highest risk-adjusted returns, they have become more willing to move their funds from one currency to another, from money market instruments to bonds, or equities, or from cash markets to derivative markets.

As the costs of settling transactions decline, as derivative contracts are better used to limit (for a price) specific risks, as information becomes more consistently available, as trading techniques and financial innovations spread, and as liquidity increases, more and more investors and intermediaries are shifting greater volumes of funds from one financial asset to another. In the process, they are directly creating tighter linkages across all globally traded financial instruments. Consequently, changes in the supply and demand for any one category of financial asset now have an impact on all others and vice versa.

By this same process, we believe equity markets will eventually integrate in accordance to the global financial law of one price. We will elaborate on this point later. However, we do not want to overstate the case. Factors other than the global financial law of one price will always affect market pricing. For example, the supply and demand for funds in the global real economy will always have a major role in establishing the global level of rates. Central bank intervention still has important effects. And external shocks of many sorts will create noise in the market. Moreover, despite all the integration that has taken place, we are not arguing that even interest rates and exchange rates are yet fully determined by the operation of the global financial law of one price. Many interruptions to the path of integration are possible including a shaking of participants' confidence in the markets, such as would take place if a series of highly publicized losses on derivatives erupted at once creating major liquidity constraints. Any such events would limit the operation of the global financial law of one price. For all these reasons, we are not proposing that integration is fully developed or could not be temporarily set back. We are arguing only that as barriers are eroded, ultimately this law will apply. In the meantime, as the transition to a fully integrated global capital market continues, rates are set by a combination of central bank action, local capital market forces, and global capital market forces. In fact, the continuing turbulence and turmoil in the global markets is an expected outcome of the integration process.

FUTURE EVOLUTION

The operation of the global financial law of one price could have other effects going forward. As the bond markets become more integrated, the notion of a global risk-free rate of return will acquire deeper meaning and can serve as a valuable indicator of the global cost of capital and relative risks. Already, we can estimate such a rate crudely. Moreover, as the global capital market evolves, the law of one price is likely to extend beyond government bonds to corporate bonds, and eventually, equities.

A Meaningful Global Risk-Free Rate of Return

Going forward, as a result of the continued interaction of the global capital market, we believe it may become increasingly possible to impute, meaningfully, a global real rate of return. This would be the minimum, global risk-free rate of return required on financial instruments, which is a well-developed theoretical construct. In reality, there are country-specific risk premiums associated with financial instruments denominated in every currency. Since financial instruments must have a currency denomination, that currency-specific risk component always will be embedded in the actual rates observed.

However, as real yields and holding period premiums for major countries with roughly similar risk profiles (such as the United States, Japan, and Germany) continue to align, it may become easier to estimate a global real rate of return. We use the rates of these three currencies as benchmark rates because these three countries are currently perceived by the market to have generally similar risk profiles. (If significant changes occurred to alter these profiles, they would no longer represent equivalent risks, and we would no longer expect their rates to be similar.) Presently, these benchmark countries have the lowest risk profile for interest-bearing instruments, and they can therefore be used to estimate a global real rate of return.

In January 1995, the real long-term government yields for the benchmark countries ranged between 5.1 percent for the United States and 3.7 percent for Japan. This was a narrow range of less than 140 basis points. If we use Japan as the benchmark rate to estimate the future risk premiums paid by other countries, this rate represents the minimum real yield required in the global capital market to raise 10-year fixed rate bonds.

At that time, the holding period premium for these countries had also converged within 20 basis points. In Japan, the holding period premium was 2.3 percent and in Germany and the United States, it was 2.1 percent. The weighted average holding period premium for these three countries was 2.2 percent, using purchasing power parity GDPs as the weighting factor.

As this holding period premium continues to converge, it will become feasible to disaggregate the global real yield further into a global real return component and a global holding period premium component. We can already make rough estimates of these components based on the January 1995 benchmark rate of 3.7 percent real yield and the weighted average holding period premium of 2.2 percent. Subtracting the holding period premium from the global benchmark rate, we obtain an estimated global real return rate of 1.5 percent. This percentage was the estimated real rate of return required to borrow funds in the global capital market that were free of holding period risk, credit risk, or any currency-specific risk, such as future inflation risk or future credit risk.

In other words, 1.5 percent was the estimated global risk-free rate of return required to produce an equilibrium in the global capital market (see Exhibit 5.7).

Before we complete the discussion of a global risk-free rate of return, we should briefly mention the countries (almost all the other countries) that are not viewed as being risk equivalents to these three major benchmark countries and that are paying a significant risk premium over the estimated global risk-free rate of return. This, itself is a change from history because at least from a credit risk perspective, almost all the sovereign governments in the developed world have

Exhibit 5.7.   Estimated Global Risk-Free Rate of Return, January, 1995

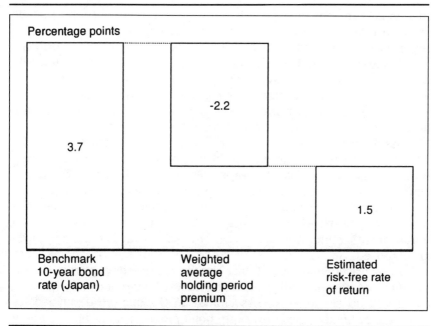

been viewed as being "risk-free." These remaining countries have been paying real risk premiums of anywhere from 1 percent to 4 percent versus the benchmark countries over the past 2 years. These risk premiums, not unexpectedly, have been relatively volatile. Canada's, for example, has varied from 1 to 4 percent. At the moment, it is impossible to say whether or not these risk premiums reflect future inflation risk, credit (default) risk, liquidity risk, political risk, or differences in the relative economic competitiveness of these nations. Perhaps the market will find a way to disaggregate these various risks and uniformly price them. At the moment, however, all we can say is that it is the most heavily indebted nations who tend to pay the highest premiums although there are anomalies.

These estimates of the global risk-free rate of return highlight two important and very interesting issues. The first is that the actual risk-free rate of return is quite low. The second is that the price of risk, as it is better understood and disaggregated, can be quite high, as the highly indebted countries illustrate.

Going forward, we would expect the market for government debt to continue to become more perfect, with the various risks better isolated and uniformly priced.

Corporate Bonds

Just as government bonds are becoming integrated, corporate bonds are also integrating more tightly. There are close price linkages between corporate bond rates and government bond rates in each national market. Indeed, the pricing of corporate bonds is typically derived as a premium above the relevant government bond rate of its home nation. Once the underlying government bonds become integrated, only the risk premiums relevant to the particular corporate bond issue remain to be uniformly priced.

As described in Chapter 3, both issuers and investors are continually pursuing pricing anomalies in corporate bonds through structured financing and asset swaps. Meanwhile, Standard & Poor's, Moody's and other rating agencies, are providing increasingly comparable, consistent information based on common analysis of information. More and more instruments are being developed to isolate and uniformly price liquidity risk and other risks to which corporate bonds are exposed. As a result, credit risk (and other risks) become more uniformly priced, and market participants pursue the arbitrage opportunities that become apparent. Going forward, more and more participants will do so. In a process similar to the one we described for government bonds, then, corporate bond prices around the world will trend toward integration.

Equities

We expect the global financial law of one price, in time, to extend even to corporate equities.

To some extent, corporate equity pricing is becoming more closely linked globally just because the bond markets are globalizing. In each national financial market, participants are always trading off investing in local bonds against local corporate equities. Therefore, to the extent that bond prices globalize, there is an indirect linkage across the world's equity markets.

Corporate equities, presently, are not very integrated. The pricing of equities of companies with similar prospects in the same industry, but headquartered in different countries, is usually quite different from nation to nation. This is not surprising. A corporate equity, particularly of a large complex firm, is a conglomeration of risks. These risks include, not just exposure to exchange risks and interest rates, but operating risks such as technological risk, industry structure change, and competitive risk. Moreover, the inadequacy of disclosure makes many of these risks opaque to the market. And the local equity markets in various countries are still very independent and are largely insider markets.

Despite these and other barriers, we expect most of these risks to be progressively disaggregated, uniformly priced, and arbitraged away.

Why do we think so?

It is simply because there is so much money to be made—particularly by investors.

As described in Chapters 2 and 3, the globalization of equities is already well started and has been led by global investors seeking out undervalued stocks in other countries and hoping to capture the benefits of diversification. These investors are now systematically searching across markets for anomalies. As their ownership grows, they are simultaneously pushing companies to disclose more information and are asking management hard questions.

Outside the United States and the United Kingdom, which already have demanding investors, companies in other countries that need to raise equity are having to adjust to the demands of global investors, which are quite different from their past cooperative relationships with local investors. And, as global competition mounts and creates needs for restructuring, and as companies contemplate the scale of investment required to convert global opportunities, more and more are beginning to consider raising equity capital from the global marketplace.

As with the foreign exchange and bond markets, derivatives are playing a critical role in the globalization process. Equity swaps are now being used to protect outside investors from insider trading practices. Equity investors are beginning to use currency derivatives, interest rate derivatives, and commodity derivatives to isolate and hedge many of those risks from the operating risks in the business. In the process, smart investors can increase their risk-adjusted returns enormously because they can overcome the higher risk premiums associated with taking risk in aggregated form.

A simplified example will illustrate this process. Assume you are an institutional investor wanting to invest in an independent oil producer that has just licensed a new oil production technology enabling it to increase its oil output by 30 percent. The company's earnings and stock price are exposed to significant currency risk, interest rate risk, and petroleum price risk. Also, the company, because of these risks, has to raise equity at three times its projected cash flows per share when these cash flows are more typically valued at nine times cash flows. You, as an institutional investor, explore opportunities to disaggregate the currency, interest rates, and petroleum risks and find that by giving up the equivalent of two times cash flow per share, you can effectively hedge these risks. You, therefore, have found a market anomaly. You can purchase equity for five times cash flows that should be valued at nine times cash flows.

Such risk-structuring tools are not just available to institutional investors. In fact, companies themselves, are already using these tools to undertake foreign direct investment. As companies seek to leverage techniques of production advantages globally, they are often willing to invest locally, perhaps in combination with a local partner, to outcompete local competitors using less efficient methods. As they do this, they too, use derivatives and structuring techniques to shed the risks they do not want and to keep the risks and the returns they do want. In the process, they too, can increase the risks and returns enormously and in the process, their stock in their home markets becomes more attractive.

As yet, the global capital market does not offer a sufficient array of derivative services to permit the full integration of the equity markets. This is particularly true of the developing countries, where the ability to hedge currency and interest rate risk is not yet available. However, as innovation proceeds and as more and more countries enact financial reforms and build their financial infrastructure, more and more of the needed financial instruments will become available.

As the equity markets globalize, the world's equity investors will increasingly push companies to perform better. Equity investors provide capital to those companies they think can make the best use of it. Local companies used to comfortable local oligopolies suddenly begin to feel the heat of outside competitors using superior techniques of production. Local companies with competitive advantages will be driven to seek out global opportunities before their competitors find them. Winning companies with higher market capitalization will take over weaker companies with smaller market capitalizations—globally.

As the pace of competition intensifies, so do the stakes. And this in turn raises the pressure to perform, which, once again, raises competitive intensity. And so on.

As this process unfolds, the equity markets are slowly integrating; eventually, the world will have uniform valuation approaches to equities.

Unlike the integration of the bond markets, which has its greatest impact on governments (but with still huge impact on the private sector), the integration of the equity markets will have its greatest impact on the private sector where it will accelerate the spread of global capitalism.

The path is clear.

It is just a matter of time.

THE APPROACH TO ABSOLUTE ZERO

We are moving toward a global capital market where the financial law of one price is completely operational. If we get to absolute zero, we will have a fully integrated, perfect global capital market. Capital, at that stage, will be completely mobile, and you will have the equilibrium pricing of risk worldwide.

We have used the absolute zero analogy throughout this chapter. However, the analogy is not perfect. To approach absolute zero, you need to create extraordinary laboratory conditions. The movement to a fully integrated global capital market, where the global financial law of one price is completely operational, requires no such extraordinary effort. It is happening naturally out of the self-interest of the world's market participants acting as individuals.

We are not yet close to having a fully integrated global capital market. We are not yet approaching absolute zero. Perhaps we will never ever get completely there. Even the physicists in Colorado only got to within a few billionths of a degree of absolute zero.

But we are headed in that direction. And the world is already changing as a result.

In particular, we believe it is now possible to observe a global capital market that is meaningfully intermediating the supply and demand of capital flows worldwide. We believe the implications of this increase in global capital mobility are profound. We believe we are witnessing the early stages of a fundamental transformation of how the world's economy works and how the power of the nation state is exercised.

* * * *

In the next part of the book, we will explore what we believe such a world will look like. We will explore a world whose economy will be driven by global capitalism.

Appendix

— 5A —

Exchange Rates and Purchasing Power Parity

In the late 1970s and early 1980s, several economists and academicians, particularly at multilateral institutions such as the International Monetary Fund (IMF), once again revisited the theory of PPP (purchasing power parity) to explain movements in exchange rates. First exposed in the 16th century by the Spanish economists of the Salamanca school, and later restated by Cassel and Keynes, PPP is a variation of the law of one price equilibrium condition applied to multiple currencies. The PPP theory essentially argued that exchange rates were determined by trade arbitrage as follows:

- In the absence of impediments to trade, all tradable goods must sell at the same price everywhere, allowing for the cost of transportation.

- Commodity arbitrage brings about the relationship between exchange rates and the prices of tradable goods.

- In the long run, commodity arbitrage of tradable goods causes currencies to trade at their purchasing power parity.

In fact, as we described earlier in this chapter, empirical evidence has convinced economists that PPP exchange rates often diverge from market exchange rates by a considerable amount and that exchange rates do not reflect changes in the prices of tradable goods, at least in the short term.

Nonetheless, it seems irrefutable that the purchasing power of a currency in the real economy is ultimately important. Over the long run, the purchasing power parity in the real economy should move toward equilibrium through the trade of goods and services, through the migration of people, and through the operation of global companies transferring best practice and technology worldwide. Over the long term, these supply-and-demand adjustments in the real economy must be very powerful.

The problem was that even by the late 1970s and 1980s, let alone today, purchasing power parity was a weak force in the short term compared with the speed and power of changes in supply and demand for a currency within the financial economy. As we explained in Chapter 4, financial markets react far faster than markets for goods and services in the real economy and, due to the growing size and integration of the financial stock relative to the real economy, financial markets dominate price movements of foreign exchange rates and interest rates at any moment in time.

Appendix

—5B—

Forward Currency Rates

The existence of covered rate interest parity is no surprise since it is ensured by the efficiency of the market in arbitraging risk-free returns. Technically, it is made possible by the existence of an extensive, forward currency market. The "profit" opportunities from covered interest arbitrage ensure the existence of forward markets whenever there are real, risk-adjusted differential interest rates. With sufficient financial stock, liquidity of financial instruments, sound counterparties, and relatively low transaction costs, the covered parity condition is likely to continue to hold indefinitely for all major currencies (and increasingly hold for other currencies joining the global capital market).

These profit opportunities are typically in the form of lower funding costs (for borrowers) or enhanced yields (for lenders), as well as arbitrage profits for market participants. For example, two companies can enter into an interest rate swap that lowers their borrowing costs because their borrowing costs are different in two markets (fixed rate vs. variable rate markets). Similarly, so long as lending rates for equivalent risk instruments are different in two currencies, lenders in one currency can enhance their yield by sharing the differential in rate with lenders in another currency.

The point can be stated more generally for two currencies A and B, each with a different interest rate structure: Any holder of a financial asset or liability currently exposed to a time-based risk in currency A can enhance the return on the asset, or reduce the cost of the liability, by sharing the difference in the interest rate between currencies A and B with another party exposed to an equivalent time-based risk in currency B. Therefore, so long as there are differences in interest rates in two currencies, and financial assets and liabilities in both currencies, there will be willing participants on both sides of the market to engage in forward exchange rate contracts. (To be complete, other conditions must also hold, such as low transaction costs, liquidity in the market, and sound counterparties.) Supply and demand for forward contracts between two currencies will be in equilibrium at only one price, which will be based on the current relative structure of interest rates and the current spot exchange rate. Forward rates, then, are nothing more than the derived price of currencies for future delivery that provides the equilibrium supply and demand given the interest rate structures in the currencies at a given spot exchange rate. Said differently, forward rates can be thought of as a family of exchange rates that uniformly price interest-bearing instruments in two currencies with different time horizons at the current spot exchange rate.

Often, in discussing forward instruments, many people assume that they are used primarily as speculative instruments. In fact, most "speculation" on future changes is undertaken by investors simultaneously borrowing and lending in two different currencies, or by entering into options agreements. In this way, they capture the profits, (the reduced lending costs or enhanced yields) of anomalies across yield curves in different currencies.

A commonly held view maintains that the forward foreign exchange rate is a forecast of future exchange rates and interest rates. According to this view, if the forward rate does not, on average, turn out to equal the future spot rate, it implies that speculators are "passing up an opportunity for profit," and that is not highly likely. In fact, forward rates are very poor predictors of foreign exchange rates, interest rates, or yield curve shapes. Empirically, an SC First Boston Fixed Income Research study (later published in *Euromoney* in 1994) provides substantial evidence throughout the period from 1977 to the present, that a projection of unchanged rates, or even of a flat yield curve, is a more accurate forecast of interest rates than that made by forward rates. This empirical outcome is not a result of the consistently inaccurate expectations of currency behavior held by speculators. Rather, it reflects that at any given point in time, it is a derived price given the difference in the term structure of interest rates between two currencies at today's spot exchange rate. As such, speculators "betting" against the forward rate are equally subject to the implied interest cost of borrowing or lending in those currencies.

Many people still believe that forward contracts should reflect expectations of future exchange rates because they think about forward contracts as settlements in the future, exposing parties to the risk of an outstanding position. As a result, they argue that if the derived rate technically resulted in a 1-year forward contract at $10 per

DM, no one would be willing to enter into that contract with another party because no one believes the exchange rate will move to $10 per DM, and no one is willing to be left holding that position. In that case, follows the argument, there will be no willing participants on both sides, and therefore no forward market. This perspective fails to acknowledge the important link described previously, which is that the forward market would only move (be derived) to $10 per DM if interest rates reflected that differential at the current spot exchange rate. In fact, forward contracts are often not really settlements in the future. Rather, they are agreements priced at today's spot exchange rate, based on today's relative term structure of interest rates, between parties with financial positions already existing in different currencies.

Part Two

Unleashing Global Capitalism

—6—

Prosperity or Devastation?

$\mathbf{L}$ike fire, the gift of Prometheus to humanity, full capital mobility can either benefit the world or harm it. Fire has the potential to provide warmth and light, but it also can cause death and destruction.

The movement toward full capital mobility likewise has the potential to benefit all of us. It has the power to unleash a wave of global capitalism that will provide prosperity to the world's citizens. But, if the governments of the world misstep, it has the potential to create financial instability that could devastate the world's economy.

We believe that full capital mobility is likely to bring us prosperity because it can cause the world's savings to be invested most productively, rather than being poorly invested, or consumed by national governments through spending on entitlements.

In an integrated global capital market with full capital mobility, the balance of supply and demand is determined globally rather than nationally. As explained in Chapter 5, we are beginning to have a global capital market that is sufficiently integrated to enable us to speak of full capital mobility as an actual, rather than a theoretical concept. No longer bound by national borders, investors of savings from anywhere in the world have greater freedom to seek their best use anywhere else in the world. Thus, changes in the supply or demand of capital in one part of the world may have important consequences for the rest of the world and the global economy. Although we are not yet in a world of full capital mobility, we are rapidly heading in that direction. And, as we will see in this chapter, dramatic changes in both the supply and demand for capital around the world, and in the allocation of that capital, already have significant implications for the world economy.

Over the next 20 years, the world's economy will see a windfall of savings due to demographic effects. The central question is, Will these savings be invested or will they be consumed by developed world governments issuing debt to finance entitlements?

Demographic changes in the developed world are likely to lead to a dramatic surge in household savings, particularly savings that are invested in financial assets. The resulting increase in capital supply probably will be greater than any we have experienced since World War II. While investment opportunities in the developed world will continue to represent a large share of global investment, they are unlikely to increase proportionately to the coming capital wave. The developing world, with enormous growth potential and numerous high-return investment opportunities, will be a major source of new capital demand, and governments in the developed world will be another source. Faced with powerful pressure to increase spending on pensions and health care as their populations age, and to keep taxes in check, developed nations are likely to continue to issue large amounts of debt. This capital demand by government, however, will be used for consumption, or dissaving, rather than for investment.

Optimistically, we see the potential for the global capital market to act as a powerful check on the tendency of governments in the developed world to issue debt. By the straightforward act of making that debt increasingly costly, the market may be able to force the recognition and correction of fiscal policies that, in any event, are unsustainable in the long run. Moreover, by instigating these policy corrections before countries reach painful limits to debt, the market will strongly encourage further increases in real household saving. Finally, the higher returns to investment made possible by the global capital market will determine the extent to which pensioners' savings provide sufficient returns for retirement, further easing the social burden on government. These potential benefits comprise the foundation of a true global capital revolution that can result in rapid economic growth.

On the other hand, there is a less likely, but still significant risk that governments will ignore the messages sent by the global capital market. Political pressure on democratically elected governments is enormous and may cause them to go so deeply into debt that the stability of the world's economy is disrupted. Countries such as Canada and Italy have already encountered some of these difficulties. The prospect for financial instability is real, based on the wealth destruction that would result from any widespread default on government debt. Moreover, any erosion in the confidence of the value of government safety nets, such as deposit insurance, could provoke a global liquidity crisis leading to extreme financial disorder with destructive consequences to the global economy for goods and services.

Obviously, there is a range of outcomes between the two extremes. We firmly believe that the potential for more beneficial outcomes is far greater than for destructive outcomes: The global capital market provides many opportunities to satisfy the capital supply-and-demand needs across different parts of the world, and across different time periods, since the peaks of supply and demand occur at different times.

Before we get into whether we are headed for prosperity or devastation, let's first examine the supply-and-demand changes we have touched on, and the needs that each implies. Then we will turn to the benefits of the global capital market. These benefits can unleash a true global capital revolution. To provide balance, we will then describe some of the concerns and fears surrounding such a revolution. Finally, we describe a range of outcomes, providing detail around the best and worse cases.

CAPITAL SUPPLY

Savings are, by definition, the source of capital supply in the economy. In theory, all participants in the economy—households, businesses, governments—can save. Households save anything they do not consume, corporations save the portion of corporate profits not paid out in dividends, and governments can run budget surpluses, and therefore save the difference between tax revenues and expenditures. Household savings are by far the most meaningful source of savings.

Our research indicates that liquid, household financial savings will grow rapidly over the next 25 years due to demographic changes in the developed world. This added supply of capital will peak between the years 2015 and 2025 but is already having a meaningful effect. Our findings are contrary to the contention of conventional wisdom that the household saving rate and with it, the rate of financial asset accumulation, will decline over the next several years as the baby boomer generation, which is viewed to be made up of "spenders" rather than "savers," gets older.

A careful assessment of the evidence dispels this conventional view. Our research concludes that far from diminished financial asset accumulation, we can expect a bonus of about $4.6 trillion from household saving in the developed economies just through the year 2000. Appendix 6A describes the model we used to arrive at our estimates. The extraordinary growth in household savings will continue until around 2020 and is driven by the aging of the populations in the developed world and concomitant economic behavior.

Why We Focus on Household Financial Assets

Savings per se include many relatively illiquid assets. For households, savings include investments in residential homes and land, and for corporations savings include corporate inventory and capital consumption allowances. These savings are not really part of the integrating global capital market because the assets are not liquid—they are not easily converted into money.

In time, sophisticated financial instruments may make residential homes, or corporate inventories, highly liquid. Today, however, that is not really the case. Therefore, the truly relevant portion of savings for discussion of global capital mobility is that which goes toward the accumulation of liquid assets, which are intermediated through the financial system and through financial markets. As described in earlier chapters, these savings directly contribute to the stock of financial assets in the global capital market.

To the extent that corporations are saving (retaining profits), they are directly impacting the equity of their shareholders, who ultimately are households with equity shares in the company. These shares are valued through the equity markets, which are increasingly integrated into the global capital market. Thus, by capturing net financial assets of households, we are capturing the relevant and liquid portion of corporate savings as well.

Finally, most governments in practice do not save at all, but instead run significant budget deficits and are major net borrowers (dissavers) of capital.

For these reasons, household net financial assets, equal to total financial assets less outstanding financial liabilities, best approximate the supply of liquid savings that are available to be allocated by the global capital market.

Socking It Away

As is generally known, household income levels and saving rates vary with age. In general, people borrow when they are in their 20s and 30s, they are in balance in their early 40s, save from their late 40s until they retire, when they then run down their nest eggs. Within that general pattern, different generations exhibit different behavior, with some generations borrowing more in their 20s and 30s and others saving more in middle age (such as those who were young adults during the Great Depression). So, a country's personal saving rate changes with the age mix of its population and with the changing behavior of new generations. Interestingly, savings are generally not very responsive to changes in the rate of return, that is, higher rates of return do not generally induce higher savings, or vice versa.

Between now and the year 2010, the proportion of the developed world's population in their high saving years (those aged 45–64) will increase dramatically, from 39 percent to 45 percent, while the proportion of the population of low savers (those aged 20–44) will fall, from 44 percent to 34 percent (see Exhibit 6.1). Moreover, this high saving group appears to be saving at even higher rates than people who were born during the Great Depression or during World War II (although not as much as those who were young adults during the Great Depression). The combined effect of a surge of people entering their peak savings years and saving at a higher rate than the people born in the 1920, 1930s, and early 1940s, produces a startling increase in personal savings. Moreover, with some variation, these patterns are similar in many developed world countries.

Exhibit 6.1.   Savers as a Percentage of the Potential Workforce,* 1950–2025

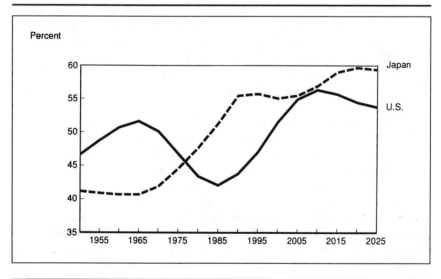

* Population 40–64 years of age divided by population 20–64 years of age.
Source: UN population data; McKinsey analysis.

Modeling Household Net Financial Assets

To estimate the magnitude of the demographic changes on the supply of capital, or on household net financial assets, our colleague Kevin Berner, in conjunction with the McKinsey Global Institute, developed a simulation model for U.S. households. The simulation model incorporates the effects of demographic changes, capital gains, and bequests and inheritances. For more details on the model, see Appendix 6A.

Because the developed economies represent such a large share of the world economy, these demographic changes are likely to result in an avalanche of savings flows into the global capital market. We estimate that from 1992 to 2002, household net financial asset accumulation will increase by $12 trillion in 1992 dollars. Of this $12 trillion, a full $6 trillion will come from the United States alone. To put this $12 trillion in context, it is equal to about one third of the world's entire stock of financial assets in 1992, which we estimated to be $35 trillion.

To make these estimates, or any other prediction about the future, we must make some assumptions about the world going forward. We assumed that the underlying growth in income that countries have experienced will continue. We also assumed that the slightly higher rates of saving observed in younger generations will continue for future generations. We then tested how various other assumptions would impact the estimates. There is almost no reasonable scenario of assumptions about the growth in income, or the saving patterns of younger generations, that does not yield a significant increase in liquid household financial savings over the next 20 years

An extreme assumption will show the underlying strength of the trend. Since the end of World War II, countries in the developed world have experienced average economic growth of 3 to 4 percent per year. Even if we assume that over the next 20 years household income levels will fall by 10 percent across the board, due to a global recession (versus the positive 30 percent which is the historical average), household financial asset accumulation would still increase substantially as a result of demographic changes. In this dismal case, the estimated increase in financial asset accumulation in the United States over the decade would be not $6 trillion, but instead $5 trillion, which is still very large.

Moreover, these estimates are probably conservative, since other drivers that were not explicitly quantified in the model may contribute even further to growth in aggregate household financial assets. For example, going forward households are likely to have greater access to higher-return financial assets, which might allow households to accumulate financial assets more rapidly. Appendix 6B describes the polarization of income and wealth and its potential impact on capital supply.

Let's, for a moment, focus on U.S. households. For most of the period since World War II, U.S. households have held the large part of their financial savings in bank deposits. What this has meant is that households have not enjoyed very high returns on their financial assets. Especially in highly inflationary years such as the 1970s, bank deposits in the United States yielded real returns (returns after inflation) that were actually negative for many years.

It is surprising that for the entire period from 1945 to 1990, real capital gains on all U.S. household financial assets were, on average, close to zero, though individual years yielded in some cases very high real positive returns and in other cases very low or negative returns particularly in the 1970s when inflation was high and returns on bank deposits were low. The problem was that only a small share of U.S. households held anything other than deposits, so most were not benefiting from high returns in equities or bonds, although many profited from the surge in the market value of their homes during this period. Even as recently as 1973, the share of household financial assets in bank deposits was as high as 51 percent, and a relatively small share of households owned any equities. Only since the 1980s have mutual funds in the United States made possible small, well-diversified, professionally managed investments in securities, which have attracted the mass market.

Now, however, more and more U.S. households are keeping a smaller share of their financial assets in bank deposits and are holding a much larger share in investments with higher returns, including money market funds, bond funds, equity funds, and direct equity holdings. The composition of U.S. household financial assets has changed sharply since 1973. By 1986, deposits represented only 40 percent of household financial assets with the remaining 60 percent being equities, fixed income securities, and mutual funds.

In 1993, bank deposits were only 29 percent of the total. More households are benefiting from higher returns on equities, and thus the average capital gain on financial assets is likely to go up. If capital gains do increase, so too will the accumulation of financial assets by households, and thus capital supply. An increase of only two tenths of a percent in the average capital gains earned by households on their financial assets would augment capital supply in the United States by an additional $300 billion over the same 10-year span (1992–2002).

Similar patterns hold for many other developed world countries. For the developed world, our total estimates amount to nearly $12 trillion. For all the reasons cited, we believe our estimates of savings are, if anything, conservative. Appendix 6C attempts to dissipate confusion about the difference between our capital supply estimate and many doomsday scenarios about declining savings.

Where Will All the Money Go?

If these savers expect to retire in reasonable comfort or to provide for the next generation, financial intermediaries acting on their behalf will need to find investments that yield high risk-adjusted rates of return.

The need for good investments is especially important since governments in many countries, which have been financing public pensions almost entirely out of current tax receipts (or debt), will find it difficult to meet their future pension liabilities as the ratio of retirees to active workers increases. It seems probable that future retirees will have to count more heavily on private pensions than has been the case in the recent past.

Sole focus on finding investment opportunities in the developed world could well prove dangerous. The rate of return on capital in the United States has been lower in the past 20 years than it was in the 1950s and 1960s. And the same demographic trends that will lead to more retirees in the future will also mean a slowly growing labor force in the years ahead, another factor possibly reducing capital needs. If significant increases in productive investment in the developed world are really unlikely, attempts to increase investment in that arena would likely run into diminishing returns, driving down the rate of return available and reducing the ability of the developed economies to provide adequately for retirees.

The experience of the 1980s in Japan illustrates the problem of having too much capital and too few opportunities. Japan pursued a monetary policy that kept interest rates low. In Japan in the 1980s, as its preretirement, high-saving age group grew rapidly as a percentage of the total population, a huge supply of capital became available for investment.

At the same time, there were limited opportunities for individual investment in assets other than domestic bank deposits because households had limited opportunities to own homes, they were hesitant to invest abroad, and regulations restricted domestic participants from offering financial instruments (e.g., mutual funds, international equities) that would make investment in other countries accessible. Moreover, most households in Japan, like those in other nations, strongly prefer to keep their savings in bank deposits or with life insurance companies.

The recipients of these funds—the banks, life insurance firms, and other financial institutions—lacking attractive returns on interest-bearing instruments, such as loans or bonds, became heavily involved in speculation in the limited markets available—primarily stocks and real estate.

The resulting combination of low real investment opportunities and cheap credit fueled what became known as the "bubble" economy: The financial valuation of stocks and real estate lost any relationship to the real economy. For example, the market capitalization of the Industrial Bank of Japan had a theoretical value of some $100 billion in the late 1980s when Deutschebank and J.P. Morgan, each with higher earnings, each had a market value of under $10 billion. Office buildings in Tokyo had theoretical values of nearly $10 billion at a time when similar buildings in Manhattan were valued below $500 million. The aftershocks of the bursting of this bubble, a full 60 percent decline in the Tokyo stock market and much greater declines in real estate values, still affect the Japanese economy today. There is a lesson here for all of us. Huge savings flow by themselves and do not create prosperity. Prosperity comes from investing savings in high return investments.

CAPITAL DEMAND

The good news for savers, and for all of us, is that if we continue to increase global capital mobility, much of their money can be channeled into high-return investments in the developing world. Expectations of rapid economic development and higher standards of living require that developing economies maintain high investment rates and acquire the skill, technology, and best practice to drive productivity increases. Despite very high saving rates in some developing countries, most of them will need to attract external capital to supplement their domestic savings. Our estimates suggest that in the next 10 years, the gap between domestic savings and investment needs in the developing world is likely to exceed $2 trillion in real terms. This gap is the minimum level of required external capital. And, as these countries join the global capital market, some of their existing capital will leave the country as "flight capital" as domestic savers seek to diversify their risks. Therefore, they will need to attract additional replacement capital.

And the need for capital is likely to increase far more significantly beyond 10 years, as growth in the developing countries accelerates.

Not only do these countries have the desire to grow rapidly, they have the opportunity to do so. There are almost unlimited opportunities to transfer best practice to the production of goods and the provision of services to China, India, Latin America, and many other countries. These markets are potentially enormous and have a large reserve of adequately skilled labor willing to work.

The opportunities in the developing world arise from low productivity levels coupled with lower wage levels. For example, recent work on Latin American productivity by the McKinsey Global Institute concludes that productivity levels in Latin America are only 30 to 40 percent of those in the United States, and labor costs are an even smaller fraction of the U.S. levels. The study convincingly concludes that these low levels are caused, not by poor labor skills or differences in output mix, but by external factors including onerous regulations, the low level of competition, and very importantly, poor organization of functions and tasks, as well as lack of capital. The opportunity for capital, accompanied by best practice know-how, to benefit from these productivity gaps is enormous.

Not surprisingly, typical returns to investment that are accompanied with best (or even simply better) practices in many of these markets range from 30 to 50 percent. These high returns reflect the richness of the opportunities available in these markets, but they also reflect the risks and difficulties of investment. As the global capital market integrates, investments in these markets are becoming more feasible, with attractive returns relative to the risks.

The global capital market also encourages governments in developing countries to create economic, political, and financial environments that will attract capital at lower costs. The large needs for capital place these countries constantly in competition with one another for external capital. They thus have powerful incentives to reduce the political and investment risks in their economies, which are responsible for a substantial portion of the high returns exacted on investments. If they want to attract external capital, these countries are strongly motivated to create a good economic and political environment for business—pursuing sound economic policies, maintaining a stable political environment, and committing to the necessary public infrastructure (e.g., education, transportation, sanitation) to ensure that these policies are successful. They must also recognize the need to develop a liberal financial policy and sound financial infrastructure that enables full capital mobility; to create an effective, competitive, and dynamic financial sector; and to enforce regulations and contracts.

Already, many countries are embarking on these necessary reforms. Over the past few years, India, China, Hungary, Korea, and Thailand have undertaken significant reforms. India is beginning to liberalize its financial system: The government is easing restrictions on private banks and permitting new institutions to open. Strict interest rate controls have been replaced by a more flexible system that allows banks some autonomy in setting rates. Foreign direct investment is increasingly permitted, and the Indian stock market has been opened to large institutional foreign investors such as mutual funds. In 1994, India announced full liberalization of the exchange rate and extensive liberalization is planned through 1995.

China is encouraging foreign investment in more areas beyond the Special Economic Zones. Even in the interior Sichuan province, for example, the government has made significant policy changes in taxation, land use, and ownership, and foreign exchange controls in order to attract investment. These policy changes are published and widely available in many languages.

Already pursuing liberal financial policies, Hungary is further opening its market to foreign investors. Since 1990, the government has reduced directed credit and subsidies. To create a more dynamic industry, the stock exchange was reopened after more than 40 years.

Korea began a slow interest rate deregulation program in 1991. In 1993, the Korean government announced a 5-year financial stabilization plan including many liberal reforms. Key among these reforms were strong incentives for foreign direct investment, such as reducing the number of sectors closed to foreigners from 224 to 94 and eliminating some approval processes.

The capital market is already responding to some of these reforms: India and Hungary received record levels of foreign direct investment in 1993.

If developing nations continue to improve their integration into the global capital market, the investment risks can be lowered. If so, companies and individuals in these countries will be able to obtain funds at a lower cost. The rate of return required to attract capital diminishes as these nations work to reduce their political risk, and so these economies will be able to absorb far more external capital since more investments will have returns higher than the costs of capital. Similarly, as these countries draw on the global capital market to finance telecommunications, roads, and utilities, they will also open up more and more attractive opportunities for investment.

While not every country will succeed in gaining full access to the global capital market, and many will have major setbacks along the way, a number of them will gain sufficient access to represent significant demand for capital that will provide relatively high risk-adjusted returns to savers worldwide.

NO DEFICIT GOES UNNOTICED

Finally, we turn to governments faced with yet another set of critical capital needs. These are the governments of developed world nations. One of the first effects of the globalization of the capital market has been to allow national governments in the developed world to run budget deficits of unprecedented size for peacetime economies.

Viewed from a certain perspective, the global capital market has provided a valuable service. In the absence of the global capital market, the large deficits incurred by the U.S. federal government and other national governments could have led to sharp reductions in the ability of the private sectors in these economies to fund investment in physical capital. By mitigating the adverse effects of running deficits in their own economies, the global capital market has allowed governments that were so inclined to continue running deficits much longer than they would have in years past. By running budget deficits, these countries are incurring debts that will have to be serviced or repaid in the future and exacerbating the problem of rising social expenditures.

To get a better understanding of the full nature of this problem, we built a model at the McKinsey Global Institute to extrapolate the debt burden of developed nations as their countries age, keeping constant current entitlement spending and tax rates. Appendix 6D describes the model in more detail. Over the next 10 years alone, this research estimates that governments in the developed world could issue between $5 trillion and $10 trillion of new debt, depending on the policies they pursue and the rates of interest rate they pay. With wide variance, we will all be much better off if debt issuance by governments is closer to $5 trillion than to $10 trillion.

We then used the model to extrapolate debt burdens and test the sustainability of current prices. The research clearly indicates that current levels of consumption with current tax revenues are unsustainable. As we said before, trees don't grow to the sky, and while the global capital market is not reaching limits to growth any time soon, government debt, particularly for highly indebted countries, does reach a true limit. Under current entitlement policies and no new taxes, many countries would reach crippling levels of debt in the coming decades as their elderly dependency ratios rise and as the interest on their outstanding debt drows. Italy, for example would reach a ratio of 700 percent debt to GNP by 2030, Germany would increase to over 400 percent.

It is safe to state that these extrapolations will not materialize. In today's global capital market, approaching these debt levels will create a market crisis. As we will describe later in this chapter, debt levels much above 100 percent of GNP are probably not sustainable for very long. Because it has a younger population and less generous entitlement programs than most other countries, the United States has the most time of any of the world's developed nations to address its structural deficit. But eventually, it too will still be subject to market discipline as the population ages.

As described in Chapter 5, the global capital market is integrating to the point where the price of government debt is market determined according to its specific and relative risk, independent of the efforts of national governments to control their own interest rates. The preceding extrapolations were calculated assuming low interest rates on the debt (real interest rates of 3 percent). As a point of fact, in 1994 and 1995 most heavily indebted nations were paying real interest rates of 6 percent or more. If we apply higher rates as countries become more indebted, countries will fall into a "debtors' trap" very quickly and will need to borrow more just to pay their interest burdens. No reasonable lender will do this indefinitely.

Thus, the global capital market (a very reasonable lender), will place real limits on government indebtedness and act as a check on the tendency of governments to issue debt for funding unsustainable

---

Projecting Government Debt

To explore the issue of changing demographics driving future government debt levels, our colleague Isobel Coleman, working in conjunction with the McKinsey Global Institute, constructed an extrapolation model of various economies out to the year 2030.

We stress that these results are designed to show how existing programs and current trends will impact the economy *unless there are changes in behavior or policy.* The model is not a forecasting or predictive tool. Indeed, we believe that policies will have to be changed as a result of the pressures created by unsustainable budget deficits. Moreover, we do not attempt to capture the short-run effects of the business cycle (our extrapolations assume full employment throughout). For more detail on the model, see Appendix 6D.

policies. The market will make pursuit of such policies extraordinarily expensive and therefore untenable.

Based on the extrapolations from the Global Institute research, countries would need to enact cutbacks of at least 30 percent of current entitlements, or increases of 30 to 70 percent in taxes, to maintain balanced budgets. Reductions in expenditures of this scale have been made only in scaling down major defense spending. None of the heavily indebted nations spend much on defense, so most of their cuts will need to come from entitlements. Such dramatic changes in entitlement benefits or taxes are unlikely to be put into effect voluntarily through the traditional political process, and thus some countries may face a market crisis in response to their unsustainable policies. At a minimum, we probably will have turmoil and unrest as developed world countries wrestle with these inherent contradictions.

This does not mean, however, that market crises due to government debt are completely unavoidable. The market responds quickly and rewards countries that move in the right direction and show a serious commitment to fiscal discipline. The global capital market can provide an important check to this vicious cycle by demanding high country risk premiums, possibly doing so in time to avoid painful market crisis later.

THE INVISIBLE HELPING HAND

We see many benefits to the world's economy from the current and future developments in the global capital market, which provides attractive opportunities to satisfy the capital supply and demand needs around the world and to alleviate the timing mismatches of the changes in global supply and demand. Adam Smith's invisible helping hand can simultaneously provide greater returns for savers, less costly capital for productive businesses, and better economic performance and discipline for governments to pursue good policies. Together, these opportunities offer the potential for a true global capital revolution that can lead to sustained and rapid world economic growth.

Greater Returns to Savers

One of the primary benefits of the global capital market is that investors can invest, worldwide, wherever they can gain higher returns with less risk. Much of the benefit from the global capital market will result even if all the capital flows are gross flows. If the net capital flows into and out of each country were perfectly balanced, many of the benefits of globalization to savers and to fund-raisers still would be possible, provided the gross capital flows were large enough to satisfy the needs of savers and fund-raisers. Additional benefits arise from the net transfer of capital, as we will describe later.

Prior to the formation of the global capital market, the only options for most investors were nationally based bank deposits, government bonds, and equities of nationally based companies. Bank deposits have been the preferred vehicle for savings worldwide, although these assets offered very poor returns and were not particularly safe in some countries. In the 1970s, many found that a low interest savings account yields negative returns during episodes of inflation. In fact, the real returns have been poor to average even at other times. The average real return on financial assets in the United States over the period 1946 to 1992 was less than 0.2 percent per year. Although this is an extraordinarily low figure, it is probably higher than the return in Europe, where an even larger proportion of financial assets have been held in low-interest bank accounts.

Government bonds have also proven to be risky, particularly during inflationary periods. They may be even riskier in the future if the creditworthiness of governments is brought into question by excesses of debt.

Finally, outside the United States, equities have generally been owned by a small group of insiders (individuals and banks in Europe and cross-holdings by corporations and institutions in Japan) and have been relatively inaccessible to most of the population.

While low or negative returns to bank deposits have been typical in the developed world, they have been even more typical in developing countries. In some countries, low rates of return to bank deposits were regulated by governments that were using these low-cost funds to subsidize targeted industries.

The potential role for the global capital market to increase returns to savers is, therefore, very large. Today's savers in the developed countries are aware that many traditional places to hold financial assets, such as bank deposits, yield very low returns. But they remain fairly risk adverse and lack firsthand information about economic conditions and potential returns outside their own countries. To bring about the transfer of funds internationally, financial intermediaries must demonstrate their ability to create portfolios of foreign assets that have tolerable risk levels. They will have to build track records that can reassure investors that international securities should be part of an investment portfolio.

This is being done today in the United States, the United Kingdom, and Switzerland. Technology has made information available much more quickly and completely. Fund managers in the developed countries can monitor events around the world and have the expertise to manage the risks using modern investment management techniques such as derivatives. Going forward, more and more savers will have better access to cost-effective international investment opportunities that offer them higher, risk-adjusted returns relative to their historic alternatives. In fact, because of the benefits of diversification, a global portfolio of investment with a similar investment mix as the investor would have maintained domestically can, in fact, be less risky than a purely domestic portfolio. Cross-country diversification of assets will lower risk until the global capital market is integrated and the global financial law of one price fully applies to the equity markets.

Beyond international investment, the forces at work described in this book are increasing returns to savers within countries through the global transfer of technology and skill. For example, as securitization proceeds and derivatives are more extensively used in Europe, risk-adjusted yields can be greatly enhanced. In developing countries, simply transferring best practice in banking from the developed world to the developing world also can improve capital productivity enormously by reducing the consumption of savings to cover the high costs of intermediation in these countries.

Less Costly Capital for Productive Businesses

The ability of business and individuals to raise capital more cheaply will also improve as the global capital market matures. For example, in Europe, the global capital market is forcing the elimination of insider markets and securitization is reducing the share of the flow of funds that is intermediated at higher costs through banks. As a result, more and more companies and individuals are gaining access to funding at better terms and conditions while investors earn higher returns. Although some of the mature companies, particularly those being cross-subsidized through national policies, may be disadvantaged by a more effective global capital market, many smaller, more productive companies are gaining access to the capital they need to grow and create new jobs.

The impact on companies in developing countries is even greater since most businesses outside those industries favored by the national government have had limited access to capital. As the global capital market matures, and the intermediation capabilities in countries improve, access to capital on more cost-effective terms will become available to more businesses. Capital will flow not only to the large corporations but also to smaller businesses such as the providers of services (e.g., medical care, legal services, accounting services) that are needed to bring the benefits of competitive market economies to the vast bulk of the national population in developing countries.

Better Economic Performance

Providing better investment opportunities for savers and more cost-effective capital sources for borrowers is possible because the global capital market allows capital to seek the highest risk-adjusted return worldwide. The result is often improved economic performance.

An important example of this result is foreign direct investment. Foreign direct investment can be beneficial at the microeconomic level, even if at the aggregate economy level, the total inflows and outflows of foreign direct investment are balanced. Through foreign direct investment, multinational companies are contributing to the transfer of production techniques from developed to developing countries and thus significantly encouraging growth in the developing world. By production techniques, we are referring not just to technology transfers but to the full range of business practices including management and organizational practices, marketing practices, distribution practices, and operations practices. If the low-income countries are to grow rapidly, the need to transfer technology and best practice business systems is probably even greater than the need to transfer capital.

The productivity studies of the McKinsey Global Institute (in 1992 and 1993) have highlighted the positive impact of foreign direct investment among developed economies. Transplants have been able to transfer best practice from companies' home countries, adding directly to average productivity in the locations where they operate. Moreover, exposure to competition from best practice producers, through trade and transplants, forces domestic industries to become more productive. The 1994 McKinsey Global Institute Latin American productivity study, which points to the need for both capital and improved business methods, suggests that direct foreign investment by best practice companies and joint ventures can greatly improve productivity and living standards in Latin America.

Direct foreign investment not only benefits the recipient countries, it is also a vital part of corporate strategy for companies headquartered in the developed world. Increasingly, the profitability of "U.S." or "German" companies will depend on their performance in the global economy. To remain globally competitive, companies cannot ignore the markets emerging in China and elsewhere in Southeast Asia, India, and Latin America. To the extent that companies headquartered in the developed world invest in developing countries, all equity owners in those companies will share in the high-return potential.

Since the nations of the world all have different saving rates, investment opportunities, demographics, and skills, the global capital market, in addition to facilitating gross capital flows, which permits capturing microeconomic opportunities (e.g., transfers of production techniques), should also result in some *net* transfers of capital to countries with insufficient savings for all the attractive investment opportunities available in a nation's economy.

The net transfer of capital must take place either through the exchange of goods and services in the real economy or through net foreign direct investment. Getting a net transfer of capital into a national economy requires that economy to give the capital provider sufficient goods and services to pay for the capital, or to pay for capital in the form of dividends, interest, and earnings. This relationship is referred to by economists as the "trade identity."

This identity says that the current account (including the net trade balance, net flow of investment income and net transfers) must offset the capital account (including foreign direct investment, portfolio investments and net government capital transactions and transfers). If a country is to receive capital, it must also be a net importer of goods and services. When a country runs a trade surplus, it must return the claims it accumulates on its trade to the country running the trade deficit. When the United States runs a trade deficit with Japan, Japan must either accept in return for that trade, financial instruments or physical assets denominated in U.S. dollars. It could also find an intermediary country to finance the U.S. trade deficit by providing capital to that country. In fact, the large difference between Japan's gross debt and net debt figures (75 percent versus 6 percent of GNP in 1993) in part reflects Japan's large holdings of foreign government debt.

The problem is that, historically, most nations and in particular, most developing countries, have tried to increase the exports of goods and services while curtailing imports and discouraging foreign ownership of assets. This means that they have been discouraging the importation of capital. Nations such as Taiwan have been massive exporters of capital. Since the United States has been running the largest trade deficits in the world, we have the incongruous situation of the United States, the richest nation in the world, being a massive *importer* of capital from other nations.

The opening up of the developing economies and their full integration into the global capital market can reverse this pattern. A number of conditions will need to hold to ensure this, including sufficient financial stock, liquidity in the market, sound counterparties, and relatively low transaction costs. If the developed world savers see sufficient opportunity for capital investment in the developing world, and if the developing world provides the right economic and financial environment (particularly unimpeded capital mobility), then both the developing and the developed world can benefit. Developing countries obtain the capital they need to grow to their full potential. The developed world increases its exports of goods and services (including capital services), and in the process increases the risk-adjusted return on their savings.

This viewpoint is the mirror image of how the trade identity is usually described. For the most part, people assume that it is the trade deficit that drives capital flows, not vice versa. But, although the relative competitiveness of a nation's goods and services is important, the forces driving capital flows can also be a powerful factor in the trade identity. For example, the capital provided by the Marshall and Dodge plans was a powerful factor in driving huge U.S. export surpluses as Europe and Japan were rebuilt after World War II. More recently, the high saving of Japan, as its rapidly aging population entered its peak saving years in the 1980s, and the consequent pressure to export capital (because domestic returns were so low), may have been more important factors in Japan's huge trade surpluses in the 1980s than were its export competitiveness or its import policies.

Discipline on Governments to Pursue Sound Policies

The political pressures on the leaders of national governments to continue borrowing to fund social expenditures are enormous. Citizens have come to expect these expenditures to continue as entitlements. Our work indicates that current policies are unsustainable into the next century. However, it will take pressures of at least equal strength to counterbalance the political pressures and get leaders to act. Fortunately, it appears that the global capital market is becoming sufficiently powerful and integrated to be able to provide this counterbalance. As the global capital market matures, it will encourage national governments to pursue sustainable fiscal and monetary policies.

The tendency of governments to run excessive debt relative to their capacity to service the debt has a long history. Financial historians can trace spectacular, cross-country defaults by governments from the time of King Edward III of England, who defaulted to Italian bankers in 1335, through the developing country debt crises of the 1970s and 1980s.

When a national government gets too deeply in debt, it has four choices:

1. It can default on its debt.

2. It can inflate its economy and then devalue through inflation.

3. It can reduce spending and increase taxes sufficiently to reduce the debt load.

4. It can pursue policies that will increase productivity, or accelerate technological change, and thereby grow out of the current debt ratios.

For major countries in the developed world, as will be described later in this chapter, the prospects of default are so terrifying as to be unacceptable. The last option, pursuing policies that accelerate technological change (e.g., deregulation and privatization), is a highly attractive option and has been successful in some cases, such as the United Kingdom in the 1980s, but cannot always be implemented very quickly.

This leaves the country with only two viable short-term options. It can issue debt in its own currency and devalue it, or it can increase taxes or reduce spending sufficiently to mitigate the debt load. The inflationary answer does not work for any country whose debt is denominated in any currency other than its own since excessive inflation in the domestic currency will cause the currency to devalue against the currency in which the debt is denominated. This policy is what led to the default on their debt by Mexico and Brazil in the early 1980s. Now, however, the emergence of a powerful global capital market is beginning to discourage governments from wanting to pursue the inflationary option even if their debt is denominated in their domestic currency.

How is this happening?

In a closed national financial economy model, such as existed prior to the removal of foreign exchange controls, domestic investors essentially had few options other than owning government bonds outright or keeping their money in national banks that, in turn, owned government bonds. Therefore, inflating the domestic economy devalued the debt relative to GDP which made the debt far easier to service. In today's open global capital market, however, investors can invest anywhere and are increasingly doing so. More and more domestic government debt, even if issued in local currency, is being owned by foreigners or by local investors with foreign investment options.

As we described in Chapter 5, this pattern suggests that investors are making more risk/reward tradeoffs on a global basis. As this happens, the market is becoming more sensitive to any sign that a government is going to become excessively indebted or to inflate its economy. We also explained that it was real interest rates, or nominal rates less inflation, that were aligning. This means that investors are now sufficiently conscious of inflation that they ignore nominal rates and focus exclusively on real rates. The market seems to be increasingly worried about the debt capacity of Italy, Sweden, and Canada. While the risk premiums they pay are quite volatile, the market sees the debt of these nations as fundamentally more risky than that of the United States, Japan, and Germany. Whether the market views this as future inflation risk, or currency devaluation risk, or credit risk of potential default, it is impossible to say, but these countries paid a real interest cost that averaged over 3 percentage points higher than the U.S., German, or Japanese rate during most of 1994 and 1995.

If we are right about the global financial law of one price, monitoring the real rate of interest the country is paying relative to other countries will provide a running critique on its fiscal policies. As we saw, the cost of long-term debt even for such benchmark countries as the United States and Germany is 4 to 5 percent (2.5 percent "risk-free" plus a holding period premium). With many highly indebted nations now paying real risk premiums of 3 percent above the benchmark countries on debt levels equal to 80 percent to 100 percent of their GDP, this translates into a 2.5 percent to 3 percent real interest rate drag on the GDP of the entire economy. This drag is particularly significant for debt held by foreigners since the interest income leaves the country.

As the interest rate that heavily indebted countries pay starts to rise, they fall into a debtor's trap and the unsustainability of their policies becomes evident. A key element in sustainability of borrowing is the relation between the interest rate paid and the growth rate of GDP. A nation with 100 percent of debt to GDP that is paying 7 percent real rates of interest, must increase its real GDP by 7 percent just to maintain its debt to GDP ratio constant *even if its operating budget (before interest expenses) is balanced.* Since most nations are hard pressed to grow by 3 percent in real terms, a nation, once it approaches its debt capacity, will find it almost impossible to avoid a continued and unsustainable rise in its debt to GDP ratio. It will be forced to maintain a large surplus in its operating budget just to remain in balance.

Small countries that run persistent deficits will face a credit or currency crisis sooner than will large countries. In 1975, the United Kingdom had to raise interest rates to support its falling currency and this had very adverse effects on its domestic economy. It was forced to change its policies. Italy, Canada, and Sweden among others are finding themselves in much the same situation now.

Large countries may be able to persist longer with large deficits. The United States especially has the power to do this. The dollar is sufficiently important to the world economy that a precipitous decline in its value would have adverse effects on many countries and therefore many central banks will want to support it.

Moreover, all the debt of the United States is financed in U.S. dollars. Furthermore, the United States is unique as the reserve currency nation in that it theoretically still has the option of inflating its way out of a debt problem. Eventually, however, even large countries are likely to find that their interest rates are rising as their debts accumulate. This will be especially true if many large countries are running current account deficits at once, as is possible given the pressure on entitlements in the industrialized countries.

Therefore, it is probably only a matter of time before the global capital market forces nations with mounting debt problems to cut their deficits. Many believe that some of these heavily indebted nations have already raised taxes to counterproductive levels—they are raising less marginal revenues than they lose in tax avoidance or tax evasion. That leaves these nations with only one real option—to cut spending. For practical purposes, this means cutting entitlements such as pensions, health care, unemployment, and social welfare, since they make up the vast majority of spending in all these nations. The only question is whether these nations cut voluntarily or are forced to do so by market crises. Either way, the market will curtail consumption making more capital available globally for investment.

In summary, the global capital market will vastly improve the global allocation of capital. The more the market becomes integrated and better able to provide frequent signals, the more these benefits will come to pass. That is, savers seeking the highest worldwide risk-adjusted returns based on their own particular comparative advantages will be able to find attractive opportunities and liquidate quickly out of deteriorating investments. Net transfers of capital will increasingly take place between countries rich in capital but poor in investment opportunities and countries rich in investment opportunities but poor in capital. Governments will consume less capital than they would have otherwise, making more available for productive, global investment.

At the end of the day, the reason the global capital market will be so beneficial to the nations of the world is that it will help improve the allocation of trillions of dollars of capital. This will translate into productive investments that can generate high levels of economic growth to benefit the developed and developing world.

CONCERNS AND FEARS

Anyone who has studied the history of capitalism has a healthy concern about the potentially destructive consequences of financial markets. Charles Kindleberger, in his classic book *Manias, Panics, and Crashes* (1978) provides a rich history of the capacity of financial markets to self-destruct and, in the process, to damage the real economy. Many people are still alive who remember the worldwide stock market crash of 1929 and the Great Depression that followed. Therefore, the thought of a global capital market beyond the direct control of national governments deeply concerns many people. Some even believe that the benefits of the global capital market are actually outweighed by the increased stability they judge it creates.

We disagree with this view, but to avoid severe market crises, it is essential that governments follow the kinds of policies described in detail later in the book.

One of the most important responsibilities of a government is to be an effective regulator of the financial system, thereby ensuring that it is not disrupted by the failure of individual institutions. For example, in the United States in the 1980s, the government was able to ensure the orderly resolution of several large banks (e.g., Continental Illinois, First Republic, Bank of New England) and a large securities firm (such as Drexel) without any eventual cost to taxpayers. Only where there is a failure of effective regulation, as in the U.S. savings and loan industry, are losses from government safety nets extensive. The eventual costs of the savings and loan crisis in the United States were over $150 billion.

Indeed, we believe the only participants who can cause real havoc in the global capital markets are the national governments themselves because they have the power to distort the market through influencing capital flows. They can do so by guaranteeing risk through regulation, by printing money (and thereby causing inflation), and by borrowing extensively. While the likely costs of an orderly liquidation of a large financial institution are probably no more than 10 percent of its assets, the costs of any government that were to default today would be immeasurable.

For example, if a nation with debt of 150 percent of GDP were to default on that debt, the loss of wealth in the affected nation would be staggering. Moreover, the default would also cause most of the financial institutions in the nation to become insolvent since the loss in value on their government bonds would, in most instances, exceed the equity capital of many institutions. Finally, any government safety nets behind each nation's banking system would be viewed by the market as worthless.

Provided, however, that governments ensure that the markets work effectively, regulate to ensure the safety and soundness of participants, and refrain from becoming excessively indebted themselves, the risks of serious instability due to the global capital market are far less likely. The forces driving growth and integration of the global capital market are strong enough to make its emergence pretty much inevitable whether or not anyone wants it to happen. Policies that attempt to reverse this fundamental trend are likely to be fruitless and, indeed, dangerous.

Fluctuations in prices and asset values are inevitable in a changing economy and are desirable as an essential part of improving the effectiveness of capital allocation. Changes in interest rates and exchange rates provide continual feedback to savers and investors that was simply unavailable under the old, fixed rate system. As economic circumstances change, it is to be expected that exchange rates, interest rates, and the market valuations of companies will also change. There is a long history of failed attempts to fix prices in the face of changing market conditions.

It is true that the volatility in financial markets has resulted in greater uncertainty for market participants. And this uncertainty could have inhibited trade and the movement of capital around the world. But the global capital market itself has created the solution to this problem through the widespread availability of derivatives. Trade and capital flows have not been inhibited.

Instead, the increased size and scope of the global capital market, its greater sophistication in valuing assets, and its enhanced ability to spread and absorb risks, have triggered a substantial rise in trade and capital mobility. Through the growth of the derivatives market and heightened expertise in risk management, the global capital market has responded to the uncertainty facing both savers and fundraisers. By precisely defining the risks different investors are asked to absorb, and by having the opportunity to use derivatives to eliminate unwanted risks, there is a far greater capacity to find the lowest possible cost for getting an investor to take a particular risk. As a result, the risk-return tradeoffs available to investors are more precisely defined than they have ever been before, and the capacity has never been greater for each investor to take only the risks he or she wants to take.

Moreover, much of the volatility of markets over the past 10 years is a result of the still ongoing transition from national markets to global markets. The global market is not yet complete and although it is becoming more efficient, it is not yet perfect—the global financial law of one price is not yet fully effective and there are some risks that are not yet appropriately priced, particularly in the newly emerging developing country markets. As the market matures and new linkages are forged, historic pricing relationships change and volatility is high.

The greatest fear of many people stems from distrust of markets and, in particular, financial markets. People are worried that their government is losing control of the nation's real economy.

In a way they are right. Governments are actually losing the ability to pursue unsustainable fiscal policies and to escape consequences (in terms of real interest paid) for pursuing inflationary monetary policies. Before the breakdown of the Bretton Woods regime, governments did not have this autonomy anyway. Essentially, all the market is doing is encouraging governments to follow policies that will benefit their economies and citizens. While yield alignment may imply some loss of the ability in fine-tuning monetary policy, and while the ability to control short-term foreign exchange rates has already been largely eliminated by the markets, governments have had limited success, for the most part, in such fine-tuning or from exchange rate management.

Governments still have huge influence on their own national economies; they simply will no longer be able to dictate how capital is allocated. As we will argue in Part Three of the book, governments can take a number of actions to help ensure that their citizens are beneficiaries of developments in the global capital market.

THE PROSPECTS FOR PROSPERITY OR DEVASTATION

While the evolutionary process is not yet complete, we can now envision the benefits of a mature, integrated capital market where capital is fully mobile emerging early in the next century. Such a market would not only be efficient, but *perfect:* The global financial law of one price would be fully operational and funds would flow from funds providers to funds users based on the prices established through the natural self-interest of all participants in the market, without regard to national boundaries. Today's market is efficient, but it is *imperfect.* We are in a transition from a series of independent national markets to a fully integrated global capital market. We still have a market with abundant market anomalies. As these are progressively eliminated, the market will become more and more perfect.

At present, the market is beginning to act as a single market but is not yet fully there. It appears that it will soon have sufficient size and power to prevent most governments from becoming excessively indebted. It also looks as if it will become sufficiently integrated to productively channel the projected surge in household saving from the aging of the developed world toward high returns in developing markets.

Prosperity

As we described earlier, this could set the stage for an extremely happy outcome. The increasing integration of the global capital market creates an unusual opportunity for the world economy over the next 40 years to benefit from the coincidence of interests between the developed and developing economies.

The following example illustrates how this could work. As described earlier, savers in the developed nations will be able to supply about $12 trillion of real capital in the next 10 years, which will be available for investment in financial instruments. For simplicity, we will assume that governments raise base case estimates of $7 trillion of debt to finance consumption, that $3 trillion is invested in the real economy of the developed world at a 5 percent real rate of return, and that $2 trillion is invested in the emerging economies of the world at a 12 percent real rate of return. Under these base case assumptions, the increase in real financial stock from now to the year 2000 would be earning some $390 billion of real returns per year or about 3.3 percent per year on the increased $12 trillion of new capital.

Assume, however, due to more responsible policies, that governments use only $4 trillion of the increase on the financial stock, that $5 trillion is invested at a 5 percent real rate of return in the developed world, and that $3 trillion is invested in emerging economies at a real rate of return of 12 percent. Under these best case assumptions, the increase in the real financial stock from now to the year 2000 would be earning $610 billion of annual real return, or about 5.1 percent on the increased $12 trillion of financial stock. With these best case assumptions, some $220 billion additional income is available annually for additional investment, or to finance retirements in the developed world.

If one projected forward the same trends to the year 2010, the cumulative impact on the developed world of a best case scenario would be tremendous, given the compounding effect of the rate of return during this decade. The impact of just a 2 percent compounding real return differential on $12 trillion of savings in 5 years amounts to about $1.5 trillion, in 10 years reaches more than $5 trillion, and in 20 years approaches $10 trillion of incremental real return on the original investment. By 2010, one would begin to see huge increases in flows available to finance the retirement of an aging, developed world population (increased flow measured in the trillions of dollars).

These numbers are highly understated because they only show the compounding effect on the 10-year savings flows we estimated earlier in this chapter (through 2002). The savings flows from 2002 to 2010 would also earn higher rates.

Under the best case scenario, government debt burdens would be much more manageable than they are today. Today, government debt is about 55 percent of OECD output and, under our base case, would rise to 66 percent of OECD output. Under the best case scenario, government debt as a percentage of GDP in the year 2000 would be 50 percent, a 16 percentage point decrease from the level under the base case.

Moreover, the increased investment in the emerging markets would be stimulating their real growth rates. If the impact of higher growth added 1 percent or more to world GDP growth rates, the cumulative impact on the world's prosperity would be considerable.

Finally, the additional $3 trillion invested in developing countries would have caused the developed world to increase its trade surplus with the developing world, or its claims from foreign direct investment by that amount. This would have either created more jobs in the developed world or increased the value of the equity of the companies making the foreign direct investment, assuming the investments were well made.

The potential for a virtuous cycle to develop is readily apparent. Increased investment in developing markets leads to higher returns to developed world savers (to provide for retirements), increasing income to be taxed and decreasing needs for government-financed entitlements. In turn, this leads to lower ratios of government debt-to-GDP output, and of the financial stock as a whole, which contributes to a less steep yield curve, lower country risk premiums, and in effect, lower interest rates for everyone (not just the government).

This outcome is obviously very appealing.

Devastation

While we do not think a disastrous outcome probable, the potential for it exists. Under this scenario, governments push the limits of their debt capacity, bowing to intense political pressures to continue borrowing to finance consumption. The surge in savings is thus not channeled to productive uses, but instead, becomes a cheap source of funding for government deficits. In effect, the opportunity of the market intermediating across geographic and temporal differences is wasted.

Under this pessimistic case scenario, by the year 2000, new OECD government debt is at the higher end of the $5 trillion to $10 trillion range. Governments are forced to pay relatively steep interest rates as the yield curve steepens, and the most indebted nations pay higher premiums relative to the rates paid by the less indebted nations. Under this scenario, the governments might consume $10 trillion of the available new stock of household saving available for investment in financial assets, $1 trillion would be invested in the developed world at rates of 5 percent, and $1 trillion would be invested in the developing world at rates of 12 percent. Under these assumptions, the increase in the real financial stock would earn only $170 billion or 1.4 percent on the increased financial asset stock (some $440 billion per year less than the best case), and the developing markets would be short of the capital needed for development. The low rate of return could have the effect of discouraging saving so that less would actually be invested (closer to the $10 trillion low end).

In this scenario, government debt burdens would become far less manageable. The government debt-to-GDP ratio would increase to 75 percent from the 55 percent ratio today. But, more significantly, some nations of the world would be in danger of falling into a classic debt trap. The collective debt of $22 trillion might then have a 7 percent real interest cost (up from the 4 or 5 percent medium range of today), which would mean a $1.5 trillion a year increase in debt to output, even if the operating budget was in balance.

While the median country would be in bad enough shape at this stage, the extreme cases could be in a very difficult situation. For example, there might be 4 or 5 countries with debt-to-GDP ratios of 130 percent or more that would be paying real interest rates of 10 percent or more. These nations would be running real deficits of 13 percent due to real interest cost per year, even if the operating budgets were in balance. It is likely that their debt-to-GDP ratios would be growing exponentially.

This could then set the stage for a worst case scenario. Shortly thereafter, several of these countries could default on their debt. At this stage the real trouble would begin. Assume, for example, that these countries were relatively small and had only 20 percent or so of the total government debt outstanding. They would still have some $4 trillion or $5 trillion of outstanding debt that could suddenly be worth 50 cents on the dollar. This loss of wealth could be significantly larger in real terms than the developing country defaults of the 1980s. While the major losses in this wealth would fall on the citizens of these nations, serious losses of wealth could be felt throughout the world depending on who held the debt.

But the real shock would be felt in the global capital market. As a starting point, all the banks in these debtor nations could suddenly be viewed as undesirable counterparties given the weakness of the country and the lack of value in government safety nets. There would probably be a liquidity run on their liabilities, and basically all short-term interbank placings to the banks in these nations would be frozen. These countries would have no choice but to reimpose foreign exchange controls. Trade would be more difficult. These countries would either have to slash their budgets or print money since there would suddenly be no market to finance their deficits. Either way, these countries would be plunged into economic turmoil, with possibly high inflation, or a deep recession. If this happened, even major nations, such as the United States and Germany, would face major difficulties. Through the global capital market, they would be dragged into this economic turmoil.

For example, any creditworthy countries still financing within the global capital market would suddenly have to pay even higher real interest rates because of the risk investors would feel after watching developed nations default on their debt. Derivatives would become less widely available. Yield curves would exhibit large differences, across currencies and national markets would begin to revert to self-containment. All these factors could combine to produce a deep worldwide recession that would exacerbate all of the debt problems with little availability of fiscal stimulus to offset it. At this stage, the worst characteristics of the financial market could come into play with reflexive demand causing the market to overreact on the downside leading to the kinds of uncontrollable bank panics and market crashes the world has not seen in the postwar era.

Under this worst case scenario, the world's economy would be devastated and could easily lead to armies marching and to massive social upheaval. This scenario, which is almost unthinkable, can be avoided if governments pursue the appropriate set of policies.

We will probably experience neither the best case nor the worst case in pure form, and certainly not immediately. Instead, we are likely to undergo a stage-by-stage process that may be resisted by many and that is likely to result in massive social changes and uncertainty in the medium term.

In Chapters 7, 8, and 9 we describe in more detail the process and the impact of the global capital revolution—the stages of economic integration, the impact on governments and on industry structures as well as other characteristics of the more likely outcome. We believe that if people understand the process and the changes it will bring about, they will be better able to embrace the global capital revolution. In that case, the optimistic outcome from this revolution will be more probable and will come about faster.

Appendix

— 6A —

Modeling Household
Net Financial Assets

We estimate that from 1992 to 2002, household net financial assets will increase by $12 trillion in 1992 dollars. To arrive at these estimates, our colleague Kevin Berner, in conjunction with the McKinsey Global Institute, developed a simulation model for U.S. households (Exhibit 6A.1). The simulation model incorporates the effects of demographic changes, capital gains, and bequests and inheritances. The details of the model are described in this appendix. Financial asset accumulation is disaggregated to the cohort level. Each cohort is assigned the average, cohort-specific personal disposable real income that is appropriate for its age, and saves at the cohort-specific saving rate that is appropriate for its age. The random capital gain for the current period is applied to the previous period's stock of assets. Bequests are made by the fraction of the oldest cohort that dies, and inheritances are added to the appropriate cohorts' assets. The initial cohort specific asset levels are taken from actual profiles based on the Survey of Consumer Finances. For each cohort, this period's assets is equal to the previous period's assets, plus saving out of current income, plus (or minus) capital gains (or losses), plus inheritances, if appropriate. Total financial assets in the U.S. economy is the sum of each cohort's average assets weighted by their total population.

Liabilities also accumulate at the cohort level. In each period, each cohort is assigned the average level of liabilities appropriate to its age. There is no cohort-specific nature to the liabilities accumulation, though, because we have no satisfactory data from which to estimate cohort effects separate from life cycle effects. Total liabilities are obtained as the population-weighted sum of cohort liabilities, and

Exhibit 6A.1.   Real Net Financial Wealth—United States

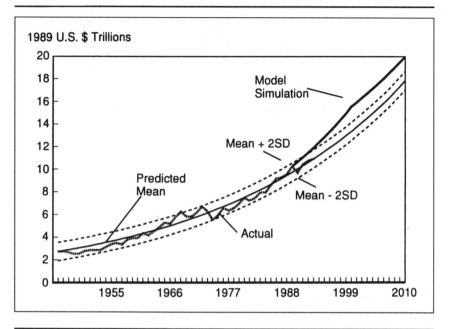

1989 U.S. $ Trillions

Model Simulation

Mean + 2SD

Predicted Mean

Mean - 2SD

Actual

1955   1966   1977   1988   1999   2010

Source: 1989 Survey of Consumer Finances; Flow of Funds; McKinsey analysis.

net financial assets are obtained by subtracting total liabilities from total financial assets. New liabilities are projected to grow at the historical average of 2.63 percent per year.

Net household financial assets are calculated as the difference between financial assets and liabilities, and are simulated for the years 2000 and 2010.

Historically, the growth is unprecedented. From 1945 to the present, household net financial assets have increased on average at the rate of about 2.7 percent. That rate will increase by 30 percent, to 3.5 percent between 1990 and 2010. From year to year, the increases have varied considerably, so that around the trend line we can estimate a band that comprises the range of annual increases within two standard deviations of the mean. Going forward, the increases we estimate are significantly greater than the range of possibilities (within the 95th percentile) suggested by the historical growth pattern. Indeed, we project a bonus growth of over $2.4 trillion for the United States alone. For the developed world, the estimated bonus would be $4.6 trillion for the years 1992 to 2002 alone.

Appendix
— 6B —
Polarization of Income and Wealth

Our estimates of increases in liquid financial households are likely to be conservative because they assume a constant distribution of income and wealth. The current income and wealth distribution may not remain constant, as there is accumulating evidence that income and wealth are concentrating worldwide. However, because of the political and social issues involved, there is much controversy around the research that has been done. Part of the problem is that the data are not consistent. For example, the Federal Reserve survey of households of 1989 is more accurate than the survey of 1986, because it oversamples the richest 1 percent of the population to account for their disproportionate share of income and wealth. These data-gathering problems are exacerbated when making cross-country comparisons. In most of the European countries, wealth statistics probably understate the concentration of national income because they undersample the wealthiest 1 percent, many of whom own the large private businesses in their countries.

Liquid financial assets are more concentrated than savings in general because the principal savings in most households is in their equity in their homes, which is an illiquid asset. Wealthier households, which are also generally older households, have proportionately greater percentages of their wealth in liquid financial assets. This leads to significant concentration of the ownership of financial assets. For example, in the United States, roughly 25 percent of all liquid financial assets are owned by 1 percent of the population.

The next 2 to 3 percent of the population also holds roughly 25 percent of all liquid financial assets. And, the next 7 percent also holds roughly 25 percent. In other words, 10 percent of the population holds 75 percent of all the liquid financial assets. Therefore, if income and wealth concentrates, it would have the effect of further increasing the flow of savings in liquid financial form.

Appendix
—6C—

Dissipating Confusion about the Savings Story

Over the past few years, there have been many reports about the future of global savings. Some articles have reported the impending capital shortage globally. Others have focused on dependency ratios or on individual national patterns and concluded that we will experience new lows in global saving rates. To dissipate the confusion about the savings story, it is important to keep in mind two important issues: life-cycle and cohort behavior, and the difference between personal savings and national savings.

LIFE-CYCLE AND COHORT BEHAVIOR

As people age, household saving patterns vary on average, as we have described in this chapter, and as the life-cycle theory postulates. Moreover, as we have also described, cohorts exhibit slightly different patterns within this cycle. Projections of savings in the future that do not allow for the life-cycle and cohort effects on savings, but focus only on overall dependency ratios, or recent historical saving rates, are likely to miss an important piece of the puzzle. In particular, they will overlook that members of the large baby boomer generation, born after World War II, are now entering their high income, high savings years and have demonstrated a tendency to save at higher rates than their parents or grandparents did. This oversight can lead to incorrect conclusions.

PERSONAL SAVINGS VERSUS NATIONAL SAVINGS

Our work on the global capital market has made clear the importance of distinguishing between personal saving rates (what households save) and national saving rates (the net for the entire economy) to understand the economic challenge and our choices. The *personal* saving rate measures saving by households and is equal to household personal disposable income less personal consumption. The *national* saving rate is the sum of net savings by the private sector (disposable income less consumption of persons and companies) and the government (general government revenue less current government expenditures).

As many articles have pointed out, the net national saving rate has slipped in many developed countries. In the United States, it is a mere 3%, down from 9% or so during most of the previous decades. Much of what is driving this decline is higher government spending on entitlements such as health care and Social Security, a form of consumption primarily funded through the issuance of debt (by governments running deficits). If these levels of consumption were to continue indefinitely, they could easily net out any increases in personal savings and result in lower (and ultimately negative) saving rates.

Making the distinction between personal and national saving highlights the improbability that we as a society should, or indeed can, continue to indulge in the high levels of national consumption to which we have become accustomed. As the global capital market grows and integrates further, foreigners are unlikely to continue funding these levels of dissaving, and it is increasingly difficult for governments to tap into their domestic savings to fund that growth. All investors, domestic or foreign, will be seeking the highest risk-adjusted return to savings and will not permit their personal savings to be consumed through government debt.

We believe current rates of government dissaving are unsustainable. The global capital market is integrating to the point where the price of government debt is market determined. Debt is being priced according to its specific risk, independent of the efforts of national governments to control their own interest rates, as described in Chapter 5. This will place real limits on government indebtedness and act as a check on the tendency of governments to issue debt for the funding of entitlement programs. The market will make pursuit of such policies extraordinarily expensive. In this way, the market will reduce the probability that the government will net out a large share of the increase in the personal saving rate.

Appendix

— 6D —

Projecting Government Debt

To explore the issue of changing demographics driving future government debt levels, our colleague Isobel Coleman, working with the McKinsey Global Institute, constructed an extrapolation model of various economies out to the year 2030. While there already exist studies drawing attention to the impact of greatly increased entitlement spending in the United States, notably the work of the General Accounting Office (GAO), our model adds to existing knowledge in two ways. First, we modified the GAO model to correct an error in its formulation that exaggerated U.S. deficit projections by using a nominal interest rate rather than a real interest rate on U.S. interest payments. Second, we explored a number of variations to our assumptions, notably that saving responds to changes in the interest rate. We also adapted the tool to apply to four other countries: Germany, Italy, Canada, and Japan. The structure of these models is similar to that of the U.S. model, with initial inputs for expenditures, the capital stock, the budget deficit, and other variables being drawn from data for each of the countries. All the countries except Japan face severe problems under the assumptions of the model. Italy and Germany's annual deficit increases lead to a rapidly escalating debt to GNP ratio. In contrast, the United States accumulates debt much less rapidly than the other countries. The extrapolations, however, indicate that several countries will face growing deficits simultaneously, adding new concerns about who will fund all of this borrowing.

In this model, each of the countries considered, except Japan, will experience expanding budget deficits, driven by increasing social expenditures on their aging populations through 2030 (Exhibit 6D.1). As a consequence, their outstanding government debt to GNP ratio will rise dramatically through 2030. Of the countries we considered, Italy has the most serious problem; its debt to GNP ratio exceeds 700

Exhibit 6D.1.   Base Case Debt Extrapolations, 1990–2030

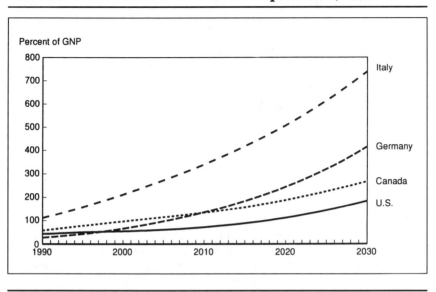

Source: McKinsey analysis.

percent by 2030. In reality, these debt ratios will not occur. Any number much above 150 percent of GDP is probably not attainable without loss of market access since at about that stage, the country enters a "debtor's trap," whereby interest expense grows faster than the country's capacity to raise revenues or cut spending. The other countries look better only by comparison. All reach unsustainable ratios that cross over the 150 percent level sometime between 2015 and 2025. Germany's ratio rises above 400 percent, Canada's exceeds 250 percent and the U.S. figure approaches 200 percent by 2030.

The outcomes described assume that each country has access to the international capital market at a fixed 3 percent real rate of interest, which as we have described in Chapter 5, is a very conservative figure for countries with such high debt-to-GNP ratios. An additional caveat is that we considered each country separately. We have not captured the interaction among them and the possible or likely competition for funds that would result if they all attempted to borrow at once. In both respects, the results reported are conservative and unrealistic, in that they are highly unlikely to take place simultaneously. Indeed, they understate the magnitude and urgency of the problem facing all the countries together.

——— 7 ———

Superconductivity

$\mathbf{A}$lthough the global capital revolution, combined with the sheer scale of capital in motion globally, is accelerating the globalization of the world's economy for goods and services, the process has been underway at a slower pace for decades.

International capital has been somewhat mobile for centuries and has long played a role in transferring new technology. For example, English stock companies financed the development of the American colonies in the 1600s. This could be regarded as foreign direct investment that transplanted English craft skills, such as blacksmithing, furniture making, carpentry, and printing into another country. And, in the 1800s, European investors (led by the English again) financed the building of the railroads and other physical infrastructure throughout much of the world. In the late 19th century, British, American, and French bankers used cross-border capital flows to finance much of the Industrial Revolution.

During the Bretton Woods era, governments laid the foundation for a global economy. After World War II, multinational corporations came into their own as they pioneered and then mastered the transfer of techniques to get large payoffs from foreign direct investments. Similarly, throughout the world, local corporations have long been importing capital as well as production techniques.

This process of globalizing the real economy has been slow, however. This has been partly because globalizing the real economy requires both infrastructure (telecommunications, information technology, jumbo jets) and a critical mass of "citizens of the world" from various nations and cultures, with sufficient language capabilities, education, and skills to operate and network in a global economy. Although it has taken nearly 50 years, most of the essentials for a truly global economy are now in place. We have much of the infrastructure needed and whatever is missing will soon be available. And, although far from complete, we have made great progress in acquiring most of the other prerequisites, such as the rule of law, for a globalized real economy.

With this foundation now laid, the increasing mobility of capital is accelerating the globalization of the real economy. What is different about the immediate future is that, up until now, the changes have been evolutionary. Now capital mobility is providing such an abundance of opportunities that the process of globalization will move much faster.

The analogy of approaching absolute zero from Chapter 5 will help explain what is occurring. At very low temperatures, many electric conductors undergo a collective transition to an ordered state with many unique properties, including in particular, the disappearance of resistance to the flow of electric current. This phenomenon is known as superconductivity, and occurs at temperatures close to absolute zero ($-459.7°$ F or $-273.2°$ C). Under conditions of superconductivity, a given amount of power would greatly increase the resulting output of a current. So, if a superconductive substance were connected to an electric current and then disconnected, the current within the substance would continue to flow on and on and could do so faster and more powerfully than otherwise.

The difficulty, of course, is creating the conditions of sufficiently low temperatures.

And this is, in a way, what the global capital market is doing as it becomes more efficient, or as it approaches absolute zero. It is creating the conditions required for superconductivity in the economy. Only instead of removing the resistance of the flow of electricity, the global capital market removes resistance of transfers of production techniques, and with them the globalization of the economy.

How is this so?

Historically, there have been great barriers, or "resistance," to transferring production techniques between nations. These barriers have included product and market restrictions, the lack of infrastructure, and the lack of skilled labor. In particular, a major barrier has been the difficulty of nonlocal producers being able to repatriate the capital that needed to be invested to transfer production techniques, and the difficulty in being able to assess the returns to be earned from the risks. Similarly, local producers were unable to attract the capital needed to import the techniques of production and, in fact, due to local oligopolistic practices often had low incentive to do so when they could. Although companies such as IBM, Coca-Cola, and Unilever were able to overcome these barriers through extraordinary commitment, skill, and patience, these companies were the exception rather than the rule.

As capital mobility advances, however, it is easier for companies in more and more countries to quantify the risks and returns on the capital that must be invested to finance the transfer of techniques of production into another country. And, when they do so, they find extraordinary opportunities to make profits relative to the capital invested because eager customers are delighted to buy locally produced goods and services at better quality and with greater variety than offered by their traditional providers. Also, these companies often have fundamental cost advantages because local players are often so much less productive. Indeed, they can either live under the "price umbrella" created by the local players, or they can price aggressively to gain market share.

Similarly, global investors are willing to invest in businesses with the assets needed to take advantage of imported production techniques. These assets can be local customer franchises or local distribution skills, or simply businesspeople who are sufficiently well connected with the government as a means to gain the required regulatory permissions.

Investing capital in technologies with known productivity advantages can produce high risk-adjusted returns and will attract capital flows. The combination of full capital mobility and high risk-adjusted returns will drive a transformation in the production of goods and services worldwide. In particular, companies with productivity advantages will seek to capitalize on those advantages through foreign direct investment, alliances, licensing, franchising, and acquisitions. This, then, is the unleashing of global capitalism to which we are referring.

However, the pace at which individual countries experience this process will vary. Let's return to our superconductivity analogy. Different substances have vastly different capacity to conduct electricity and become superconductors at different temperatures. Just as substances vary in their conductive properties, countries, too vary in their ability to conduct a flow of new techniques of production. In fact, no country can yet be said to be truly superconductive.

As capital becomes more mobile, however, conditions are created that resemble approaching absolute zero. More and more economies will become "superconductive substances." As the global capital market grows in size and power, and as capital mobility speeds up, the resistance to the flow of techniques of production will decrease. Suddenly, the profit drive that is unleashing global capitalism will create changes so rapidly in country after country that the process will no longer be evolutionary, but instead will be discontinuous and the entire local economy will abruptly begin to work differently.

Because this process is so important, we will examine step by step what happens to a nation's economy as it is exposed to global capitalism. Then, we will take a step back and view the economic transformation from a global perspective.

NATIONAL VIEW

Until recently, the world consisted largely of closed national systems where the local inputs to production, labor, capital, and technology, were primarily determined at the national level. External competition and the dissemination of nonlocal forms of production or technologies occurred primarily through international trade. Such trade, therefore, represented the principal window through which companies in different countries competed with one another.

A major share of the national economy—that portion which is not internationally traded goods—was largely protected from competition with global, best-practice producers both by historical government regulations, including capital controls, product market restrictions, labor restrictions, and by other cultural differences such as language and customs. Most governments maintained nearly complete control over the majority of the economy by limiting the entry of certain products, declaring the inconvertibility of local currency, imposing onerous approval processes for acquisitions of companies by foreigners, dictating very high labor costs through minimum wages and benefits, and even setting constraints on the hours stores were allowed to remain open.

Governments also controlled their financial systems: Through their banking laws and other regulations, they influenced the allocation of capital in the economy and had a primary role in setting interest rates. Moreover, the governments had enormous resources—a monopoly on printing money and the ability to raise taxes—with which to exert their direct control. And they did so in a variety of ways, including price controls, interest rate intervention, direct entitlements, and direct subsidies.

These barriers created powerful resistance to the mobility of capital and the transplant of best practices to the majority of the economy, the 80 percent or so that does not participate in international trade. In these closed national economies, the domestic businesses and citizens enjoyed a relatively high degree of certainty and stability from knowing their way of life would be protected, that certain industries would be protected, that certain practices would be protected, that certain jobs would be protected—even if the protection came at the expense of greater productivity and economic growth.

The agricultural industry in France prior to the signing of the General Agreement on Trade and Tariffs illustrates these conditions. Despite low levels of productivity, and high costs of produce, farmers in France were protected from competition for decades. By protecting that industry for so long, the government was able to ensure social cohesion and avoid the disruption of displacing large numbers of people who had been in farming families for centuries. The effect on the economy was simply that foreign produce was kept out, and therefore French people paid much more for their domestic produce than was necessary because best practice produce was available outside France.

Japan represents a more general example of this same type of situation: Across a large number of industries, onerous restrictions have kept competition to a minimum. The low level of competition, in turn, has resulted in many large undynamic, highly unproductive sectors. According to work from the McKinsey Global Institute, (covered in more detail in Chapter 9) the overall service sector productivity levels in Japan, for example, are a mere 60 percent of U.S. levels, and are lower than those of West Germany at 77 percent of the United States, France at 70 percent of the United States, and the United Kingdom at 67 percent of the United States. Only in some export-based industries, such as the steel or auto assembly, are Japanese productivity levels high by global standards, and a very small share of the labor force works in those industries. The vast majority of the labor force works in unproductive, uncompetitive industries such as processed food, with productivity levels only 33 percent of U.S. levels. As a result, the cost of living in Japan is excessively high by world standards, and consumer satisfaction is very low.

Over the long run, this type of "protection" not only leads to lower standards of living or lower purchasing power, it can also lead to lower employment in the economy. Eliminating this protection can actually create jobs because although increased productivity means fewer workers will produce the same output, they can also trigger price cuts based on lower costs. This, in turn, will improve the competitive position internally, increase the attractiveness of products internally and externally, and drive greater aggregate demand and standards of living. The relationships between productivity, output, and employment were carefully explored in another large-scale McKinsey Global Institute effort on employment performance.

In that report, the authors examine why employment growth has been much faster in some countries than in others. After many years of very low unemployment, Japan is experiencing a rapid rise in joblessness; Europe's unemployment has been increasing for 25 years and is reaching postwar highs; and the United States has experienced cyclical unemployment, with the average below that in Europe for the past 10 years. The report also highlights that the United States, in contrast to most developed world nations, has experienced rapid job creation, particularly in services. It provides strong evidence across countries in Europe that the existence of product market restrictions, which limit advances in productivity, can lead to poor employment performance. For example, if government regulations prohibit stores in Spain from staying open past certain hours, or on Sundays, these same regulations will inhibit the jobs that would be created by store owners who wanted to provide that service. Strict zoning regulations can have the same effect by dissuading new construction and therefore limiting the potential for new jobs in the economy.

Evading Barriers

The unleashing of global capitalism alters this traditional picture very quickly. At the microeconomic company level and at the industry level, nonlocal producers with clear competitive advantages find ways to expand directly within the existing rules of most countries. They do so by using new technology, setting up joint ventures, creating alliances, taking advantage of risk management techniques, and participating in any variety of ways that will enable them to get capital into these markets. No longer limited to the one "window" of international trade, the global capital revolution has created multiple windows, or contact points across economies. These contact points occur everywhere that international capital can flow—and there are fewer and fewer limits to where capital can now flow.

The more innovative the approaches participants develop to enter these markets under existing constraints, the more pressure is put on those constraints. The breakdown of Bretton Woods was a key example of how this happens. Through the use of technology, innovation, and creativity, highly motivated, resourceful profit seekers find "holes" in the existing barriers. This was precisely what Japan did in the United States in the 1980s, investing in transplants to access the market, when quotas and tariffs prevented them from doing so through exports. Similarly, when onerous policies prevented foreign institutions from participating in a highly attractive market such as India, many companies quickly found local joint venture partners to act as nominal fronts for the operations they would have set up there had they been allowed to do so. In other cases, from mass-cookie production to flower delivery shops, local companies sought out new approaches, or processes, in other markets and "imported" them to their own country, where they could compete as aggressively as external competitors could have done had they been allowed to enter.

Consumers, too, can abet the process of undermining restrictive regulations. For example, during the early 1980s, when most Latin American countries had strict controls on imports of most foreign goods, a large number of wealthy citizens were known to fly to Miami at least once a year and bring back with them the goods they wanted, finding ways (legal and otherwise) to get through local customs. In some cases, these same individuals imported best practice processes to a local operation, allowing them to make the higher quality goods at home. In some countries in Europe, such as Germany and Italy, excessive taxation and overregulation of the financial system have created a direct traffic route to Luxembourg and Lugano, where many wealthy Germans and Italians have invested their capital in a less restrictive financial environment that, in effect, permits them to evade taxes and earn higher returns on their savings. Over time, these activities subvert attempts to protect local markets and, in conjunction with the activity of powerful global capitalists, quite effectively undermine regulatory and legal barriers to competition.

The Process of Economic Transformation

As participants find more and more ways of entering these markets, highly competitive nonlocal producers begin accessing the local customers, who stand to benefit most directly. Americans can buy higher quality cars at a lower cost and actually desire that more of these less expensive foreign cars be made available, through transplants or otherwise; Europeans obtain less expensive financial services and welcome the option to bank with a more efficient foreign bank operating domestically; the Chinese become able to purchase the locally produced, canned vegetable soup all year-round and soon want to purchase low-cost, locally produced, canned fruit as well. The local customer base thus starts to become a pulling force that acts in conjunction with the companies' pushing force to open up closed markets. Such large-scale activity, in greater and greater volumes as the global capital market grows, puts pressure on existing barriers and begins to break down the insulation of a closed economy.

At the same time, even as some customers desire further opening up of the economy, other entrenched interests feel threatened by these developments and oppose them. As local producers and local labor are faced with these large threats from external competition, they lobby the government for protection. For example, even after capital controls were removed and Barclays, a UK bank, was allowed to participate in the French market, its attempt to offer interest-bearing checking accounts to French citizens was vehemently opposed by the officers of the local banks, who perceived it as a threat to their healthy margins, and promptly lobbied the government to put an end to the threat. There are also those who oppose the infiltration of external best practices as anticultural or as a core threat to the domestic nationality and exert pressure on the government to protect these vital national interests. And there are those who oppose the changes simply because change is disruptive. All of these entrenched interests solicit the government to protect them, to put an end to the threat.

Governments, long used to being in control, often try to appease these interests. In many cases, the relationships between politicians in government and the leaders of business are very strong, developed from days together at university, or through family connections. Together, they represent a powerful, cohesive group, and many in this oligarchic group fear any change to the status quo that may reduce their current high levels of influence. Among them, politicians and business leaders can rally strong political support and significant resources in this endeavor.

Nonetheless, the power that comes with many of these changes—in effect, the power of enormous global capital and all the other interests associated with it—makes it difficult for most government and oligarchic groups to prevent the changes from taking place. The typical response of governments then is to continue dipping further and further into their resources to provide protection and subsidies even when they are highly uneconomical. As mentioned in Chapter 6, citizens in most countries will have little appetite for higher taxes, particularly at a time when the economy is confronted with so much change. Instead, governments will tend to increase their issuance of debt, thereby plugging the ever-greater gap between rising expenditures and stagnating revenues. And they might try to continue doing so indefinitely.

But they cannot do so.

Governments have definite limits to debt imposed on them by the growing power of the global capital market, on which they have become highly dependent. Already, a large number of countries are approaching those debt limits. This means that the power of the government to appease the local, entrenched interests is limited in the long term, and for some countries is limited even in the short term.

What happens as these various tensions are played out?

The answer depends on the actions of individual countries, their governments, and the local producers.

Although some countries can stave off these changes longer and more easily than other countries, all countries will eventually be exposed. We have seen this most recently with Mexico in 1995, but in a number of other countries, such as India or Indonesia, over the past few years, the global capital market has weakened the government's control. These governments have been forced to accept economic changes and embrace the capital market. Countries that are already heavily indebted (e.g., Canada, Italy, Belgium) or those that are fast becoming highly indebted (e.g., Sweden) are in the first stages of this confrontation between government and market. Soon, other countries with high unemployment and low productivity levels, such as Spain, or even France, will need to begin addressing these issues. Even relatively productive countries with enormous resources, such as Germany or the United States, will eventually feel these pressures, unless they curtail their appetite for debt.

Embracing Economic Transformation

If governments recognize that the events taking place are largely inevitable, they can accept the changes, and proactively take the actions necessary to reduce their dependence on the debt markets and allow their economies to prosper. This way, they can avoid being exposed to the types of market discipline that the global capital market will bring to bear on them, and their economies can flourish. For governments, this means curtailing entitlement growth, reducing subsidies for underproductive sectors, clearing up burdensome restrictions in product and labor markets, and very importantly, committing to balanced budgets.

Similarly, if local producers recognize and accept the threat of competitors with clear advantages, they can move quickly to respond and adapt to those threats. They will capitalize on their own critical advantages, which could include a long-standing client base, strong distribution channels, or specific local knowledge. Rather than try to resist or find ways to build protective walls against more productive competitors, these local producers can pursue a well-planned response to emerge as winners. This was the challenge faced by U.S. auto makers, as we will describe in Chapter 9.

The benefits to the economy if governments and local producers accept and adapt to the changes are enormous because they will enhance the "conductivity" of the transfer of best practices. Companies will become more competitive, and exposure to competition increases the productivity of all participants in the market. Across the full range of industry sectors covered in the McKinsey Global Institute productivity studies—a total of 14 sectors in the United States, Japan, Europe, and Latin America—a strong relationship is evident between the level of exposure to best practice and global competition and the level of productivity. Long-term job creation is also likely to improve; the McKinsey Global Institute Report on Employment Performance makes clear that heavy product market and labor market restrictions historically have had a negative impact on the ability of the economy to provide jobs.

These increases in productivity and job creation will translate into greater economic growth potential. Customers will also benefit directly, as their incomes will have greater purchasing power and their markets will offer more cost-effective, high-quality goods and services.

The longer this process is in place, the more the self-interest of the local participants switches to ending the remaining restrictions to retain the customers they have or take advantage of possible cooperation with external, competitive producers through alliances or joint ventures. In this scenario, an attractive virtuous cycle develops that can bring long-term economic prosperity.

But as we have outlined before, a much less optimistic possibility can come about if governments resist these changes or try to

---

McKinsey Global Institute
Employment Performance Study

The McKinsey Global Institute, along with a prominent advisory board of academics including Nobel laureate Bob Solow, reviewed employment performance across economies in the United States, France, Germany, Italy, Spain, and Japan (see Exhibit 7.1). To do so, they examined eight service and manufacturing industries across these economies. The report, released in 1994, concludes that significant employment performance differentials exist across economies that are caused not only by labor market regulations, but also by product market restrictions. The findings provide strong evidence that the existence of labor and product restrictions inhibits job creation in the economy, and that the removal of these restrictions can contribute to growth in employment.

Exhibit 7.1.   Employment Performance, 1980–1990

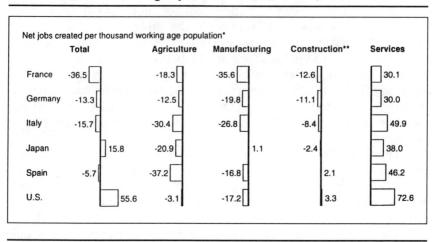

Net jobs created per thousand working age population*

	Total	Agriculture	Manufacturing	Construction**	Services
France	-36.5	-18.3	-35.6	-12.6	30.1
Germany	-13.3	-12.5	-19.8	-11.1	30.0
Italy	-15.7	-30.4	-26.8	-8.4	49.9
Japan	15.8	-20.9	1.1	-2.4	38.0
Spain	-5.7	-37.2	-16.8	2.1	46.2
U.S.	55.6	-3.1	-17.2	3.3	72.6

* Adjusted for growth in the working age population.
** Including mining and utilities.
Source: OECD Labor Force Statistics; national household surveys; McKinsey analysis.

impose further regulations. Where entrenched local interests that have the most to lose resist the changes, the government may become an accomplice to that effort. Because so many countries have already become dependent on the global capital market, this could lead to market crises and shocks.

Economies pursuing this tack not only will expose themselves to potential market crises but will severely limit their growth potential. Eventually, when governments reach their debt limit, they will be forced to make most of the changes anyway. They will of necessity cut entitlements, reduce restrictions, and commit to balance budgets. In the long run the economy will be exposed to much of the same global competition.

Because many governments have not responded earlier and have strongly resisted change, adapting will likely be much more painful and difficult than if it had been done over a longer time. Local producers who have relied on oligopolies and government subsidies will face similar difficulties. Because they will be responding late to the challenges from more productive competitors, they will be less able to capitalize on their unique advantages, which will have been eroded. They will have to scramble to adjust, and in many cases, it may be too late.

In either case, whether through a less painful process, or a more painful one, the benefits will come eventually: Productivity will increase along with competitive intensity; customers will benefit and increase their purchasing power; and there will be growth in employment and in the economy.

While these benefits will represent much fundamental change, they are likely to be accompanied by other, less attractive characteristics even for the most attractive scenario of economic prosperity—great volatility and a high degree of uncertainty. Strong political and social tensions are likely to emerge, as entrenched interests are uprooted and new interests defined.

The range of conflicting interests that have a stake in these changes is wide, and their interaction will drive much of the uncertainty and turmoil. World-class, competitive producers, pressured by their own shareholders and backed by their governments, will expand into new markets seeking high-return opportunities and growth. The economic incentives for these players are phenomenal, given their relatively competitive positions and the often-untapped potential markets. Thus, many are likely to be extremely aggressive in seeking resourceful and creative ways to push resistance aside and capture the opportunities. Local customers who stand to benefit from cost-effective, improved goods and services will also seek out ways to access these producers. Both directly as citizens and voters and indirectly through their economic choices, they will be a powerful voice and source of activity creating change. Moreover, in just a few years, a liquid stock of global financial assets amounting to more than $80 trillion will provide powerful pressure for these interests, as any single country's currency becomes illiquid against the stock of assets moving in response to new information. The power of this global capital market will be applied in full force in response to the broad range of economic opportunities.

At the same time, all those who benefit or are protected under the status quo will resist these changes. Local labor interests that are threatened, either directly for the jobs or indirectly for their benefits such as extended vacations, short working hours, or greater coverage will oppose the threat. In many countries, these interests are powerful and politically active. Voters who want to maintain their growing entitlements to pensions or health care, or those who have come to feel that promoting the welfare state is a right and duty of any civilized, industrial nation, will reject many of the necessary changes. Producers who do not want to face up to the competitive threat, who have grown accustomed to stable, if not spectacular, returns and use of resources will fight to maintain their way of doing business, and in many cases, their ability to do business altogether. And politicians who benefit from the status quo, whose support base consists of these powerful interests who would stop change, will also resist many changes. These detractors are extremely powerful in most nations. The interaction of these conflicting interests within each nation will create unstable situations and turmoil.

As different nations respond in their own way and at their own pace, as the conditions for superconductivity are created in more and more countries what global picture begins to emerge?

GLOBAL VIEW

At the same time that individual economies are undergoing such enormous changes internally, they are also experiencing new linkages and dynamics with other economies externally. The unleashing of global capitalism on a major scale creates strong integration and interdependency across economies. It is also likely to create strong competition among countries, as they seek to attract capital, and with it increases in productivity, employment, and standards of living.

Previously, when only the traded goods component of the economy participated internationally, any one country had limited exposure to events in other parts of the world. So for example, because the United States was the major export market for many countries, including Japan, Korea, Mexico, and Chile, a recession in the United States could have an impact on their heavily export-driven economies. But the impact was felt only on the portion of the economy that consisted of traded goods.

The most extreme case of the previous interdependence was felt during the embargoes of the Organization of Petroleum Exporting Countries (OPEC) in the 1970s and 1980s, when the decision of the oil cartel to limit supply and increase prices translated into enormous economic difficulty for many countries that relied heavily on imported oil. The reason that the oil embargo was so dramatically felt around the world was that the price of oil was an important input into production throughout the economy in all countries.

As global capitalism extends beyond a single border and affects economic activity not just in traded goods, but in services and most all local production, individual companies, their shareholders, and their customers will be increasingly affected by events taking place in other parts of the world. So too, therefore, will the governments that have as constituents those customers and shareholders. Global capitalism will create linkages across economies that will become more transparent as more and more economic participants understand the high stakes they individually have in the events that take place, and as they seek to understand and influence those events.

The potential for rapid transmission of both financial and economic prosperity or shocks and devastation is ever greater. Citizens in one country can no longer limit their understanding of events to what is happening in their own economies, to their domestic prices or to their own government debt interest rates. As we have described earlier, changes in the supply and demand in one part of the world will affect all other parts of the world.

Greater global awareness on the part of economic participants, and a desire to influence the outcomes, will likely lead to "beauty contests" among countries. Countries will compete in creating a desirable economic environment to attract the capital that will increase productivity, employment, and economic growth. Countries will feel competitive pressure vis-à-vis other countries with respect to their economic policies, fiscal policies and monetary policies, and importantly, their financial policies. In particular, countries, whether they realize it or not, are in a race to reduce product market restrictions that inhibit best practices from being applied across industries, to clear up onerous labor regulations that inhibit job creation and discourage others from setting up operations with local labor, to maintain balanced budgets and control over inflation to ensure greater financial stability, and to liberalize financial regulations to ensure the most effective and efficient allocation of capital.

In the developing countries, this type of cross-country competition already is evident. Many developing countries, such as Argentina, Brazil, India, Indonesia, and Korea, have adopted more liberal economic and financial policies in response to the need for capital to drive economic growth.

But this dynamic is not limited to developing countries. Not at all. As more and more countries become superconductors, pressure will be increased on those countries who resist. Developed countries will also face the need to make a choice: Take the leadership in enacting economic, fiscal, monetary, and financial reforms or limit the potential of their own citizens and their own economy to improve their standards of living and benefit from the enormous opportunity ahead of us.

END STATE: AN INTEGRATED GLOBAL ECONOMY

As the global capital revolution and global capitalism proceed at an accelerated pace, companies within industries, industries within national economies, national economies within the global economy, and the global economy itself will undergo major transformations. Countries that resist will lag behind, which in turn will put pressure on their governments to embrace the market. Over time, more and more will become superconductors. As more countries embrace the market, the process feeds on itself and the pace of change continues to accelerate. In a relatively short period—a couple of decades at most—we will find ourselves in a truly global economy for goods and services.

What will this global economy look like at the end of the day? Will individual national markets for goods and services merge into one enormous market that is so tightly integrated it behaves as a single market?

No, we believe that the real economy, even though it will be transformed, will be enormously rich and diverse, with separate markets for goods and services in nation after nation. To some degree, this is self-evident. Even in single national markets like the United States, where people share a common language, common national laws, and common media, there are enormous variations in demand patterns in different cities, states, and regions. Even in the United States, the markets for goods and services are segmented.

The global capital market can integrate very tightly only because at the end of the day, money as well as anything easily convertible into money, is a pure commodity. Any asset in the global financial market can be converted, usually at a minimal transaction cost, for any other asset in just a few moments.

In contrast, most goods and services are not commodities. A meal in Shanghai cannot be traded for a meal in Oklahoma City.

Moreover, excepting physical commodities, most markets for goods and, in particular, services, are relatively inefficient. It can take hours of work, even by a knowledgeable medical person, to compare the relative value of one health-care provider against another, even if they operate in the same city. Even then, considerable judgment is required to determine whether the services being priced are truly comparable. Comparing relative value across countries is harder still.

But, the primary reason global markets for goods and services will remain segmented, rather than be integrated into a single global market, is that buying preferences for goods and services vary enormously from one buyer to the next. Buying preferences are diverse within any given nation and are far more diverse across countries.

Anyone who has conducted business internationally understands that the first requirement of success is to cater to local tastes. And this requirement is not going to change. If anything, markets will become more diverse as more goods and services are produced with the ever-wider variations in techniques of production that become available through globalization. The range of choice available to customers will expand, and the critical skill will be to more highly tailor products to the individual buying preferences of a diverse market while taking full advantage of the state-of-the-art production techniques (including state-of-the-art marketing techniques). Market segmentation for goods and services will become more, rather than less, important.

On the other hand, while consumers' diversity of choice will be growing, producers will find a convergence of opportunity across nations. Although any given national market will be increasingly segmented, when your perspective is the world, all those individual segments will look like an integrated global market opportunity.

The globalization of the automotive industry is a good example of simultaneous segmentation and integration. As the per capita income in the developing countries increases, as product market restrictions are liberalized, and as advanced techniques of production are transferred, it will become possible for hundreds of millions, if not billions, of people to own automobiles in country after country over the next 20 years. This, in turn, not only will affect global manufacturers of cars but will also create numerous global opportunities in country after country for a variety of services related to the car, from gas stations to automobile distribution, to repair, to pollution control, to traffic engineering, to highway design, to highway construction.

From the consumer's point of view, choice will be increasing. For example, rather than having to deal primarily with state-owned oil companies, they will be able to choose among many different, globally branded retail outlets as well as a host of repair specialists in transmissions, or mufflers. The number of outlets offering service will expand, service levels will both expand and segment (with segments ranging from no frills to full service), and prices will fall.

From a producer's point of view, opportunities will increase. If you are concentrating on any service segment (e.g., automotive repair), the global opportunity in just that segment will dwarf the full range of service opportunities in any single nation. Simply repairing cars worldwide will be a bigger global market opportunity than selling cars, fueling cars, and servicing cars in any single nation.

Going forward, the scale of the global market will create opportunities to develop large firms from small national participants. A wide variety of global firms will be created in very narrow specialities. For example, there will surely be firms that wind up specializing in such areas as relieving the traffic-flow problems of large, developing world cities.

This, then, is the essence of capitalism. Adam Smith and other economists discovered this essence centuries ago. Global capitalism merely accelerates the process of creating an incredibly dynamic, diverse global market for goods and services. There is nothing new about this process; it has been underway for centuries. But, the superconductivity of the global capital market and the greater mobility of capital will fast-forward the process.

We asked earlier, What will the global economy look like at the end of the day? Our answer is, We see a never-ending process that drives the increasing satisfaction of individual preferences at lower and lower costs. The more that nations become superconductors, the more dynamic and accelerated will the process become.

Making the right choices to benefit from an integrated global economy involves understanding the magnitude of the changes that have started to take place and that are likely to accelerate dramatically going forward. It involves an understanding that our traditional framework of closed national systems is flawed in the context of these changes. Many of our assumptions about economics and, particularly, the role of governments, are simply wrong and we must fundamentally rethink them.

CHANGING ROLE OF GOVERNMENTS

As these national and global changes evolve, governments will face new and difficult challenges. Until recently, the resources of most major governments were very large relative to the market. Governments had the greatest level of power to affect change and to influence their own national economic outcomes. The large body of economic literature was developed under the fundamental assumption that this was, as a matter of course, true. As the power and size of the market grows, these assumptions are no longer valid, and governments find themselves much less in control of traditional levers for managing the economy.

Governments have had at their disposal a wide range of levers to control and manage their economies. They have adopted restrictive trade policies and declared high tariffs on imported goods. They have imposed product market restrictions, and they have had control over wage and labor regulations. They have had the power to impose and raise taxes. Governments have also enjoyed a high degree of control over their financial systems, and have used these systems to channel resources within the economy, or to influence interest rates. Finally, governments have been able to pursue relatively independent fiscal policies and monetary policies.

However, the global capital revolution and the rapid expansion of global capitalism have systematically reduced government's controls over each and every one of those levers.

Challenge to Economists:
Keynesians and Monetarists Alike

Keynesian economics, based on the theories exposed by John Maynard Keynes (1883–1946) in *The General Theory of Employment Interest and Money* (1936), differs from neoclassical economics in its focus on aggregate behavior, particularly the effect of total expenditure on economic income and the role of investment in determining economic activity. As noted in Chapter 2, Keynes was also a principal architect of the Bretton-Woods system. Keynesian economics centers on three interrelated issues: the stability of a market system and its ability to maintain full employment, the role of money in such a system, and the long-term dynamics of growth in the market economy. Keynesians proposed that because of the existence of a "liquidity trap," in which an increase in the money supply does not lead to a fall in interest rates but only to unused liquidity, and because of the inelasticity of investment, fiscal policy is more effective than monetary policy. Unfortunately, when these theories were later proposed by "Keynesians" and taken into practice by governments, particularly from the mid-1980s onward, they were translated into a willingness to run deficits and a justification for doing so, with no parallel appetite for or tendency to run surpluses when economic growth was strong.

Monetarism, a term first introduced by Karl Brunner in 1968, and most frequently associated with Milton Friedman and the Chicago School of Economics, argues that changes in the level of aggregate money income are a result of changes in the stock of money. Monetarists emphasize the unique role of money, a commodity that was substitutable for a wide range of other commodities and financial assets. As a result, they argued that monetary policy would have a direct impact on aggregate demand, in contrast to Keynesian analysis, which argued that it would have an impact primarily on financial assets, and only a weak and uncertain impact on aggregate demand. The monetarists' view, while still largely national, permitted a more open economy.

Initially, the central debate between the Keynesians and the monetarists was the relative efficacy of monetary versus fiscal policy. Over time, almost all economists have come to agree that both fiscal and monetary policy can effect aggregate demand, although they still differ on their relative importance. These differences have come to be mainly an issue of degree.

(continued)

(continued)

Today, the major area of disagreement among economists concerns the principal source of instability in the economy. Monetarists argue that the private economy is basically stable and that fixed policy rules are necessary to insulate the economy against ill-conceived and badly timed government actions which cause instability. Nonmonetarists argue that the private sector is the source of instability because private investment decisions, in particular, are unstable, and that therefore an active government role as a countercyclical influence is required to achieve stability.

In important ways, both points of view are challenged by the unleashing of global capitalism and the forthcoming economic transformation. Both views still assume, primarily, a closed national model in which governments have the full choice either to have an active countercyclical role, or not to have such a role. We have argued that while governments are still powerful and their actions greatly affect the world economic outlook, their choices are becoming limited as they confront the growing power of the global capital market and the forces driving it. Moreover, opportunities for worldwide investment, domestic and cross-border, cannot be offset easily, nor should they be, because they offer enormous growth potential. Instead, we must learn to adapt to and manage the often beneficial, often unstable and volatile, patterns of global private investment.

In *The General Theory,* Keynes stated, "Practical men, who believe themselves to be quite exempt from any intellectual influences, are usually the slaves of some defunct economist." In this rapidly changing world, we must throw off all such bonds.

Outright tariffs and restrictive trade policy are giving way as multilateral pressure from governments around the world increases, and as the costs of restricting free trade are better understood. The successive rollout of multilateral pacts such as the General Agreement on Trade and Tariffs (GATT), now the underpinning of the World Trade Organization, is but one example. Many other multilateral or bilateral free trade agreements are taking hold, such as broader participation in the European Union, Mercado Cono Sur (MERCOSUR) among Brazil, Argentina and Uruguay, and North American Free Trade Agreement (NAFTA), between the United States, Mexico, and Canada.

The ability of governments to erect product market restrictions is likewise being eroded by the resourceful and innovative approaches that highly motivated participants are taking to circumvent the restrictions. We have described numerous examples of this type of erosion, first in the financial markets, and increasingly in the product markets.

Mandated wage rates or burdensome labor regulations put enormous pressure on the economic system, inhibiting the ability of the economy to generate more jobs. The response to date, to subsidize or fund these practices through high levels of entitlements, is increasingly untenable as the global capital market gains power and governments approach their debt limits. This traditional lever is also ineffective.

Governments' control over their financial systems is already dramatically weakened against the global capital market. This trend will continue, as more and more of any nation's financial stock is in liquid, highly tradable assets and less and less is in the money supply, which is the bank-dominated portion of the financial stock. Similarly, as the global stock of liquid assets has grown, the ability of any government to sustain fiscal policy that is fundamentally unattractive to the market, or to use monetary policy to inflate its way out of debt, is being undermined.

—8—

Heroes to Lead Us
(Not Politicians)

Throughout the world, people have become cynical about their political leaders. And, most politicians have earned that cynicism. They have made promises they could not keep. In particular, they have promised their nations economic prosperity. They have promised their citizens that they would provide them with economic security. And, they have promised to maintain social stability.

To their credit, many politicians have tried to honor their promises. Worldwide, political leaders have borrowed money as a fiscal stimulus to animate stagnant economies. They have used the money to provide subsidies to uncompetitive industries and to maintain generous entitlements. They have used the considerable powers of the nation state to restrict competition in financial markets, in markets for goods and services, and in labor markets to protect domestic businesses and jobs, and to maintain social stability.

Their actions have often had perverse effects because by trying to manage their economies directly, they were stifling the very market forces that could have provided them with the promised prosperity. Now, many of these nations are approaching the limits to their debt capacity and feeling the constraints of over regulation. Nations are increasingly unable to afford the costs of guaranteeing personal economic security to their citizens through entitlements and economic protection. At the same time, the regulatory barriers they erected in their domestic financial, goods and services, and labor markets to protect social stability are crumbling under market pressure, despite government attempts to resist this pressure.

These political leaders are caught in a trap. The historic policies are not working, but they are scared of unleashing the full power of the market completely. Many of them, moreover, do not fully understand the futility and danger of trying to continue to use the tools designed for a closed, national system as the whole world shifts toward an open, global system. Their instincts for what actions to take are not only wrong, they are dangerous.

And this gets to the heart of the issue. We have greater need for national political leadership than we have needed since the end of World War II. But instead, we have confused politicians making promises they cannot fulfill to a confused electorate. The risk is that our political leaders will take actions that would have worked in a closed, national system but will have destructive effects in an open, global system.

Rather than look at the challenge generically, let's look at the kinds of issues real political leaders face. Let's examine the dilemma a real nation faces. Let's look at Japan.

JAPAN: A CASE EXAMPLE

From near destruction during World War II, Japan rose from the ashes. From the late 1940s into the 1980s, Japan flourished under sustained growth built on the export of internationally traded manufactured goods to become the second largest economy in the world. By the late 1980s, there was serious talk, worldwide, that Japan was going to displace the United States as the preeminent economic power in the world. By 1995, Japan's plight was a quite different one: stagnant output, unstable deflation, an impending banking crisis twice the size of the U.S. savings and loan crises in a country half the size of the United States, and insufficient political leadership.

At the heart of Japan's quandary is its difficulty in accepting transition to the age of the global capital revolution and global capitalism. Under the closed, rules-based systems developed at Bretton Woods, governments were able to fully control the economy. Japan did so to an extreme: Powerful, centralized ministries such as the Ministry of Finance (MOF) and the Ministry of International Trade (MITI) were involved in nearly every major economic decision affecting the country. And in this closed system, the government effectively controlled economic priorities and allocation of resources.

The core of Japan's post–World War II strategy was to become the world leader in internationally traded manufactured goods. After World War II, the Japanese government developed a financial system to bootstrap the recovery of Japanese industry. With a devastated economy, Japan needed foreign capital and high domestic savings to support the manufacture of goods, particularly for exports. To facilitate this, the banking system ensured that there was no risk of default by corporate borrowers. As a first layer of defense, all loans were secured by collateral. As a second layer of defense, most large corporations were part of industrial groups, which had their history in prewar Japan, with a bank at the center committed to backstopping all members of the group. Behind the banks stood the Ministry of Finance and the Bank of Japan.

This structure enabled large Japanese manufacturing companies to operate with debt leverage ratios even higher than those being used in the leveraged buyout and junk bond takeovers in the United States from the 1980s. For example, as recently as 1990, the net worth ratio (the ratio of net worth to assets) for all industries in Japan was 26 percent. In other words, about 1 yen of equity for every 3 yen of debt. In contrast, the average for publicly traded U.S. corporations was 55 percent, only $1 dollar of debt for each dollar of equity.

The banks themselves were highly regulated and were divided into narrow categories of competition, such as "city" banks, regional banks, foreign exchange banks, and trust banks. In effect, this created government-sanctioned oligopolies. Banks also were encouraged to own directly the equity in the corporations to which they lent funds. Much of this equity stock was bought, very cheaply, right after World War II.

Another feature of the Japanese financial system was the official encouragement of savings. In particular, the tax system has strongly encouraged savings because 70 percent of personal savings was tax-free. In addition, taxes on corporate dividends were as high as 78 percent. Corporations therefore retained and reinvested most of their earnings, rather than paying them out as dividends, and this too, added to national savings.

Yet another feature of the Japanese financial system was the encouragement of high stock prices. From right after World War II, until the late 1980s, the Japanese stock market was managed by Japanese banks and insurance companies with government support and encouragement to maintain high prices. When it faltered, in 1965, a special corporation was actually set up by the government to buy stocks until the sell-off passed!

The continued rise of the Japanese stock market over a 40-year period was made possible by maintaining a limited supply of stock for trading. A "thin" market is easier to manipulate than a "deep" market. Corporations issued little equity (given the use of extensive bank debt funding and the encouragement of retained earnings due to the high taxes on dividends). And, perhaps as important in limiting stock availability, roughly 75 percent of all Japanese stock is cross-held (by banks or insurance companies or by other members of the company's industrial groups).

The Ministry of Finance has historically worked closely with banks and insurance companies to intervene, supporting the market through encouraging stock purchases and discouraging the sale of holdings. This strategy worked. An investment of $1,000 in the TOPIX index in 1949 was worth $183,426 by 1988.

This stock market manipulation also led to very high stock prices relative to earnings. Multiples of 50 to 60 or more have been typical. Modest returns on equity had huge stock market valuations placed on them. That is, companies could target low returns on capital, enabling them to keep prices low to build market share, without paying any penalty in the value of their stock.

Finally, the government used various devices to discourage investment in residential housing, which effectively meant an unusual proportion of the nation's savings was channeled into business investment. This glut of capital available to industry kept borrowing costs low. The Japanese government manipulated its entire financial system to make Japan more competitive in traded manufactured goods.

The combination of high debt leverage, the support of stock prices, and the high savings rate enabled Japanese corporations to raise, cost-effectively, the capital needed to build strength in the international traded goods (of steel, cars, heavy equipment, consumer electronics, chemicals) until Japan became the most productive, cost-effective competitor in the world in many of these industries. It also enabled Japanese corporations to offer trade finance to buyers at terms more attractive than those offered by other nations. These cost and sales advantages, when combined with high commitments to quality, hard work, skillful marketing, and the discouragement of imports through trade and product/market restrictions, led to large Japanese trade surpluses year after year.

The financial policies that had been designed to bootstrap the postwar financial economy in Japan remained in place long after the circumstances that led to their creation had disappeared. By the early 1980s, the combination of high Japanese productivity in internationally traded goods and the overvalued U.S. dollar led to the creation of unbelievably large Japanese trade surpluses—particularly with the United States.

Meanwhile, Japanese companies in the internationally traded goods arena ran out of domestic investment opportunities in the mid-1980s. Economists call this the "seventh shovel" effect, which means that if you give a worker one shovel to use, the returns are high. However, the extra returns earned by giving the worker additional shovels with which to work diminish rapidly.

At the same time, changes in Japanese demographics led to a huge surge in savings. This all combined to create the financial asset bubble described in Chapter 6. As a result of this bubble, the value of stocks and real estate lost all relation to their underlying value. In real estate, 1,200-square-foot apartments, worth $350,000 in New York were worth $6 million in Tokyo. American companies with Japanese subsidiaries were able to sell their subsidiary for more than the entire company was worth on the U.S. market.

This bubble signaled the beginning of the end for Japan's closely controlled system. Just as the Nikkei index continued to set new highs and just as the rest of the world began to view Japan as the ultimate winner in the global economy, the seeds of trouble were beginning to sprout.

The bubble had been created primarily by the banking system, awash with cash, lending massive amounts of money, often through other intermediaries like credit cooperatives and finance companies to individuals and corporations speculating in stocks and real estate. With the thinness of available supply, such lending only fed the market mania in stocks and real estate that was already underway.

When the bubble burst in the late 1980s and early 1990s, the collateral underlying these loans evaporated. However, over the past several years, in cooperation with the Ministry of Finance and despite enormous economic losses, banks did not write these loans off. Rather, they continued to lend the borrowers more money to pay the interest on the loans and continued to pretend that the loans were valuable assets. Naturally, this solved nothing. By 1995, official estimates put "bad loans" in Japan at over $400 billion, but unofficial estimates are as high as $1 trillion. No one knows the eventual losses that will be realized but they will be staggering and will probably dwarf the U.S. government's losses on the savings and loan industry.

Only the confidence that the market has in Japan as a country has kept this credit bomb from exploding into a financial panic. The market has good reason to have confidence in the Japanese government since, almost alone among major nations, Japan has not yet become heavily indebted on a net basis. The government and its agencies hold hundreds and hundreds of billion dollars worth of U.S. government paper.

Nonetheless, the Japanese banking system is in poor shape. In 1995, Moody's issued new credit ratings for banks worldwide that rated banks on a stand-alone basis, without government support.

These ratings were issued in conjunction with a normal rating that takes into consideration government safety nets. On a scale of A to E, Moody's rated the average large Japanese bank as a D with no banks being rated higher than a C+. A "D" bank, according to Moody's, is a bank with adequate financial strength but limited by a vulnerable business franchise, weak financial fundamentals, or an unstable operating environment. Because of their weakness, Japanese banks have been unwilling to lend for the past several years. This has contributed to a sustained recession and an unleashing of powerful deflationary pressures, particularly in real estate.

Meanwhile, the productivity of the sectors of the Japanese economy protected by heavy product/market and labor restrictions (in reality the majority of the economy) remained very low. As a result, Japanese standards of living did not rise anywhere nearly as rapidly as did their dominance of the internationally traded goods sector. Therefore, despite the despair created in Detroit, the average Japanese worker maintained a far less prosperous life than did the average worker in the United States. Japanese workers tend to work harder, commute longer distances, live in smaller homes, and have less purchasing power to acquire things than their U.S. counterparts.

Understandably, Japanese citizens are unhappy with their government. The Liberal Democratic Party was thrown out of office in 1993 for the first time in nearly 40 years due to a series of financial scandals related to the Japanese stock market bubble. Since then, coalition government after coalition government has failed. The instinct of Japanese politicians and the bureaucrats is to resist change.

Meanwhile, Japan is severely exposed to market pressures: externally, from those who seek to compete in this domestic market served by heavily protected, inefficient local producers, and internally, from those dissatisfied with their standards of living. Pressure is growing particularly from people who understand that embracing globalization will help end the sustained, painful recession. These pressures are becoming so strong that they are creating an awareness in the broad population of a need for change. Many understand that systematic deregulation of the closed, national economy is essential. As yet, however, the will and ability of the existing leadership to drive the change is not apparent.

And these are the core issues that all of us, not just the Japanese, face. We need leadership from our politicians. Global capitalism can provide prosperity relatively quickly. But for the prosperity to come about, national governments must embrace global capitalism rather than resist it. They will need to work to make their economies better conductors of global capitalism.

EMBRACING GLOBAL CAPITALISM

It is critically important for national governments to realize that the global capital market is now a powerful force of its own and that it will be progressively less possible for an individual government to pursue policies under the assumption that it can directly control its own domestic financial market. This will be true even of the largest nations, including Japan, Germany, and the United States. This does not mean that nations are powerless to influence their economies. This book has emphasized the critical role that governments will play in the outcome. Instead, it means that governments will be less able to use traditional levers and the direct control of their domestic economic and financial markets to achieve their objectives.

It does not matter whether a national government or a particular political party likes or dislikes the development of such a powerful global market and the loss of direct control of its domestic financial economy any more than it matters whether a national government likes or dislikes nuclear weapons. The global capital market, like nuclear weapons, has become a reality that is too big to ignore and policy must reflect this reality.

The critical issue each national government must face, then, is what policies to pursue that will enable the global capital market and global capitalism to further the interests of its citizens, its economy, and its own national purposes.

MAKING MARKETS WORK BETTER: PRINCIPLES OF FINANCIAL REGULATION

National governments need to play an essential role in making the global capital market work constructively rather than destructively. The only reason the Japanese banking crisis has not developed into a full-blown global financial panic has been because the market still has confidence in Japan and the willingness of the government to stand behind its banking systems. If we want to prevent the worst case scenario from Chapter 6 from becoming a reality, we had better pay attention to how governments regulate and protect their financial systems.

Hundreds of years of economic history prior to World War II tell us that the social costs of unregulated banks and financial markets are profound. Therefore, it is not a question of regulation or no regulation. It is a question of what kind of financial regulation and government safety nets will be the most constructive.

We need a new regulatory approach that is based on neither the essentially unregulated model of the pre-World War II era nor the rules-based, controlling approach developed during the Bretton Woods era. We must fundamentally rethink financial market regulation.

The governing thought behind this new approach is that the purpose of financial regulation should be to improve the effectiveness of competitive and economic forces as they operate in the global capital market. We should do our best to create a perfect global capital market and with it more perfect real economic markets. As defined earlier, a "perfect" global capital market would be one in which the global financial law of one price is fully operational and in which funds flow from funds' providers to funds' users at prices established through the natural self-interest of all participants without regard to national boundaries.

As described earlier, people often confuse efficient markets with perfect markets. A market is efficient if it quickly and cost-effectively reflects, through changes in market prices, all available information. However, efficient markets can be destructive if they merely reflect changes in speculative demand fed by market distortions created by governments. Earlier in this chapter, we described how the Japanese government's deliberate distortion of the market led to a massive financial bubble and a greatly weakened financial system. Similarly, during the 1980s in the United States, the banking markets became far more efficient, but also far less perfect, because the government assumed risk through the deposit insurance system that should have been absorbed by participants in the market. These government distortions led to massive misallocations of capital, the destruction of the savings and loan industry, and the near bankruptcy of the U.S. commercial banking industry. Efficiency is necessary, but is not sufficient to create a perfect, or effective market.

To create an efficient, effective, global capital market, we must first recognize that financial markets are different from the markets for other goods and services and therefore require specific regulation. For a long time, governments have been tempted to use their regulatory powers over financial institutions to achieve objectives unrelated to sound monitoring. Under the regulatory approach we propose, regulation would not be used in such a manner. Such a proposal to separate financial institutions and market regulation from politics may seem naive. For many of us, financial institution regulation and politics seem to be hopelessly joined together. However, if we fail to make this separation, we will also fail to reform the system.

Why is this so important? It is simply because politically backed use of regulations to achieve policy objectives can be dangerous in an integrated global capital market.

Let's provide an example to illustrate the dangers. In response to rising interest charges, a heavily indebted nation can either work on fundamentals (like cutting spending) or can simply become more creative in issuing more debt. When faced with this choice, most government's first inclination is likely to become more creative in issuing debt. Governments have various devices, including taxes, reserve requirements, and capital requirements, to provide banks and other nationally based financial institutions with incentives to hold government debt. If a government increases the use of such incentives when pressure mounts, it may escape the full costs of issuing debt in the short term, but it also deprives itself of the market feedback that it may be approaching its debt limit. Eventually, the nation may get over-indebted relative to the long-term capacity of the nation to handle the debt. Then, if it gets into trouble, not only does the government lose the world's confidence, but the losses in the value of the debt can also cripple the capacity of the institutions holding the debt to help the country recover from the crisis.

Distorting capital flows almost always causes problems. For example, developed countries have often used a subsidized savings industry to cause an overallocation of capital at too low cost to the real estate market, which inevitably leads to overbuilding relative to real economic demand. The experience of the United States in letting the government safety net be used by savings institutions to subsidize real estate development in the 1980s illustrates the perils of such policies.

These perils exist in developing countries as well, where it is often said that protecting and controlling infant financial markets is necessary at an early stage of development. Financial systems that subsidize favored industries that are not truly creditworthy inevitably lead to much of the nation's scarce capital being tied up in large portfolios of nonperforming loans, or curb markets developing outside regulators' control.

The case of Korea illustrates this forcefully. Korean banks, under direct control of the government, were forced to lend, at reduced rates, to favored sectors, such as chemicals and heavy industry. These "policy loans," which were being subsidized by more productive businesses that were forced to pay higher rates than their creditworthiness alone would warrant, amounted to up to 50 percent of all loans. Not surprisingly, Korean banks ended up lending a full 10 percent of their entire assets to companies that could not meet their debt obligations. Even at the peak of the U.S. savings and loan crisis, the ratio of nonperforming assets to total assets in the United States was under 2 percent. The cost to the economy, particularly a developing economy, of so much misdirected investment potential is enormous.

In other words, in an open system, governments' attempts to channel capital cause capital to be misallocated while denying participants the information they need to adjust to changing conditions in the world. It is like trying to drive a car blindfolded.

In general, using regulation to prevent the spread of financial innovations such as securitization or derivatives, or to protect existing institutions, will also hurt the nation's long-term interest by allowing financial institutions from other nations to gain skills that domestic institutions will not have. Once the regulations are liberalized—and they will be liberalized through the power of market forces—domestic institutions are then at a clear competitive disadvantage. In the meantime, these restrictions will have deprived the country's citizens of the benefit of those innovations. For example, financial institutions in the United States and United Kingdom have been operating under more liberal regulation and greater competition in their home markets, and have developed extensive skills and competitiveness. As a result, the global investment banks and commercial banks in these nations are far better prepared to take advantage of the opportunities available in the global capital market. In addition, their home markets are better served.

We believe the global financial market is fundamentally more effective at making risk-and-reward tradeoffs, and at allocating capital, than are governments. Financial markets participants have the self-interest of putting their own capital at risk and this drives them to ensure that capital is invested well. Politicians making promises are less interested in finding where capital is best invested. Rather, they are largely concerned with how many votes they can collect. This means that they are often inclined to make bad economic decisions. Inevitably, the nation is hurt from the resulting misallocation of capital.

We believe that national governments that want to regulate their financial economy to help their own nations should use the global capital market to the nation's advantage by following three principles described in the following sections.

Principle 1. Create Effective and Efficient Local Financial Systems and Capture the Benefits of Globalization

Regulation should be designed to increase transparency: to improve financial disclosure; to ensure accurate accounting of assets, liabilities, income, and expenses; to prevent fraud; to prevent insider trading; and to ensure that contracts are effective and enforced with predictable regularity. The government should help make the markets work better. Conversely, domestic financial institutions or financial markets should not be regulated to achieve social objectives that the government is unwilling to finance through taxation or other independent resources.

Nor should regulation provide an unfair competitive advantage to preferred industries, to a particular institution or class of institutions, or (especially) to state-owned institutions. Most importantly, regulation should not be used to force or motivate regulated institutions to fund the government's own debt.

To capture the full benefits of global capitalism, governments should take a proactive role in facilitating global capital market activity, removing restrictions on domestic ownership of foreign assets and foreigners' ownership of domestic assets, assisting companies that seek to invest abroad or at home, and encouraging innovation in product offerings and services that allow savers the full benefit of global, risk-adjusted, high-return opportunities.

Principle 2. Provide Essential Safety Nets but Prevent Their Abuse

Financial markets will only work effectively if they are orderly. Bank panics benefit no one, and they can be terribly destructive. Therefore, safety nets are essential. Specifically, market makers in financial instruments need access to central bank liquidity in times of crisis, the deposits of unsophisticated savers should be insured against loss, and the payment system should be protected. However, it must be recognized that such safety nets are market anomalies (they provide depositors or investors with the potential for risk-free returns from institutions that are exposed to risks). Therefore, they offer significant potential for abuse. The stronger market forces become, the more market forces will cause any anomalies to be completely and fully exploited. Therefore, the government must also play a role in preventing the market from exploiting market anomalies created by safety nets.

In particular, the government should not influence risk-reward decisions or absorb significant risk because such actions will distort the market and create market flaws. Government also has a role in ensuring that failing financial institutions are liquidated, dismembered, restructured, or sold off in an orderly manner. In this way, they help minimize market disruption, ensure that losses from closure, liquidating, and restructuring are borne by private capital, and enable nonproductive capacity to be eliminated quickly from the system. Under this concept, no financial institution should be too big to fail and individual financial institutions should add value to customers or perish.

The natural consequence of competition is to separate winners from losers. It is extremely important that the capacity of losers be eliminated from the system. Overcapacity is not economically sound, as the protected steel industry and airline industries in Europe have shown. Because of the unique role of financial institutions in the economy, care needs to be taken to ensure that society is not disrupted by the precipitous failure of individual institutions. Over the long term, however, economic forces, not regulation, should determine the role of financial institutions in a nation.

Principle 3. Maximize the Direct, Long-Term Financial Self-Interest of the Government Itself in Any Financial Undertaking

If governments follow the first principle and do not influence the institutions they regulate to hold government debt, they will have to issue debt based on terms the market finds attractive. To the extent that governments are major borrowers from the global capital market, they have a direct self-interest in funding on the most cost-effective terms possible. This means that governments like any fund-raiser, should structure their funding to minimize costs. This would include adapting the terms of borrowing to meet the needs of different investors, possibly altering rate terms, maturities, or even currencies.

For example, governments could consider using more floating-rate debt in their mix of debt issuance. Governments have issued such a large amount of fixed-rate debt that the overall mix has shifted heavily in that direction (government debt increased from 18 percent to 25 percent of the total financial stock in the past decade), more heavily, possibly, than the willingness of savers to hold that debt. As a result, governments at times are charged a significant market premium on their long-term, fixed-rate debt. They can reduce this premium either by shortening the maturity (and continuously reissuing debt) or by issuing floating-rate debt. Issuing debt at floating rates places inflation and interest rate risk on the government, which has the best ability to control these risks through its policies.

There is considerable resistance to this idea. The market is more familiar with fixed-rate government debt, governments are not used to the relatively credit-insensitive floating-rate market, and most importantly, floating-rate debt exposes governments directly to inflation or other risks. However, asking the market to continue taking these risks may prove to be very expensive, since the market is charging governments for the perceived higher inflation and other risks anyway. So long as governments intend to keep a lid on their debts, and do not intend to monetize their debt (for which they will pay a heavy penalty as soon as the market detects the possibility), they should be more willing to take the risk than to pay the market directly for it. Such an approach could also lower the cost of fixed-rate debt to the private sector and to developing countries, and could possibly stimulate investment. While the United Kingdom has begun experimenting with this approach, most other countries have not.

Finally, governments should act like other participants in the market, pursuing profitable activity and refraining from unprofitable operations. A government with aligned policy objectives and market opportunities may consider intervening in foreign exchange markets if it can reasonably expect to profit from such an action. It should not, however, attempt to oppose the market in defense of its currency. The only possible outcome will be enormous losses of reserves, as demonstrated by case after case—United Kingdom in the 1970s, Spain during the ERM breakdown, and the United States in 1994 relative to the yen.

In summary, individual governments should act with the same kinds of financial self-interest exhibited by other global capital market participants. In so doing, the market will become more perfect since governments—major market participants—will become rational participants pursuing their own financial interest.

Moving to such principles will take time, particularly for heavily indebted nations or for those geared to operating within a tightly closed system. The required challenge is the least in the United States, but could be very large in Europe, in Japan, and in many developing countries. It may well be necessary for some nations to experience a series of financial crises before they are prepared to change. If they resist too much, for too long, however, the consequences to the individual nation could be severe. And, if too many nations resist for too long, the consequences to the world's economy could be disastrous.

PUTTING THE HOUSE IN ORDER

Over the past 20 years, the various nations of the world have used the freedom of floating exchange rates to pursue widely divergent economic strategies.

The United States used the freedom of the global capital market and the liberation of its own national financial economy to incur enormous trade and fiscal deficits and to keep its real economy growing for almost the whole decade of the 1980s. In effect, the United States used its trade deficit to attract capital from both the developed world and the developing world to help it finance its fiscal deficit. Japan, on the other hand, used its financial system to gain a competitive advantage in trade markets, but kept domestic inflation moderate despite high growth rates and high saving rates. Japan achieved this end by channelling the resulting excess liquidity into the real estate and equities markets, rather than into domestic demand for real goods and services, and the result was the bubble economy. Not only did the unwinding of this economy lead to recession in Japan, it also involved financial scandals that toppled many political leaders. Germany also pursued an export strategy during the 1980s to stimulate its economic growth. Germany kept domestic inflation moderate by exerting heavy regulatory control over the money supply and its domestic financial economy. Neither Japan nor Germany could have pursued these strategies if the United States had not been running its massive fiscal and trade deficits.

Now, this process of Japanese and German capital funding U.S. deficits is coming to an end. During most of the 1980s, Germany maintained a relatively low debt-to-GDP ratio. Now, as a result of German unification and Germany's generous entitlements programs, the country is also headed down the path of deficit finance at a pace that is unsustainable into the next century. Other smaller nations have been far more aggressive, relative to the size of their economies, in using debt to finance consumption. Some of these nations will be the first to test the capacity of the global financial market to finance their debt. Even in Japan, the era of fiscal surpluses is seemingly over and that nation will also be running deficits.

By running budget deficits that have spilled over into current account deficits, many developed countries are doing exactly the opposite of what they should be doing. Instead of running current account surpluses and building up a stock of foreign assets whose profits will then finance future retirees, deficit countries are incurring foreign and domestic debt that will need to be serviced or repaid in the future, exacerbating the problem of rising social expenditures. As we have seen, this will lead to unsustainable levels of debt.

What is a sustainable level of debt?

The answer to this question is not simple and will vary for each country; it is a function of the level of debt as a percentage of output, the rate of increase in the debt, the real rate of interest, and the economy's growth. A 55 percent debt-to-output ratio, at a 4 percent real interest cost, places about a 2 percent drag on the economy. Such a debt level may be sustainable given recent rates of growth. An 80 percent debt to output ratio at an 8 percent real interest rate, which is the current situation in several countries, places about a 6.5 percent real debt service drag on the economy and builds a major, long-term debt service issue. Such an interest rate drag is not sustainable even with a highly optimistic growth forecast. Indeed, if yield curves steepen further, the problem could become severe very fast.

At the very least, developed nations of the world must stabilize their debt to national output ratios. It is most important that the large nations, particularly the United States and Germany, get their fiscal affairs in order since their absolute share of the debt being raised is so large (in our base case, we project these two nations will issue close to 60 percent of all government debt from now to the year 2000).

Governments must consider creative solutions. Some countries have moved toward greater reliance, or even complete reliance, on private pension funds. Programs to encourage (or require) more widespread use of private pension funds would provide for future retirees even with lower government pension benefits. The private funds would be much more likely to be invested productively through the global capital market.

There is also the potential to mitigate the budget deficit by reducing government funding of health-care costs, particularly in the United States where these costs will overtake Social Security payments in the next four years.

Among all nations, the actions of the U.S. government are the most important because of its size (the United States alone accounts for about half of all government bonds issued today), the role of the U.S. dollar as a global reserve currency, and the nation's historic leadership role. As our projections show, the unique circumstances for the United States will insulate it from discipline for a while. It is likely that other nations will face a debt crisis long before the United States faces one. On the other hand, because of its unique circumstances and relative insulation, the United States has a powerful opportunity to be a leader in restoring fiscal imbalances that will enable the global capital market to lead us toward prosperity and away from devastation. The United States is far and away the nation that can most benefit from the unleashing of global capitalism and has the greatest capacity to take the lead role in ensuring that the world heads down the right path.

We stress that we are not taking an absolute position on expansionary fiscal policy per se. It may make great sense for some nations to make investments in the economy: in infrastructure, health care, and education through government programs. But they must think through how these investments will be paid off, and commit to following that plan. Most nations in the developed world have been using their debt capacity to fund consumption for social expenditures and low-return subsidies of unproductive industries, and consequently, they have little debt capacity available to finance public investment with potentially higher return.

The nations in the developed world are moving closer to the limits of their absolute debt capacity than is wise. Further movement in this direction will not only become progressively more expensive, it could be disastrous. The global capital market is able to function only because of the confidence it has in the various major governments and the safety nets they provide to their financial institutions. Undermining that confidence could be dangerous to the entire global economy.

BECOMING A SUPERCONDUCTOR FOR GLOBAL CAPITALISM

Beyond maintaining sound fiscal and monetary policies, governments must also pursue liberal economic policies to capture the enormous economic opportunity offered by global capitalism. This path leads to greater economic growth and, ultimately, to greater growth in jobs. Becoming a superconductor for global capitalism means opening up the economy so that it can access and benefit from the vast global store of existing innovations and processes known to increase productivity. Doing so involves a rethinking of policies on trade, limitations on foreign direct investment, new entrants' participation in markets, unnecessary codes and restrictions in the product market, and onerous regulations in the labor markets.

As a first step, many governments must embrace more fully the developments in international trade that are taking place. Despite much progress on bilateral and multilateral open market agreements, many developed world countries still limit the benefits of trade to those sectors that are internationally traded. But, as we have described, this is not enough. Countries must also open up the remaining portion of the economy, the 80 percent or so that is not internationally traded, the locally produced and locally consumed portion of the economy, so that these sectors can benefit from the increases in productivity that are possible through the transfer of best practices. This involves lowering restrictions on foreigners' investing directly in a country, as well as facilitating the licensing of external technology or techniques of production by local players, or simplifying the process of domestic-foreign company alliances. Going further, it also involves facilitating the process by which highly competitive companies access local distribution channels and direct marketing to customers.

Moreover, becoming a superconductor requires rethinking many rules and codes that govern product markets, but are not really necessary, or that give uncompetitive and underproductive companies unfair advantages.

Similarly, in many countries, it will be necessary to rethink the commitment to certain labor regulations that severely limit the long-term job creation and overall growth in the economy.

Becoming a superconductor also means ensuring the quality of the labor. While the transfer of innovation and best practice can take place even across countries with very different labor skills, as shown in the examples of transferring best practice from the United States to Latin America, the benefits of having a well-trained and educated labor force are clear throughout the world. Better educated and trained labor forces are more adaptable, an important characteristic in a rapidly changing global economy. And they are more likely to continue improvements and refining processes, which can further enhance productivity.

Finally, other traditional roles of government are ever more necessary, if ever more challenging. These include maintaining law and order, ensuring the validity of contracts and the respect of property, and maintaining social cohesion without excessive debt.

PREPARING FOR TAKEOFF

Until a few years ago, many developing countries pursued economic policies that repelled the global capital market; in many cases, governments imposed restrictions that made foreign investment very difficult. Because large levels of investment are required for growth, and people have high expectations for improving their standard of living, developing countries will be in great need of external capital to supplement their domestic savings. To attract this external capital, they will have to pursue economic policies that enhance the environment for business and, importantly, develop financial policy and infrastructure that are attractive to the global capital market.

The pattern of capital flows indicates that to access the global capital market, countries need to create a good economic and political environment for business. Such an environment will include some of the same characteristics noted for developed countries' policies: a manageable fiscal budget, an exchange rate that is neither overvalued nor undervalued, and a relatively low and controlled inflation rate. Historically, many developing countries have followed policies that are not market-oriented, that have instead restricted markets, granted private or public monopolies, and reduced competition through trade restrictions. A strong market orientation, competent government, and a stable order are elements of an attractive political environment.

We are not taking an absolute position on economic policy in developing countries either. Some countries may choose to provide basic infrastructure, health care, and education through government programs and others may choose to minimize government involvement even in these activities. We do not believe that the global capital market will condition its willingness to lend based on such choices. Rather, we are arguing that economic policies in developing countries that have often worked to repel the market have also reduced productivity and discouraged efficient allocation of resources. The global capital market will not channel funds toward the countries that hold on to such impediments to economic growth. For developing countries, economic reforms that make their economies more attractive to foreign investors will also stimulate economic growth for the countries' own citizens, as will the external capital itself.

Such a business-oriented economic and political environment is necessary but not sufficient. Liberal capital policy and an effective financial infrastructure are also needed. Liberal financial policies enable capital mobility and market allocation of funds. These policies would encourage the elimination of exchange rate restrictions, a simplification of approval processes for foreign direct investment, and the facilitation of capital mobility, including the repatriation of capital and dividends. As we have described, market allocation of funds is possible only when interest rates are not heavily regulated and the government does not direct large amounts of credit to targeted industries or regions.

A critical feature of financial management for a developing country is its foreign exchange rate policy. Once foreign exchange and capital controls are removed, which is an essential step in joining the global capital market, a developing country's exchange rate is subject to extreme market pressures. Moreover, it will be years after removing controls before a developing country can provide the conditions that enable forward foreign exchange derivatives to become deep enough to be useful. Foreign exchange uncertainty, with the absences of forward foreign exchange cover, creates real risks for investors that can discourage the importation of capital.

One approach a country can take is to try to peg exchange rates. But, as Mexico amply demonstrated in late 1994 and early 1995, this can be disastrous when market pressures force a revaluation. When even the central banks of Europe, working together, could not make the ERM work, what chance does a single foreign developing country central bank have in standing up to market pressures?

One response, used by nations such as Argentina, is to adopt a currency board approach. Under a currency board system, the domestic currency is set at a fixed rate against a foreign currency, typically the U.S. dollar, and is issued only if it can be fully backed by foreign reserves. In the extreme, then, a currency board system would not require a central bank, only a central monetary authority that would exchange domestic currency against foreign exchange at a set rate. Thus, this rules-based system creates high confidence: It prevents governments from printing money to finance deficits (and thereby creating inflation) and it limits the damage speculative attacks could have.

In practice, as in Argentina, countries with currency board systems do have central banks, and they use not only foreign currency reserves but also foreign currency denominated government bonds. The base money is only partially backed by these bonds though, and the basic system is highly transparent and strict. Even in this less strict form, a currency board system can be a sound way to stabilize risks.

In addition to good financial policy, countries must develop a good financial infrastructure with a competitive industry structure that encourages innovation, with limited state bank presence, and where possible with foreign participation that brings in healthy competition. A good financial infrastructure also requires reliable physical systems, such as bond and stock exchanges and reliable custodial services, and sound regulatory systems, overseen by impartial supervisors, to ensure accurate business accounting and to provide sound legal backing.

How rapidly can and should these changes take place? In Korea, changes are being implemented very slowly, while in India a full liberalization plan was launched in 1995. Of course, the answer will vary significantly by country. However, the existence of the global capital market actually provides developing countries with a much higher chance of success through liberalization than was previously the case. They are now able to benefit sooner from the benefits of a more effective, more perfect market and be the recipients of net flows that will help them grow faster and attain higher standards of living.

Despite the incentives for developing countries to adopt market-oriented policies, there is no guarantee that these policies will in fact be followed, or that once followed, that countries will stick with them. The case of Venezuela, from late 1993 to 1995, is an example of thwarted economic and financial reforms. The rapid deterioration of the economy in this example illustrates, however, that once the genie of economic reform is out of the bottle, it is hard to get it back in, and the negative consequences of being excluded are much greater. The pressure from the global capital market is increasing, making it more and more costly for unwise policies to be followed.

Developing countries can continue for some time to isolate themselves from the global capital market. But developing country governments have strong incentives to participate in global capitalism by allowing capital to flow freely and by letting international financial institutions operate in their economies. The high stakes for economic potential and the vast range of local investment opportunities in developing countries make the strategy of importing capital and know-how superior to the strategy of export-led growth. It allows much greater access to external capital accompanied by best practice, and thus to more rapid growth.

SOCIAL CHALLENGES

The benefits to developed countries of putting their house in order and capturing the opportunity, and to developing countries of preparing for takeoff, are enormous and probably unprecedented. In effect, the benefit to the world will be to enlarge dramatically the global pie of prosperity. But the social challenges that result from these changes are likewise enormous and probably unprecedented. While the pie may be bigger overall, the allocation of shares of the pie will not be easy.

We described in Chapter 7 the range of powerful conflicting interests that will oppose the changes. And it is not surprising that they should do so because many of them will be seriously disadvantaged by these policy shifts particularly in the short term.

Workers who spent a life in toil, even if it happened to be in underproductive enterprises, worked under an implicit contract that the employment and social system would take care of them. When this contract is broken, grave displacement can occur in society. Retraining or relocating workers after major industry restructurings is never easy, and seldom is it done rapidly. Cutting back on entitlements, such as pensions and health care, that individuals had always expected to receive, means that many will be severely unprepared when sickness or old age approaches. Particularly for older workers, the simultaneous rupture of the employment contract, such as a guaranteed job for life or continuous pay increases, and the social contract, including entitlements to pensions and health care, can be truly devastating.

On the other hand, the economic rent to those who are highly skilled, or to those who own the innovations and best practices across industries, has probably never been greater. In a globalizing economy the value of skill and know-how is multiplied over and over. In a closed economy, having a 1 percent better operating margin than all other competitors as a result of a better process or product yields the producer the value of 1 percent applied to the one closed market; in a global economy, if the process or product represents a truly sustainable advantage, a 1 percent better margin yields the producer the value of 1 percent applied to multiple markets throughout the world.

The dichotomy between the losers and the winners is likely to be enormous and to be the source of major social conflict and regional strife. Some of this is already apparent in several countries around the world. China, for example, as it has allowed some of its peripheral provinces to "prepare for takeoff" has created enormous prosperity, but the Special Economic Zones, where the wealth and growth are concentrated, stand out now in stark contrast to the poverty and backwardness that is evident in much of the rest of the country.

In the process of change, many critical social norms and structures will be put into question before new ones can be developed. This will put severe strain on the same mechanisms that are needed to alleviate the social conflict and find viable solutions that will not destroy the opportunity altogether.

A major challenge for individual countries and for the world as a whole will be to find a constructive framework for the resolution of social conflict that does not rely unduly on mortgaging and overleveraging countries by issuing unsustainable levels of debt. The more countries are able to capture the opportunity and achieve greater economic growth in their economies, the more resources they will have (including a greater ability to sustain moderate levels of debt) to develop these frameworks and find solutions to these difficult problems.

HEROES WHO CAN LEAD US

We are headed into turbulent times. We need heroes to lead us, not politicians who make promises they cannot deliver. We need leaders of the stature of a Churchill, a Roosevelt, or a Bismarck to coalesce nations around making the fundamental changes required to bridge to an open, global system. In recent times, however, with a few exceptions such as Thatcher in the United Kingdom, Gorbachev in Russia, and Menem in Argentina, leaders of sufficient stature and vision have not come into power.

It seems leaders of such stature only emerge in crises. Perhaps it is because the populace resists true leadership when they are satisfied with the status quo and are only willing to be led when it is apparent that the current situation is becoming untenable. If so, then the conditions are being created in many nations where true leaders can emerge. The existing pillars of economic and social stability are crumbling. With the possible exception of the United States, which faces the least change to integrate into an open, global system, most of the nations of the world are ill prepared for the changes ahead.

While difficult times can enable heroes to emerge, they can enable a Hitler, or a Lenin, to emerge as well. What kinds of leaders emerge will depend on how well the citizens in each nation state understand where their true interests lie.

At this moment in time, given the discrediting of socialism and communism, there is a real opportunity to get much of the world's population to embrace capitalism and work to address the challenges that it poses. The critical issue will be whether or not leaders emerge who will tell the population what they need to hear as opposed to what they want to hear. Churchill's promises of "blood, toil, tears and sweat" were far more accurate, and inspiring, than promises of an easy path to victory which no one would have believed anyway. We need heroes who can tell people that real prosperity to the nation can come from embracing global capitalism, but who will also tell that achieving that prosperity will require that unsustainable entitlements be cut, that industry subsidies be cut, that unproductive jobs be eliminated, and that individuals who want security take responsibility for creating it for themselves.

At the same time, we will need heroes who do not ignore social issues, but who use the power of the nation state to create incentives for people to help themselves and who find ways to ensure the remaining money available for entitlements flows to those who are truly incapable of helping themselves. This will often involve taking on powerful political elites and the broad middle class.

The United States can occupy a special role in helping heroes emerge. Much of the world still looks to the United States for leadership even though it led the world away from fiscal responsibility in the early 1980s.

If, going forward, the United States can willingly close its fiscal deficit, it can set the stage for other governments to follow. Closing the deficit is easy for the United States in comparison with most other nations. If the United States can curtail the growth of its health care and Social Security entitlements to its middle class and its affluent citizens, through market based health-care reforms and through greater reliance on private pension systems, its deficit could be reduced sharply by early in the next century.

While faced with slightly greater challenges in making the necessary changes, Japan and Germany, as the economic powers that they are, also have important global roles to play. In addition to its current financial difficulties, Japan must address the massive overprotection of its product markets. Fortunately, it is the only major developed world country that has not let its fiscal house get out of order. It must continue to be a leader of fiscal responsibility (especially given the most recent trends toward indebtedness in its economy) and must assist the world in providing the necessary backstops.

Although Germany has maintained a sound financial structure with no major credit exposure, it will face serious fiscal problems related to the unsustainability of its entitlement policies. It must also address the extreme extent of product and labor restrictions that inhibit the benefits of global capitalism (including product restrictions even in their financial sector). Given the size of its economy, Germany must become a major European leader driving the necessary changes toward a truly prosperous global economy.

If they confront their challenges, the United States, Japan, and Germany, working through such agencies as the Bank for International Settlements, the World Bank, and the International Monetary Fund (IMF) can have the financial strength to provide the essential safety nets required to protect the world's financial system. The real potential for the devastation scenario outlined in Chapter 6 suggests that it is in the enlightened self-interest of the United States, along with other major nations such as Germany and Japan, to be prepared to deal with defaults on debt by major developed world nations. Indeed, it will probably take major crises to get some nations to make the required changes. However, rather than arranging a unilateral bailout such as was done with Mexico, the financially secure nations should consider backstopping the banking system (perhaps through injecting capital and through temporarily taking over key management roles of troubled banks in the event of a crisis) rather than bailing out the entire government. A beefed-up Bank for International Settlements could potentially take the lead role.

Should such backstopping be required, there could also be a role for the major nations of the world, perhaps working through the IMF and the World Bank, to help political leaders in developed countries going through such crises make the necessary broader changes in economic policy.

Beyond helping contain global financial crises, the United States has the opportunity to be the champion of global capitalism and to lead by example rather than by rhetoric. If it has the will to put its fiscal house in order and to complete the liberalization of its product market restrictions and financial regulation, the United States has the opportunity to become a true superconductor for global capital flows. In reality, the United States needs to make relatively fewer changes in policy and regulation, relative to other countries, to be a full beneficiary of global capitalism.

Will the United States find heroes to lead it? Will Germany? Will Japan?

Much will depend on the willingness of the nations' citizens to be led. All of us must get our minds around embracing global capitalism:

politicians, journalists, businesspeople, voters. We all must understand that the forces at work are unstoppable and that the faster we
make the required changes, the better we will all be.

If we continue to elect people who promise prosperity without
change, income without hard work, and social stability at the cost of
failure to adjust to economic reality, not only will we lose a more prosperous future, we risk having serious crises as well. Nation after nation will be forced to cut back on entitlements to the point that the
truly helpless are irreparably hurt. And, nation after nation may experience major social instability, caused by economic devastation, such
as we have not witnessed since the 1920s and the 1930s.

* * * *

Up until now we have been taking the perspective of a "citizen of
the world." We have been describing the unleashing of global capitalism from the perspective of the political leader, the economist, the social scientist, the journalist, the historian.

Now, we will shift perspective. In Part Three, we will focus on
global capitalism up close and personally. How, specifically, are capitalists capturing global opportunities? And, how can corporate leaders
and investors ensure that they capture their share of the opportunity?

Part Three

Capturing the Opportunity

— 9 —

The Unfettered, Unrelenting
Search for Profit

The driving force behind global capitalism is not hard to understand. Just as the woolly mammoth hunters in the global capital market have found opportunities to exploit anomalies in financial markets, global capitalists have found opportunities to exploit anomalies in the markets for goods and services. And, in the worldwide markets for goods and services, the principal anomaly is that barriers including product market restrictions, labor restrictions, and—perhaps most importantly—the lack of capital mobility have prevented the efficient transfer of product offerings and superior production techniques.

Consequently, the increasing mobility of capital, in combination with the crumbling of product market and labor restrictions, is creating a massive opportunity to earn extraordinary returns on capital, not from new innovation, but simply from the transfer of existing products and techniques of production. Although this process is not new, what is new is the sudden emergence of millions upon millions of these opportunities at the microeconomic level as capital has become more mobile in virtually every industry, from consumer packaged goods, to construction materials, to retail banking, to funeral services. The result has been to attract a vast number of individual participants seeking profit. And, by their very actions, these individual participants are overwhelming the remaining product market and labor restrictions, which in turn, creates even more opportunities for global capitalists with literally trillions of dollars to finance transfers of products and techniques of production. An unfettered, unrelenting search for global profits is now well launched.

Again, let's go from the generic to the specific. Let's examine how the Japanese automobile industry captured enormous opportunities in the U.S. market.

THE AUTOMOTIVE INDUSTRY IN THE UNITED STATES: A CASE EXAMPLE

When we think about industrial capitalism, few stories carry as strong associations as does the story of the automotive industry in the United States. Dating back to the 1920s with Ford's Model T, the American car has been a symbol of industrial capitalism in general, and of American enterprise in particular. Interestingly, the U.S. world share of automobile production peaked in 1947, at 82 percent of total production, and declined continuously after that year until the early 1990s, when it started rising again. Non-American cars, particularly Japanese cars, began appearing in the 1950s and 1960s, offering differentiated value and gaining market share. As has been documented extensively, from the 1950s through the 1970s open competition against foreign imports led to sharp reductions in the sales of all U.S. cars, motorcycles, and heavy trucks.

But the really rapid decline in the fortunes of the American car industry came in the 1980s. Most everyone knows that fierce competition from abroad drove down the U.S. share of world production. But the nature of the competition is often poorly understood. It was not only the continuing increase in the number of imports of foreign cars, which rose almost 5 percent between 1979 and 1990 (from 21.9 to 26.4 percent of sales), that was at the heart of this competition. More importantly, it was the output of transplants—foreign car manufacturing plants located in the United States—(which increased from zero in 1982 to 22 percent of sales in 1990) that really undermined the U.S. car makers' position. This kind of competitive threat was ultimately responsible for the rapid restructuring of the U.S. industry. Between 1980 and 1990, the Big Three U.S. auto makers closed or converted a large share of their North American assembly plants: Ford closed or converted 40 percent; Chrysler closed or converted 38 percent; and General Motors closed or converted 24 percent. The Japanese "auto invasion" was also responsible for producing a vast number of high-quality cars for U.S. consumers at a relatively low cost.

This U.S. auto industry story is an early example of global capitalism at work: External capital (in this case, Japanese capital) accompanied by better techniques of production (in this case, production of high-quality cars at a lower cost) seeks high returns worldwide, and hunts down opportunities to profit from the existence of lower productivity around the world. The opportunity took the form of making large investments in major U.S. plants, employing U.S. workers, and organizing according to Japanese techniques of production, all of which provided attractive growth and returns to capital. These transplants represented fierce competition and posed dramatic challenges to local producers. It was this global capitalism that so fundamentally restructured the U.S. automotive industry and ultimately drove the Big Three to take the actions necessary to become more productive and lower cost producers. They have now become largely competitive with the Japanese transplants.

The global capital revolution and the unleashing of global capitalism will lead to innumerable cases of more intense competition and similar industry restructuring. The global economic transformation described in Part Two of this book will be driven by the unfettered, unrelenting search for profit. As capital mobility accelerates, more and more opportunities for capital to profit by hunting down differences in productivity will be exploited. More powerful market pressures, from competitors, consumers, and shareholders will result in dramatic changes to industries and short-term turmoil. While these changes will be resisted by many, ignored by some until it is too late, and cause much tension, the opportunities are so large, and the participants so resourceful, that the changes will ultimately take place.

In this chapter, we will define global capitalism at the microeconomic level, and explain what barriers have prevented it from extending rapidly until very recently. Then, we will explore industry transformations and how global capitalism is likely to affect industry structures, the specific opportunities created for some and the threats created for others, highlighting the new challenges for all. We will also describe the critical role of the equity shareholder in driving the changes. Then, by providing a cross-section of specific examples covering most aspects of the economy, we will illustrate how dramatic and fundamental this change will be at the company and industry level and how it will affect very large portions of the economy.

GLOBAL CAPITALISM AT THE INDUSTRY LEVEL

By global capitalism at the industry level, we refer to the process by which industry leaders seek to profit from a competitive advantage by pursuing opportunities globally, beyond any national boundary or by importing competitive advantages globally to compete locally. As we described in Chapter 7, global capitalism has existed for a long time. It was, in fact, a major force behind the Industrial Revolution. But the speed and force with which global capitalism will now proceed, given the development of the global capital market, is unprecedented. It is truly driving a transformation of the world's economy without parallel, in scale or scope, in human history.

Until very recently, the boundaries around an industry were typically national, defined primarily by the country boundaries and the national government's laws and regulations concerning products and services, labor practices, taxes and trade. Local culture and history, as well as language and religion all helped define the development of the economy and particular industries.

While many industries were exposed to trade, and therefore to some extent best practice from elsewhere in the world, international trade affected only a portion of the economy. Up until now, the global economy was limited primarily to goods and services that could be internationally traded. However, in most nations, tradable goods account for less than 20 percent of GNP, and in many nations less than 10 percent of GNP. Most goods are locally produced and consumed. As capital becomes fully mobile, the stage is set for rapid globalization in nation after nation of the 80 percent of world's economy that is locally produced and consumed.

What has prevented this lucrative process from fully taking place? Why is this happening now?

Although some transnational opportunities have been captured from some time—Coca-Cola expanded internationally during World War II—the barriers to pursuing them on a large scale were formidable. Not only did companies have to contend with insufficient information and complicated capital controls, they were often unable to remit their dividends or make investment and divestment decisions without burdensome approval processes. Even when they were able to have sufficient control over their investments and the returns to those investments, they were often exposed to enormous risks—currency risk, interest rate risk, and liquidity risk—that they were unable to manage or hedge. Moreover, in many markets, restrictive regulations in the product markets and the labor markets significantly blocked productive competitors from introducing products or innovative techniques of production. They often had trouble finding local labor with sufficient skills or language capabilities. In addition, cultural and historical preferences and traditions have resisted many changes. Despite these barriers, many profit seekers found innovative ways to tap into the potential opportunities.

The developments in the global capital market provide profit seekers in the product markets myriad new approaches to pursue opportunities creatively and to overcome the difficult barriers that have existed for so long. By taking advantage of the relentless liberalization of financial regulation worldwide, by leveraging the much greater information that is available for servicing global capital flows, and by proactively managing risks, more and more companies are becoming global capitalists. Particularly important to this process is new risk-management techniques that allow market participants to take the risks they are best able to take (e.g., operational risks) and not take risks they are unable or unwilling to take (e.g., interest rate or currency risks). Just as aggressive profit seekers led to the dismantling of financial regulation, so too those seeking to profit from clear global competitive advantages will find ways to get around any barriers and will drive the ultimate dismantling of any remaining barriers.

Once unleashed, global capitalism—driven by the vast liquid, highly mobile, financial stock—will continue to extend far beyond the traditional production of manufactured goods. Global capitalism will extend to food production, consumer goods distribution, legal services, health services, consumer financial services, restaurants, and even haircuts. It will take place around the world, in developed countries and, even more dramatically, in developing countries and will involve every industry in the world. And it will take various forms, including capital investments that involve direct transplants, alliances with local partners, joint ventures, or licensing agreements.

INDUSTRY TRANSFORMATIONS

Let's start with a concrete view of an industry as a group of companies, all of which create a specific value for customers that the customers perceive to be generally interchangeable. A simple example to keep in mind is the soft drink industry, most clearly personified by the Pepsi versus Coca-Cola competition over the past 40 years but with gathering global intensity over the past 10 to 15 years. Despite their spending millions of advertising dollars to achieve differentiation in the market, Pepsi and Coca-Cola, as well as multiple other colas, are rough substitutes for one another. The products themselves are generally locally produced (bottled) rather than exported and are essentially nothing but carbonated water, flavoring, and packaging. The industry structure is a relatively stable one defined by the head-to-head battles of the two dominant players.

Every place these competitors have entered, they have pushed aside local producers of nonalcoholic drinks while simultaneously building primary demand. They have displaced not just local producers of carbonated beverages, but also other forms of nonalcoholic beverages such as juices, tea, coffee, and even bottled water (particularly in countries where potable water is hard to find). They have competed particularly hard in the techniques of marketing (market research, promotion and branding, distribution, pricing, etc.). They continually invest in new products (e.g., new flavors of soft drinks) technology improvement (e.g., new packaging) and new product lines (e.g., expanding into juices) and roll out these new products, technologies, and product lines globally taking full advantage of scale. In the process, every place they operate they have stimulated the development of innovative, new competitors (from juices to "premium" carbonated water) seeking out niches sometimes globally, in the marketplace dominated by Coke and Pepsi. They have spawned a global industry as they continually strive to gain competitive advantage over one another.

Although the globalization of soft drinks has been well underway for decades, the process is now being repeated in industry after industry, in country after country, worldwide, not just in manufactured goods or consumer goods, but in every product and service being offered.

Innovation and Technological Improvements

It is generally well understood that innovations and technological improvements are a source of competitive advantage that can lead to major industry restructuring. A classic business school example is the "category killer" case of Wal-Mart in the United States. Almost every state in the United States has seen the pattern: a relatively stable set of small, independent, local mom-and-pop stores that offer health and beauty aids, household cleaning supplies, or packaged goods are wiped out in a matter of months (in some cases, a matter of weeks) by the entry of a full-service, low-cost provider of all these products. The innovation or new technology that gives Wal-Mart a competitive advantage in this case is an integrated, well-executed, warehouse-type delivery and distribution system that is technically superior, and radically more productive, than the existing practice in these small towns. A snapshot of Wal-Mart's financial success reveals that growth and returns over the period of rapid expansion were truly extraordinary. Net sales for the company skyrocketed from $4.7 billion in 1974 to $67 billion in 1994. There are now well over 2,100 Wal-Mart outlets in the United States.

And Wal-Mart is not alone; indeed, there are many such examples. Domino's Pizza, by streamlining the process and timing of pizza making and delivery transformed another mom-and-pop industry into a national one, in the process taking thousands of small operators out of business. Staples has become the leading office supply store, rapidly replacing a large number of regional distributors. First USA has recently shaken up the credit card industry by becoming a leading provider that leverages systems technology to maintain a low-cost position. Yet another example is Mrs. Fields Cookies, which through superior information systems for processing, communications, and other management functions, including operations of the stores and hiring sales employees, created a highly lucrative worldwide franchise in an industry that had only highly local appeal. In the process, Mrs. Fields Cookies has significantly transformed that market as well.

The Wal-Mart case, like many of the other examples cited, is important for two reasons. First, these companies are not in the manufacturing sector. Services comprise the lion's share of total output, 60 percent (or more) in most developed world economies. Second, they are all examples of "innovation" taking place through the transfer of existing techniques of production, not the transfer of physical goods. Traditional models of competition rely exclusively on the notion of physical goods arbitrage as the vehicle of change. The more subtle form of competition is the introduction of a process or innovation that might include the organization of tasks and functions, or real advantages in quality control, or specific organizational strengths such as recruiting and training, or systematic approaches to selling and distribution. This subtle form of competition is a critical dimension of the economic growth that is possible through global capitalism and a critical feature of the dramatic transformation of industries that is likely to take place.

Watching Water Boil

The vast amounts of research and investment on the topic of innovation inform us that breakthroughs in technology, management techniques, or product developments are hard to come by or to plan on a continuous basis. Moreover, undertaking any innovation can be risky and terribly expensive. Technology innovations usually follow an *S*-curve with a very long, slow start-up before entering a rapid growth phase. Waiting for these innovations can be a bit like watching water boil. Moreover, the risks of investment loss by betting on the wrong technology at the wrong time are large. Therefore, the real opportunity presented by the birth of the global capital market and the unleashing of global capitalism is that now the large stock of proven, existing "best" techniques of production and processes can be transferred around the world, to less productive areas.

With a proven technology, you have many advantages. For example, you are less likely to drill "dry holes," you better understand the relevant economics, you can anticipate likely competitive responses by local producers (because you have seen them before), and you can focus attention on the key sources of competitive advantage (which you understand but which your local competitors do not).

Therefore, with increasingly mobile capital, these proven technologies will be transferred globally because they represent enormous risk-adjusted returns on operations, provided the risks to capital can be mitigated. Now, in country after country, innovation can simply be a transfer of best practice, rather than new invention. And, as the rapid growth in global foreign direct investment suggests, much of this is beginning to happen already (see Exhibit 9.1).

The extension of global capitalism around the world is therefore providing enormous opportunities for those with clear advantages in productivity and techniques of production.

Exhibit 9.1.   Summary—Global Patterns of Foreign Direct Investment

$ Billions, Annual Averages

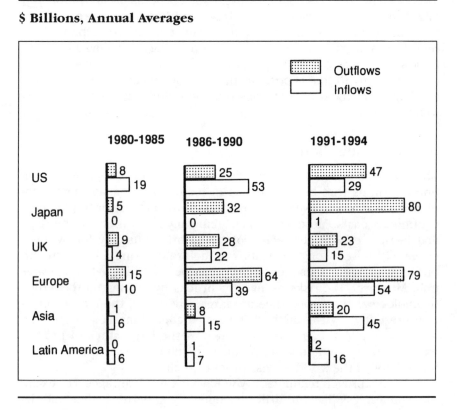

Source: BIS.

The perspective from the local player under attack is much different, particularly for those who have been exposed to little or no competition. In country after country, participant after participant is complaining about the difficulty of growing revenues and protecting margins.

While with a global perspective, the world seems awash with opportunity and an overchoice of possibilities, local businesses see a grim future precisely because nonlocal competitors are entering the market and are gaining share with innovative (to that local market) techniques of production.

Many of these players, ostrichlike, are trying to pretend it isn't happening to them. Others, under attack from global competition, are cross-subsidizing uncompetitive businesses from the returns earned on healthier businesses and are thereby failing to make the investments needed to protect the still healthy businesses. In some businesses, multi-year wars of attrition are being waged, that no one will win, between local competitors cross-subsidizing a favorite business and global players, lacking distribution, trying to enter directly.

For all players, global capitalism opens up a wide range of new strategic choices. It also is creating whole new sets of risks for all participants.

All these changes, in turn, are driving changes in industry structures and economies. The turmoil that is likely will affect all participants as they are forced to operate in an uncertain and rapidly changing world. Importantly, the principal owners of major companies, the equity shareholders, will respond to these changes, demanding globally competitive returns to their investments on a risk-adjusted basis. And, as the equity markets integrate, these pressures will be felt more and more uniformly worldwide. Sleepy companies and sleepy industries, worldwide, will become a thing of the past.

GLOBAL OPPORTUNITY

The source of the global opportunity will be the globalization of the best techniques of production from around the world, and the access to more and larger markets, which enables companies to achieve economies of scale.

Opportunity from Transferring Best Practice

Even within the developed world, enormous productivity differences, or market anomalies, persist in the production of goods and services. If the various regulatory and risk barriers can be overcome, an industry player operating at best practice can translate its competitive advantages into high return. We opened this chapter with the example of the U.S. auto industry, but even since the restructuring of the U.S. plants, large productivity gaps persist outside Japan and the United States. Germany's productivity levels in the automotive sector were only about two-thirds of U.S. levels (in 1992), and Germany, Italy, and Spain all have cost positions that are at least 75 percent higher than the U.S. cost position, which is not yet at Japanese levels.

Pursuing such woolly mammoths in the economy of goods and services takes more time than in the financial markets, but the returns are enormous. As they are pursued, they will cause restructuring in industry after industry worldwide.

The work of the McKinsey Global Institute demonstrates productivity gaps, which could be largely closed through the transfer of best practice, exist across a wide variety of sectors, including auto assembly, auto parts, metalworking, steel, computers, consumer electronics, processed food, beer, and soap/detergents, airlines, retail banking, restaurants, general merchandise retailing, and telecommunications. For example, productivity levels in Japanese food processing, or general merchandise retailing, are but a fraction of the U.S.

McKinsey Global Institute Productivity Studies

Since 1992, the McKinsey Global Institute, along with a prominent advisory board of academics, including the Nobel laureate Bob Solow, has been exploring differences in productivity around the world and the reasons for those differences. In 1992, they released a report on Service Sector Productivity that examined five service sectors across the United States, Europe, and Japan. In 1993, they released another report on Manufacturing Sector Productivity, which covered nine manufacturing sectors, also across the Triad. In 1994, they applied the methodologies from the two earlier studies to examine productivity across four industry sectors in five countries in Latin America—Argentina, Brazil, Colombia, Mexico, and Venezuela. Across all these industries, a few critical themes emerge. Very large differences in productivity exist within sectors in different economies. A primary determinant of the level of productivity in any given sector is its exposure to competition, particularly, its exposure to global best practices. Exhibits 9.1, 9.2, and 9.3 summarize the productivity differentials from the three reports.

**Exhibit 9.1.   Summary—Labor Productivity Comparison —
United States versus Germany, France, United Kingdom,
and Japan**

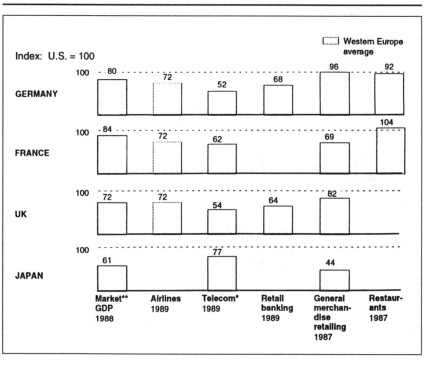

* Total factor productivity shown for telecommunications.
** GDP excluding government, education, health, and real estate.
Source: McKinsey analysis; McKinsey Global Institute.

levels, 33 percent and 44 percent respectively. In the United Kingdom, the productivity level in the telecommunications industry is only 54 percent of U.S. levels. And Germany's beer producers are only 44 percent as productive as American beer makers.

In the developing world, there are even more extreme cases where the transfer of best practice transfer can lead to highly profitable investments. (Again, based on the work of the McKinsey Global Institute, we can document other productivity gaps in Argentina, Brazil, Colombia, Mexico, and Venezuela. In steel production, none of these countries achieve even 45 percent of U.S. steel productivity levels; in processed food, none achieve more than 52 percent of U.S. levels. And anecdotally, the list continues, with consumer goods packaging in

Exhibit 9.2.   Summary—Labor Productivity

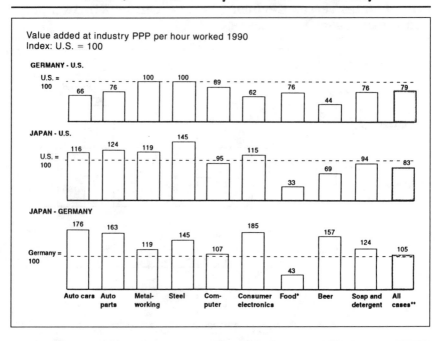

* Based on shipment.
** Weighted by employment, only 1990.
Source: McKinsey analysis; McKinsey Global Institute.

China, credit card servicing in India, airlines in Venezuela, chemicals in Colombia, pharmaceuticals in Sri Lanka, banking in Russia, and so on.)

In addition to the opportunity from the huge productivity gaps in the developing world, exciting possibilities stem from the low levels of penetration for many goods and services. Banking services in Latin America showed very low levels of penetration—fractions of U.S. levels—even when the proper market, only those earning high incomes, was taken into account. Likewise, low penetration levels are evident in telephone access: Whereas the United States has 52 lines per 100 inhabitants, Brazil has only 7, Mexico has only 9, and Colombia has only 10. Similar low levels of penetration hold for almost all services in these economies: computers, airlines, or food. As the economies of these countries prosper, the number of households able to purchase such goods and services will increase, further expanding the opportunities

Exhibit 9.3.   Summary—Labor Productivity Comparison—United States versus Argentina, Brazil, Colombia, Mexico, and Venezuela

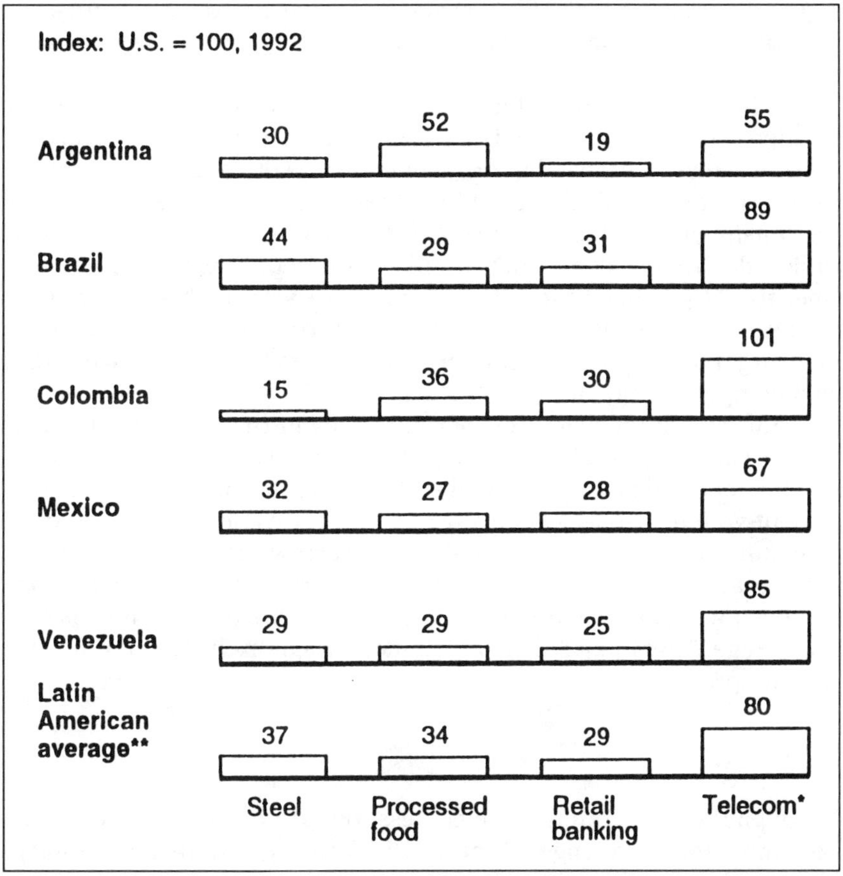

Index: U.S. = 100, 1992

	Steel	Processed food	Retail banking	Telecom*
Argentina	30	52	19	55
Brazil	44	29	31	89
Colombia	15	36	30	101
Mexico	32	27	28	67
Venezuela	29	29	25	85
Latin American average**	37	34	29	80

* Total factor productivity shown for telecommunications, unadjusted for quality differences.
** Weighted by employment.
Source: McKinsey analysis; McKinsey Global Institute.

for market penetration. At the recent average growth rates of developing countries over the past decade (a decade which included the debt crisis), world GNP would increase from $29 trillion on a purchasing power parity basis to $88 trillion by the year 2020, when the developing countries' share of the total would increase from 45 to 69 percent.

Opportunity from Scale

The transition toward full capital mobility, by providing greater access to more markets, multiplies opportunities to benefit more directly from large economies of scale. Such scale economies could come from a variety of sources: production, logistics, marketing, distribution, or purchasing.

A few examples will illustrate the value of a global market versus a national one. Large advertising campaigns are critical for many industries, such as branded goods, consumer health aids, or cosmetics, but up-front expenditures to build a brand name can be exorbitant. In the consumer health-care market, for example, it can take over $50 million dollars of advertising to create a brand. The greater the volume, the larger the base over which these very high costs can be amortized. Companies that can effectively leverage their fixed costs over larger volumes by expanding into new markets will have a distinct competitive advantage.

Earlier, we touched on other examples in the financial markets, foreign exchange trading and swap transactions. These already take place in enormous volumes daily at a global level. In this industry, without volumes greater than any one country could demand, it would be impossible to survive profitably the narrow margins that characterize that business. However, since the market is now defined globally, even with a margin of only a few basis points (or hundredths of a percentage point) per dollar of volume, foreign exchange trading can be quite profitable.

Challenges

Although the opportunities are endless, the participants also will confront numerous challenges. Precisely how to capture the opportunity, whether through licensing, joint ventures, alliances, or foreign direct investment, become critical questions that are not always easy to answer. There will be many more risks to manage, including political risks, legal risks, risks that contracts are not upheld, interest rate risks, currency risks, operational risks, partner default risks, contingency risks, and quite possibly, a greater likelihood of catastrophe risk. New methods will be needed to break into entrenched and possibly loyal client bases in new markets. Having proper distribution or access to local sales forces in new markets may become a thorny issue.

Less productive local players face the additional challenges of how best to respond, how to adapt to the changes while leveraging unique strengths, such as an entrenched client base, unique relation-ships, or well-established distribution systems. They also face critical questions of the timing of the response. The companies that manage these challenges successfully will define the new industry structures that emerge.

INDUSTRIES UNDER SIEGE

Global capitalism and the worldwide transfer of the best tech-niques of production will transform industries around the globe, just as traditional innovations have transformed domestic (and in many cases global) industries in the past.

Local competitors that are unproductive on a world scale, and that have benefited from protection (government regulation, high tar-iffs, oligopolistic structures) will be faced with the threat of new com-petitors in the form of capital financing better techniques of production who can draw upon almost limitless funding from the global capital market. Local competitors will be subject to all the industry pressure that comes from direct competition against players with clear com-petitive advantages—more demanding customers and pressure on costs. And, very importantly, they will face pressures from sharehold-ers for improved performance.

When Wal-Mart opens a store in a new region, the local stores must respond by cutting their prices significantly. To maintain their levels of profits, or simply to make a profit, many local shop owners are forced to keep their stores open longer than usual, reduce the number of employees, and cut expenditures on sourcing and opera-tions. Wal-Mart's pursuit of huge opportunities puts enormous pres-sure on the traditional way in which these local shops conduct business and, in many cases, forces some out of business altogether.

Similarly, as world-class productive competitors seek out the myriad opportunities described earlier, less productive local national competitors will feel the pressure on their less productive operations and, in some cases, may be pressured out of business. The pressure will come in the form of customer demand for better service, price competition, expense reduction, and ultimately, unsustainably low re-turns to investment.

THE GLOBAL CAPITALIST: THE EQUITY SHAREHOLDER

If less productive companies do not adapt, and are not able to match their new competition by delivering greater value, lowering cost, offering new product, or providing better technology—if they do not respond to the competitive threats to which they are exposed—they will lose customers, and ultimately profits. This can quickly lead to dramatically lower profitability and lower returns to the shareholders' capital. If lower returns persist while higher return opportunities exist in the market, shareholders will vote with their feet, and unproductive companies will be divested, or be acquired by others, who are willing to make the necessary changes.

At the core of global capitalism, then, is the equity shareholder and the investor market that owns equities. Equity investors will demand globally competitive returns to capital. For companies with clear global competitive advantages, productivity-driven, scale-driven, or otherwise, this will mean stronger and stronger pressure to pursue the vast range of global opportunities that yield high returns. In a world where Procter & Gamble aggressively profits from its competitive advantages by pursuing opportunities around the world, Colgate-Palmolive cannot compete effectively if it does not also profit from those high-return opportunities. For those companies that are exposed to the competition of companies with competitive advantages, the pressure from equity investors means pressure to adapt to the competition, to become more productive, less costly, or adopt new technology; otherwise, they will perish by liquidation or by being taken over. Such was the pressure that the U.S. auto makers faced, and that drove them to adapt to the competition, transforming the industry through those changes.

As companies across a wide array of industries respond to the pressures of equity investors, they will find innovative ways to circumvent any existing barriers to greater economic performance. Through the use of technology, the greater access to information, creative risk-management techniques, new delivery channels, joint ventures, alliances, and any number of other ways, companies will eradicate the multiple barriers that have enabled the less productive, less efficient industries to persist. In this way, government regulations, product market restrictions, labor restrictions, and other constraints will be undermined by the vast levels of highly motivated, resourceful economic activity.

This very process of equity holders demanding globally competitive returns, from companies with a competitive advantage as well as those without it, will drive the globalization of the equity markets. This will happen much in the same way that the bond markets and exchange rate markets were globalized by traders around the world seeking globally competitive risk-adjusted returns, and exploiting any market anomalies for profit. Equity investments are increasingly held in the hands of institutional investors, and these investors are becoming more sophisticated and global in scope. As they seek to compare returns for alternative investments, they will drive convergence in valuation approaches, equity issuance, and trading practices across equity markets.

AUTOS, HIGH FINANCE, CONSTRUCTION, SOUP, AND FUNERALS

Global capitalism will transform companies and the industries in which they participate. Specific examples can be found across all kinds of industries, from auto assembly, to financial services, to construction materials, to packaged goods, even to funeral services. Across these industries, as well as many others, we can expect significant changes worldwide.

Autos

Turning back to the automotive industry, we can explain in more detail what happened in the 1980s, and what might happen going forward. To illustrate this case, we will draw from the McKinsey Global Institute work on manufacturing productivity. According to that work, in 1980, the United States had a relative cost position twice that of Japan, and somewhat higher than Germany. This reflected the substantially less productive practices of auto makers in the United States relative to either Japan or Germany. The introduction of Japanese transplants into the United States and the heavy competition to which that exposed American auto makers, put enormous pressures on domestic car makers to increase productivity by improving quality and reducing costs.

Throughout the decade, this is precisely what happened: Over the period 1981 to 1991, the real hourly wages of auto makers actually decreased, by 0.4 percent, annually, while the growth in the productivity of labor increased by over 4 percent annually. Achieving these changes entailed dramatic numbers of plant closings, as mentioned earlier. It also entailed fundamental changes in the organization of car assembly plants. Not surprisingly, by 1992, the U.S. cost position relative to Japan had improved dramatically—from 2 to 1 in 1980 to 1.4 to 1 in 1992. According to the McKinsey Global Institute work, some of the most dramatic changes in plant organization, and some of the most successful ones, were made with a unionized, highly seasoned workforce (average seniority of 15–20 years). The Ford Atlanta plant, for example, was able to achieve over twice the productivity of the average U.S. car maker and even greater productivity than some of the Japanese transplants.

But the story doesn't stop there. If we take a look at the situation in a few other developed countries outside the United States, many are currently exposed to the same set of pressures that the U.S. auto industry faced in the 1980s. As recently as 1992, Germany, Italy, and Spain each had a relative cost position of more than twice that of Japan and over 75 percent higher than U.S. levels. As Japanese and U.S. auto makers continue to find ways to enter those markets and compete aggressively with their competitive advantage, the German, Italian, and Spanish auto industries are likely to experience the types of fundamental changes that the United States experienced in the 1980s.

Wholesale and Retail Banking

Similar fundamental changes are taking place in the financial services industries worldwide, where differentials in financial performance across countries vary dramatically.

A case in point is the investment banking industry in Germany, where the battle between highly innovative U.S. firms such as Lehman, Morgan Stanley, Merrill Lynch, Goldman Sachs, and J.P. Morgan and the locally entrenched German firms such as DeutscheBank AG and Dresdner Bank is in full force. In an article published in August 1995, *The Wall Street Journal* reports, "U.S. Investment Banks Are Making Hay in Germany." They point out that U.S. firms, entering the market with their lower cost, "American style" financing techniques, such as structured notes or leveraged buyouts, are putting the German banks on the defensive. Increasingly, highly productive, innovative American firms are leading the cream of the crop of financial deals; for example, the Bavarian electric utility turns to Lehman Brothers for the $4 billion sale of its electric utility and the German government turns to Goldman Sachs for the major privatization of Deutsche Telekom AG, the largest telecommunications company in Europe.

The German banks, faced with this threat are responding by building similar capabilities to those of the American banks, and even hiring the very bankers previously at the American institutions. There is no doubt that at the end of the battle, the investment banking industry in Germany will be transformed.

Or, consider the case of retail, personal financial services in Latin America reported in the McKinsey Global Institute study on Latin American productivity. In the United States, the performance of a typical personal financial service provider is as follows: Average revenues, estimated as the total net interest margin (interest revenues less interest expenses) plus fees, are roughly 5 to 6 percent of assets, where average noninterest costs are just under 4 percent of assets. The difference between the average net interest revenues and average costs serves as a quick proxy for profits. In this case, then, U.S. personal financial service providers average pretax margins of less than 2 percent of assets. The economics in Argentina, on the other hand, are quite different: The typical financial service provider enjoys a net interest spread plus fees, or revenues, of 14 percent of assets, of which over 10 percent are eaten up in noninterest costs. Pretax margins, therefore, are nearly 4 percent of assets in Argentina, much higher than in the United States, even though the participants are far less productive than in the United States.

What happens when a U.S. player comes to Argentina with better practices, or a potential cost of 4 percent of assets versus 10 percent?

With a revenue umbrella of 14 percent of assets and a cost of under 4 percent of assets (or possibly even lower, given much lower labor costs), pretax margins for a U.S. player could be as high as 10 percent of assets. Even if they can only capture half of this productivity difference, they have enormous competitive advantages. The leading U.S. players in Argentina, Citicorp and Bank of Boston, do not disclose results at the country level, but their operations are thought to be highly profitable.

Such margins in developing world countries translate into huge return opportunities to any such players and their equity investors. And the growth potential is also great because the penetration levels for financial services in such nations are only a small fraction of current U.S. levels. The cost structure makes banks so expensive that only a small portion of the population can afford them. At the productivity levels of a U.S. bank, a far greater percentage of the population in a developing nation would be able to afford banking services.

Many factors contribute to these large performance gaps. Internal practices such as corporate leadership and performance culture, marketing and sales competence, differentiated and efficient distribution, efficient (and often automated) processes, and credit policy and skills all contribute to performance, but vary significantly across retail banks. Moreover, external market restrictions exist in many countries. Nonetheless, in market after market, the leaders are able to outperform the laggards, and are finding ways to enter more and more new markets. In the process, they undermine any remaining barriers and will expose the less competitive, driving fundamental changes in the retail banking industry.

Cement and Other Construction Materials

Once the epitome of a local operation, cement production is also undergoing dramatic change as it encounters the forces of global capitalism. The construction materials industry is among the most local imaginable: There are cement batch plants every 10 to 15 miles and the distance between plant source and the final destination is seldom farther than 25 miles. In most markets in the world, such operations are still highly fragmented and terribly inefficient. The typical supplier was for decades the local farmer who found gravel on his property but had no access to high-quality machinery nor capital to acquire it, and thus never achieved scale economies or developed world-class process management.

However, superior practices in this industry are already in operation in some parts of the world. Best practices in this case were developed primarily in Europe, by Swiss and U.K. firms. Important strategies for world leaders have included developing targeted acquisitions of key reservoirs of natural resources to gain dominance in the market and finding creative ways to access the capital market to fund these acquisitions. Best practice leaders have also developed specific management expertise to contain transportation costs, often the single largest share of expenses; to tailor sales and marketing expertise; and to achieve precise, high-quality control.

Companies from around the world, with these superior techniques and with access to capital, are driving consolidation in all major economic markets, from Europe, to North America, to Australia, forever destroying the traditional structure of the industry.

Packaged Goods

The list of industries likely to be transformed by the unleashing of global capitalism goes on, almost indefinitely. The leading consumer goods companies have significant productivity advantages, stemming from highly efficient processing and scale economies in marketing and logistics. Already, the opportunities are being hunted worldwide. An internal McKinsey survey of a sample of 36 consumer goods companies conducted by our Consumer Goods practice, indicates that at least 103 separate, new ventures in emerging markets were undertaken by consumer goods companies over the period July 1993 to September 1994. This includes over 20 ventures in China and 14 in India.

International sales account for over 50 percent of total sales in the companies most aggressively seeking these opportunities throughout the world. As a case in point, international sales at Nestlé have grown over 14 percent during the past few years. In fact, Nestlé's presence in Latin America alone is extensive: Total sales are nearly $4 billion across all major markets, including Brazil, Mexico, Argentina, Chile, Venezuela, and Colombia. Many other companies such as Campbell, Ralston, Sara Lee, Quaker, Unilever, Heinz, and Kellogg are also getting in on the action, with international sales now representing as much as 30 to 40 percent of total sales. Moreover, there are still many that have barely started: Gerber's sales are still only 10 percent international, despite compounded annual growth of 35 percent in international sales over the past few years.

Although the entry of these companies into many markets, particularly the emerging markets, will stimulate primary demand, it will also threaten the market shares of existing suppliers. The introduction of these highly productive consumer goods companies into relatively unproductive markets will shake up the existing structures and drive forth fundamental change.

Funeral Services

Even the funeral service industry is likely to be transformed as best practices in providing high-quality, cost-effective funeral services are transferred around the world. For example, a friend working with a leading funeral service company, the Service Corporation International, has helped acquire funeral service providers in the United Kingdom and France. They are in the process of transferring their best practice management of costs (e.g., uses of limousines, drivers) and marketing of services (e.g., flowers, caskets). This transfer of best practices provides for a large improvement in profit margins. There is hardly any industry that is more local than funeral services yet even here, some consolidation is already evident. Not surprisingly, the consolidation is taking place across borders, and, over time, will transform the industry globally.

— 10 —

Leading a Corporation in a Superconductive World

How should corporations respond to the challenges posed by these industry transformations?

A few years ago, one of us was at a dinner party with the author Tom Wolfe. He had just written his first novel, *Bonfire of the Vanities,* which was on its way to becoming a major best seller. He was asked what it had been like to write a novel long after having been successful as the nonfiction author of *The Right Stuff* and *The Electric Kool-Aid Acid Test.* He replied that it had been much harder than he expected. He said he had always assumed that fiction was easy because there were no constraints. You could write whatever you wanted. When he sat down to write, though, he discovered that the lack of constraints was the problem. In writing fiction, you have to make all the decisions about what to write and, therefore, you have an infinite range of choices.

Leaders of corporations now face this problem. In a world suddenly without any real barriers, they have an overabundance of options and choices. Which of these options do they exercise? Which choices do they make?

From the perspective of the CEO, the transformation of the global economy by the unleashing of global capitalism is both exhilarating and terrifying. All at once, it seems that all the rules of competition are changing. From a global perspective, a world filled with potential opportunity emerges. At the same time, all the company's carefully erected protections from competition seem to be under attack and without warning, the world seems filled with risk.

The exhilaration comes with the potential opportunities that suddenly appear. Companies in mature industries as diverse as consumer goods, publishing, or financial services are being presented, in just a few years, with a range of choice that was unthinkable in the past. All at once, no industries are dull or stodgy.

With the world as your perspective, formerly mundane skills become potentially valuable weapons to capturing profits globally. For example, as developing countries make the transition from an agrarian economy to processed food, basic marketing and branding skills built up in the home nation can be converted into virtual long-term annuities in those markets. Publishers of business information in a single country, used to stagnating revenues, suddenly see their market opportunities expand in all directions as businesses worldwide begin seeking out information and as the Internet opens up new global distribution channels through World Wide Web sites. With a shift from a national to a global perspective, the credit card opportunity is transformed. No longer just a consolidating national business with saturated demand in the United States, it becomes a global industry taking off in Europe, or an industry just at the start of a generation or more of unbelievable growth as literally billions of potential cardholders from developing countries begin to come into view.

The terror comes from the sudden threats of attack on the company's core businesses that seemingly emerge from everywhere. State-run oil companies find themselves confronted with outside independent producers, armed with capital raised in the global capital market and with advanced techniques of production, ready to deliver higher output at less cost to the same national governments that own them. Local retail chains find themselves confronted with large store formats that drain off their customer base with remarkable speed. Local corporate and investment bankers discover that their carefully cultivated relationships become meaningless as they prove unable to serve their clients' needs to raise new equity capital, cannot expand to new markets, or fail to find means to manage the new risks to which they are now being exposed.

And, most of all, the terror comes from these new risks. Chief executives picked for their skills in competing in the closed, national economies, under the protection of regulation, find themselves being asked to expand into countries they barely know, to work with alliance partners they do not necessarily trust, and to place large capital bets on technology investments they hardly understand.

The challenges are immense. The competitive landscape is being transformed from a series of segmented national markets, with defined, protective regulation, established loyal customers, known competition, and known technology into an open, integrated market with multiple, complex uncertainties. Rather than operating within the constraints imposed by national boundaries, chief executives now see a world emerging that is almost without boundaries.

Simultaneously, the very industries themselves collide. Starting from different home countries, different industries, and different skill bases, different participants see the same opportunity and begin to pursue it. Electronics companies, telecommunications companies, cable television companies, publishing companies, and media companies from different countries begin to compete in a global multimedia industry. Banks, insurance companies, securities firms, software companies, and the financial arms of industrial companies throughout the world all begin to compete in a global personal financial services industry.

In such a world, capital changes its role. Rather than being an ally of the entrenched interests, which use capital to muscle local competitors, capital becomes available to any global competitor, with production technique advantages, that is able to exploit those advantages. In the process, small companies can become larger very quickly. Their success provides them with capital that they can use to take over slower-moving companies, with attractive but underutilized customer franchises and other assets.

As this process takes place, the meaning of scale changes. Companies that were once thought to be too big to acquire turn out not to be too big at all. The power to deploy capital globally becomes more important than any conventional scale economy. Sales size, asset size, even book capital are no longer meaningful measures of scale in this sense. Market capitalization becomes the only real measure of size and power. In just the past 20 years, the market capitalization required to be among the 20 nonfinancial companies with the largest market capitalization in the world has gone from about $1 billion in 1975 to well over $43 billion in 1995. At that rate (and the forces at work seem to be accelerating it), by the year 2005, it may well take over $100 billion in market capitalization to be among the 20 largest.

At the same time, the capital market will increase the pressure on companies to sell assets for which they are not the best owners. If a company is unwilling to spin off those assets or to sell them, then someone will acquire the company and do it anyway. Consider the size of some of the divestments in just the last few years: Dean Witter, with a market capitalization of over $5 billion was divested, while General Motors spun off EDS at a market capitalization of $22 billion.

Over time, the pressure of the global capital market on management is becoming more and more unrelenting. It will reward companies that provide it with consistently high returns and will punish those with consistently low returns thereby forcing them to sell their assets into stronger hands.

The unleashing of global capitalism, then, becomes an unleashing of the strong to displace the weak, worldwide. It raises the stakes. The opportunities for winners become unlimited. The costs of mistakes escalate. The spoils go to the global capitalists. What will it take to win in such a world?

To prosper as a global corporation, the firm must undergo transformation. The mind-set must change. The notion of strategy must be rethought, the way capital is deployed must be rethought, and, the way the firm is managed, and led, must be rethought.

After we describe these mind-set changes we will conclude this chapter with an example based on the perspective of a global commercial bank.

STRATEGY AS A PORTFOLIO OF OPTIONS

As global capitalism proceeds, strategic thinking and strategic action become continuous and dynamic rather than episodic and static. In this environment, flexibility and the timing of actions become critical.

Continuous Flux

We believe winners will be those firms who anticipate the future continuously. They will see the world as being in flux. They will use "war gaming" techniques to maximize their reaction time as they strive to understand how industry structures and competitive advantages are changing.

Rather than defining their world as a portfolio of business, they will see their world as a portfolio of options and choices. They will seek attractive options and choices to add to this portfolio while eliminating those that no longer seem attractive.

Out of this portfolio of options and choices, they will choose to play where they are advantaged and will avoid expensive battles where they lack advantages. They will particularly try to avoid engaging in wars of attrition with a number of other global players and "deep pocket" local players on highly visible battlefields. Rather, they will use the lack of boundaries on the global battlefield to redefine the problem. In place of head-on assaults, they will seek opportunities to outflank, outmaneuver, or leapfrog.

In general, they will concentrate on defending and building core businesses where they have productivity advantages over a majority share of the world's participants. They will avoid big bets on noncore businesses or in core businesses in which they are competitively disadvantaged.

Winners will take multiple, low-cost bets on potential future core businesses or businesses that naturally leverage core business strengths. This, in turn, will require understanding, deeply, what those core skills are and then thinking through how to leverage those skills, and how others could leverage them, as the global landscape changes. Out of such thinking will come opportunities, not only for direct expansion but also licensing, alliances, and acquisitions.

Flexibility

Making an options approach to strategy work in practice requires that the corporation build flexibility along key management dimensions. In particular, this means thinking explicitly about ways to make key investment decisions marginally, step by step, as more information becomes available and as uncertainty on key issues dissipates. In this way, new information feeds the decision process and continuous fine tuning is possible. In addition, the corporation avoids inappropriate or unnecessary risks. To do this effectively, management needs to build a high degree of flexibility into all key decisions.

For example, successful manufacturing companies exposed to the rapidly changing world of technology have realized the importance of designing modular processes, so that an individual piece can change as new technologies that affect it evolve, without throwing all pieces into disarray. These same companies have also learned to design inherently expandable or contractable systems, that minimize specificity to any one activity, and that are upgradable. In some cases, this results in somewhat higher up-front costs, but it is often a small price for flexibility, for the option of being able to incorporate new information as it becomes available.

More broadly, in thinking about strategy, corporations will need to take a similar approach. They will need strategies that are capable of incorporating feedback along the way, from test marketing, from prototypes, from customer responses. There are some solid examples of best practice companies, such as First USA in credit cards, or Sony in new product development, that have made use of this type of strategic feedback by incorporating specific performance measurement into key triggers for decisions.

Another critical element of successful strategies will be that they have individual components, or modules, that are replaceable without disrupting all elements of the strategy. For example, Nucor's expansion of minimills was one such strategy. These were replicable, generally standardized approaches to a major rollout applied in a number of different markets. As such, failure in one market did not translate into failure in all markets, but did provide valuable information for future decisions. Compaq's approach to developing new computers is quite similar: basic, replicable, standardized units are combined with new features, increasing the flexibility of dropping or adding any one feature.

Finally, successful strategies will be creative, finding ways to keep options open until full commitments are made. This involves considering all the components of a strategy, from options on sourcing (e.g., outsourcing to reduce in-house investment, or multisourcing to reduce exposure to any one supplier) to options on partnering up with other players who are better positioned to take risks through alliances or joint ventures.

Being able to change direction at various points over time is a highly valuable attribute of the global strategy, made possible by an explicit commitment to flexibility.

Consider the case of a hypothetical large consumer packaged goods company, Worldwide Foods, that is developing an entry strategy into India. The more traditional approach would begin with the understanding that the sheer number of Indians, close to a billion people, will make India one of the largest markets for processed foods in the world. And history has demonstrated worldwide that early entrants who establish brands maintain those brands as the markets develop. To avoid being shut out of a market that represents nearly 20 percent of the world's population, Worldwide Foods decides it must make a full-fledged investment of several hundred million dollars in an Indian operation using the single approach most likely to lead to success. Settling on which approach is the most likely to succeed is done on the basis of the best available information at the time of the launch.

A more sophisticated approach, based on the notion of options and flexibility, might be quite different. Instead of making one large investment on the single most attractive approach, Worldwide Foods might decide instead on starting with two or three smaller approaches, possibly each with a different product or a different brand name. One might be in the form of a fully owned direct foreign investment to capture the broad-based market through traditional channels. Another might be licensing the same process to a local producer and securing an option to acquire a majority share at a specified time (and at a currently attractive price to the partner). And a third might involve setting up a joint venture agreement with a local producer that has a unique distribution channel. In each approach, Worldwide Foods makes an explicit investment to pay for options to liquidate or to expand down the road. Then, as the years pass, when the path of economic and financial liberalization that has just started in India becomes clearer and its unique traits discernible, Worldwide Foods can make new decisions on each approach, reinvesting in those that continue to look promising and divesting from those that are at that point riskier or less promising and adding other options that become apparent. If any one option becomes a clear winner, Worldwide Foods stands ready to invest whatever capital is necessary to take full advantage of the opportunity. This type of approach can help Worldwide Foods allocate resources to cover the potentially enormous, yet risky and unclear, opportunities in multiple markets, not just India, but China and Indonesia as well.

Timing

In addition to the classic strategic choices of where to compete (which customers, which products, which geographies) and how to compete (what techniques of production to employ), many of the critical strategic choices will revolve around when to compete. It will become far more important to think through the timing, pacing, and sequencing of actions. This will be particularly valuable to maximize the value of options and flexibility purchased. This means thinking through in advance whether or not to be a "first mover" or a "first follower" and identifying the windows of opportunity as well as how to capture them. It means weighing the possible consequences of taking a particular action, the range of competitive responses, and the actions that will be appropriate for different competitive responses. It means thinking through in advance when to make choices and when to exercise the options available to you.

Some of the hardest choices on when to compete will be over how long to invest in protecting or trying to transform core businesses and when to give up and get out of them. Very few leaders can be dispassionate about the businesses that they grew up in. The continual tradeoffs will involve how hard to defend the domestic core versus attacking, globally in more promising, but less familiar, businesses. This, in turn, challenges the capacity of the firm to compete on multiple fronts. Of critical concern in making the tradeoff will be the willingness of the global capital market to continue letting existing management make decisions. Giving up too soon on a core business can sell short a company's principal asset. Giving up too late can waste that asset. The problem is often compounded when in many cases, the only real way to exit the core business is to sell the entire company.

THINKING LIKE A GLOBAL CAPITALIST

To succeed in the world we've been describing, the trick is to think as if you are a global principal investor investing your own money, becoming a global capitalist, if you will.

Pursue options with the best risk-return outcomes rather than always assuming that direct expansion is the only option. For big opportunities, take out multiple options rather than placing one big bet. In particular, be willing to overpay (as an option premium) to gain corporate control of a bet with a high upside or the potential to be a future core business, if in return you can minimize your downside risks while preserving the upside returns.

Overmanage the risks and returns from business choices aggressively. This will require disaggregating and structuring the risks in any major business venture and taking only those risks where the returns are large relative to the risks and where you have a relative comparative advantage. It will often make sense to place risks with others, including alliance partners, or employees, where you lack comparative advantage in taking a particular risk.

While the global landscape requires keeping many options continually open and delaying decisions until the timing is right, once a decision is made, overmanage its outcome. Don't take aggregated risks that require leaps of faith. Track outcomes against expectations. If industry structures are changing differently than you expected, if competitors are behaving differently, if customers are responding differently, make adjustments, rather than let the momentum take you to an unhappy outcome.

Once it becomes obvious that an investment is turning into a "dry hole," cut your losses rather than worrying about losing face. This works well if you have a portfolio of options. If you have several ventures in your portfolio that are suddenly succeeding beyond expectations, it is less painful to stop or sell the ventures that are falling behind.

Barring a global financial catastrophe, the world over the next 20 years should be full of opportunities for the global capitalist. If you work hard at extracting the most value from the capital you deploy, your base case should be to expect to find numerous possibilities to earn large returns, relative to your risks. For the foreseeable future, the global markets for goods and services will be sufficiently imperfect for you to find an abundance of large, woolly mammoths. The key skill will be to overmanage the process of hunting them down.

Our advice is to think like a global capitalist is not new advice. Academics and consultants have long advised managers to put shareholders first. Almost all business leaders, at least in the United States, give lip service to "shareholder value" whether they actually believe in it or not. What is new, though, is that the opportunity costs of not putting shareholders first are far larger now that the limiting constraints on global capitalism are disappearing. There are larger returns to be earned. If your company does not seize opportunities, another company will. This changes the consequences. With the unleashing of global capitalism, managers who do not put shareholders first will not keep their jobs for very long.

LEADERSHIP

Among the senior management of one of our favorite clients, the following saying is frequently heard: "Leaders Must Lead." While at first this may sound obvious, and in some ways it is, true corporate leadership, from the corporate office to individual middle manager, is becoming more and more difficult just at the time that it is becoming more and more imperative.

Leadership is difficult because the need to be open to the world of opportunities, to perceive the range of threats, and to set high aspirations for global competitiveness has become more important than ever, as the range of attractive choices multiplies. Leaders of a winning global firm will have eyes and ears everywhere. As the world's economy moves from the closed national model to the open, global system, so must the corporation. As competitors emerge from other countries and other industries, corporations that are not fully aware will be blindsided. If a company's board and management team are all from the same country, or the same region, or the same industry, and think with the same perspective, they can be unpleasantly surprised by the initiatives of other competitors. Furthermore, as major opportunities develop, leaders must have a sufficiently open mind to recognize them and pursue them successfully. Leaders must be able to perceive that what might be a maturing, staid business in one market is an emerging, high-growth opportunity in another, newly liberalized market. In an open economy, leaders must anticipate and ward off threats, but they must also set high aspirations to become and remain globally competitive.

Leadership has also become more difficult because of the sheer scale and complexity of information that must be mobilized, the skill and capital that must be adequately deployed, and the faster pace of change. In a national, single-industry business, the information, skill, and capital are controlled by relatively few people who are typically colocated. In a large global firm, the marshaling of information, skill, and capital to surface an opportunity, to create a range of viable options to capture that opportunity, to structure the risks so that only those the corporation is most advantaged to take are kept, to raise and deploy the capital, can easily be spread over large numbers of people in multiple markets around the world. Much of the information, skill, and capital needed may not even reside within the company, but may involve mobilizing alliance partners, board members, and outside experts including lawyers, accountants, investment bankers, and consultants.

Major challenges arise because the information, judgment, skill, and authority to make decisions do not often reside in the same location or with any single individual or group of individuals. Often, critical decisions cut across organizational boundaries so that only the CEO has the mandate to make decisions. Yet, no one CEO can make even a small fraction of the critical decisions for an entire global organization. Similarly, to act like a good principal investor, you should vest the risks of implementation and the accountability for results in an individual or team. Yet, the scale and complexity of a global firm and the sheer number of people involved in making decisions work against clear accountability. Unless the corporation ensures accountability through strong leadership, dynamic risk management, and adequate performance measurement, the allocation of critical resources, including information, people, and capital, will be undermanaged. Seemingly attractive risk-adjusted opportunities then can become highly risky and unattractive.

Finally, leadership is difficult because in a world that is in flux—in which many corporations have large labor forces from different countries and cultures—instilling and maintaining strong corporate values is a serious challenge. And yet, it is more important than ever. Where societal values and traditions are under attack, strong corporate ethics and responsibility are critical to the economy. In a world where many safety nets for employees, traditionally provided by governments, are disappearing, corporations must take on a larger and more responsible role with respect to skill building, career management, and retirement management. Winning global corporations will distinguish themselves because of their strong corporate values and people management in an increasingly uncertain world. The guardians of these values must be strong leaders in the corporation.

CASE IN POINT: AN EMERGING GLOBAL COMMERCIAL BANK

To make these notions less abstract, we will describe how a particular firm in a particular industry might rethink its strategies, its deployment of capital, and its leadership style as we move to the new age of global capitalism.

Almost any industry would do to illustrate our point. We could pick electronics, or publishing, or petroleum, or telecommunications, or consumer-packaged goods, or pharmaceuticals, or automobile repair, or legal services, or frankly, even funeral services.

However, since both of us are consultants to the financial services industry, we will pick one that we know quite well—global commercial banking. Let's take the perspective of the CEO of a global commercial bank headquartered in the United States, First Global, with some $150 billion in assets, some 30,000 employees, and a market capitalization of $10 billion. First Global has three major broad-based business arenas, each of which account for roughly one third of its profits. First Global's three business arenas are the delivery of branch-based banking services primarily in its home region where it is the dominant bank, the direct distribution of retail financial services nationally, such as credit card, mortgage, mutual funds, and the corporate banking and capital markets businesses with major presences in New York, London, and Tokyo and with minor presences in a dozen other countries.

First Global is a composite bank that roughly fits many of the largest commercial banks in the United States, excepting Bank of America, Citicorp, Chase-Chemical, and J.P. Morgan, which are all more global and larger than our hypothetical composite. Moreover, among Australian, British, Canadian, French, Dutch, German, Spanish, and Swiss banks, not to mention Japanese and other Asian banks, there are at least 50 others with roughly the same profile.

But, let's return to First Global, our hypothetical U.S. bank.

Like most large, global commercial banks, roughly 50 to 60 percent or more of the costs of running First Global are shared costs such as corporate overhead, operations, technology, and distribution that are not unique to individual businesses. As a consequence, the CEO has difficulty ensuring accountability for business results and strategic flexibility is limited.

Each of its three business arenas represent different opportunities and challenges. In its branch-based retail banking and payments business, it has become worried that its branch system is becoming an albatross. While branch-based banking is still quite profitable, revenues are simply not growing and they continue to lose market share to mutual funds, retail securities firms, credit cards, mortgages, and consumer loans through non-branch-based channels by players as diverse as Merrill Lynch, Fidelity, GE Capital, AT&T, Countrywide, and Household International. Even more worrisome, Microsoft and Intuit, among others, seem intent on using the personal computer to deliver interactive home banking services including "electronic commerce," or use of electronic methods to pay for goods and services that bypass the normal payment system. These methods are likely to be particularly appealing to the upscale, top 20 percent of the bank's customer base that accounts for some 70 percent of the branch system's revenues. At the same time, the bank is being approached, on multiple fronts, to see if it is interested in alliances with some of these same nonbank competitors. Moreover, the bank is being approached by banks in countries from Hungary to Brazil to Thailand asking for help in improving productivity in everything from branch management, to check processing, to consumer loan underwriting.

In just this one business arena, the branch-based banking businesses, the CEO is faced with an overabundance of critical issues. How much should be invested in defending fully the core business? Is the answer replacing smaller branches with downsized automated branches and using the larger branches to cross-sell more products? Or, longer term, should the bank try to migrate its best customers through an alliance to a home banking platform and sell off most of its branch system to another player while the branch system still has value? What are the shared cost implications of these different options? Or, should the bank try to reinvent its physical distribution systems while simultaneously seeking banks in other countries where it can license its production techniques? Or, should the bank explore direct entry into other countries?

In its second set of core businesses, the U.S. national direct, non-branch-based distribution of retail financial services (including mutual funds, credit cards, mortgages, annuities, consumer loans, and trust), the bank has different opportunities and challenges. In these businesses, First Global is competing both against other banks and nonbanks nationally. In these half-dozen different businesses, which are also very profitable, revenues are still growing but are growing more slowly than in the past as the bank continues to lose share to more focused players. While First Global is a player in each of these businesses, it is a leader in none of them. Direct marketing to customers in these businesses is becoming saturated, and share and profitability are moving away from players with conventional direct marketing skills to players with advanced proprietary and technology-based techniques of production that give them real advantages in distribution, risk management, and servicing. These in turn enable players to reinvest in otherwise maturing businesses. Meanwhile, much more rapid growth is occurring in Europe in some of these products as some of the direct product distributors are beginning to make real headway against the universal banks, just as they did against U.S. banks in the 1980s. Meanwhile, in developing countries, a few players, such as Citicorp, are beginning to leapfrog the inefficiency of the local banking systems through direct distribution of these products. And, in each of these businesses, the technology-based investments to be a major global player over the next few years could be in the billions of dollars.

In this set of core businesses, the CEO is also faced with multiple critical issues. How many of the several different direct distribution businesses should the bank aspire to be a major player in? Will "me too" investments be enough or will it take major billion-dollar-plus investments, or major acquisitions, to continue to be a player? What is the balance between defending each of these core businesses, expanding into Europe, or leapfrogging into developing countries? Is the bank prepared to take on the risk management challenge of being in these businesses in developing countries, particularly in the lending businesses? If the bank misses the "window of opportunity," will it be locked out of the global opportunity forever? Is a war of attrition likely in any of these businesses as deep-pocket participants go head to head? Will these wars destroy the profits in the domestic core business, which will then require cross-subsidization from other businesses for its defense to fund global expansion?

In its third major arena, the global corporate banking and capital markets businesses, still different opportunities and challenges face First Global's CEO. In these businesses, the 50 largest global commercial banks, plus investment banks, and hundreds of niche players, are already engaged in a war of attrition.

In this business, although revenues are growing rapidly, expenses for both labor and technology are growing more rapidly still. As these large players compete globally in the capital market we described earlier in this book, the best investment bankers and traders (the woolly mammoth hunters) are in heavy demand and have been able to extract extraordinary returns. Moreover, competition from securities products and among the banks themselves has eroded the returns on corporate loans to the point that the risk-adjusted returns are well below the costs of the equity capital required to absorb the risk. In combination, these factors cause First Global to earn only about 10 percent on its equity in these businesses, while it estimates its costs of equity, given the volatility of those businesses, to be nearly 20 percent. In other words, while these businesses are profitable, they create a major drag on market capitalization. On the other hand, at stake, probably after shakeout over the next decade, is becoming one of the 5 or 10 players who will wind up dominating the global capital markets businesses as the "trees grow to the sky." The problem is that there are at least 25 players who aspire to being one of the leaders and many of them seem willing to cross-subsidize these businesses from returns earned in the retail businesses.

In this corporate banking, global business arena, the CEO also must deal with critical issues. How much can the bank afford to cross-subsidize this business in the future? Should the bank exit or downsize this business to concentrate on the retail opportunities? Does the bank need to be a player in this business simply to acquire the risk management skills (e.g., risk structuring, derivatives) and capital market skills to compete globally in its other businesses? Can the business be reinvented to make the returns on capital more attractive?

With businesses and the issues facing First Global, what should the CEO do to take the advice we outlined earlier in the chapter?

The CEO of First Global should begin by exercising leadership. The kind of situation we described is typical not just of large global banks, but of many large, global companies in multiple industries. Everyone in management is aware of the issues but no one really knows what to do with them. Without leadership, most managers tend to wallow in them. They take the safe way out. They focus on "making budget" versus proposing bold options.

The starting point for a leader is to establish aspirations, probably very stretching aspirations. Then, with every action, the leader has to reinforce behavior that moves the firm toward those aspirations and to curtail behavior that obstructs positive movement. A critical part of these aspirations should be targets for increasing returns on capital.

One of the critical leadership tasks is to reframe all the issues facing these various businesses in terms of options and choices. To do this, the CEO might organize "war games." For example, in the direct distribution retail business arena, different teams of managers might assume the role of different competitors thinking through their global business strategies in each of the core businesses. In the credit card business, First Global could organize a team called First USA, American Express, and the AT&T Universal Card to compete against "First Global card." Such war games can go through several moves.

Through these maneuvers, new, creative options will be identified, competitive response can be better anticipated, and the timing of when to make decisions can become clearer. The same process will cause managers to open their eyes and ears. As they go from move to move through the war game, they will seek out more information on competitors, on potential new markets, on potential new technologies, and other critical issues. They will also open up their minds.

Whether discovered through war gaming or through other strategic thinking exercises, some of the options identified can then be more fully fleshed out to see whether they are truly viable and how the returns can be enhanced and the risks minimized. Out of such effort, multiple new options will be available and those that appear to be especially attractive can be funded and managed.

Leadership is also required to stimulate flexibility. For example, one of the difficulties facing First Global in being flexible is that the various individual businesses are wedded together by a huge shared cost structure that restricts flexibility. Decisions to divest businesses or outsource functions are limited because, while the revenue can be shed, the costs cannot be. At First Global, the lion's share of the cost structure, whether central staff function, central operations and technology costs, or distribution, is shared. This makes it difficult both to understand real economics because costs must be somewhat arbitrarily allocated. It is also difficult to have sufficient information to make real business choices and assign real accountability for results. Therefore, a major leadership need is to determine which businesses and functions are so clearly integrated that sharing cost is appropriate and which are not. From our experience, we believe that many banks share the wrong costs among the wrong businesses. Like many other businesses, banks assume static conditions and make incremental cost decisions based on marginal cost analysis. This always leads to the decision to share costs. What this approach misses is the value of having a more flexible cost structure, and the potential to manage risks and returns better through having better accountability for results. In rapidly changing environments, the option value of having a more flexible cost structure can be very large.

Coming back to First Global, it is almost impossible to address some of the return on capital challenges facing the corporate banking/capital markets portions of the bank if that business arena is, like a Siamese twin, integrally connected to the cost structures of the branch-based retail businesses and to the direct marketing businesses.

Leadership is also critical in making timing decisions. Large firms like our global bank have real inertia. Decisions, once made, tend to go forward, despite changes in market conditions. First Global's credit card group might have committed to compete nationally in the credit card business, without major investments in new systems. The decision was to invest in marketing and distribution. All of a sudden, many other competitors who have made investments in new technology platforms begin to take major share from First Global and to explore international expansion. Unless the decision on the technology platform is resurfaced in a timely fashion, the "window of opportunity" might close down to the point that First Global loses the option to compete in this business forever unless it is willing to make a major acquisition.

To avoid such problems, corporations like First Global need processes to ensure that its leaders visit, revisit, and revisit again critical business issues until appropriate decisions are made. At First Global, the drain on returns to capital from the corporate banking/ global capital markets business needs to be continually revisited until a clear path forward becomes apparent.

Leadership is also required to get the institution to think like a global capitalist. In the First Global bank example, one of the sources of low returns in the global corporate banking/capital markets businesses is that often managers of those businesses are measured and evaluated on absolute profits rather than risk-adjusted capital returns. This, in turn, causes loan officers to want to book as much loan volume as they can on the bank's balance sheet. However, if the institution begins to think like a global capitalist, the mind-set changes. All of a sudden, the bank looks to structure and disaggregate the risks and returns from lending; the bank begins to look for aggregated risks that can then be disaggregated, structured, and placed, while only retaining those risks where the returns fully compensate for the risks taken. For example, in a project loan to an independent oil producer, the various project risks can be disaggregated into risks such as oil price risk, reservoir risk, and production risk. For some of these risks, the bank may not be the participant with the best capacity to take these risks. Once these risks are disaggregated, the bank can then keep only those risks that provide a comparative advantage and place all other risks with other institutions and other participants.

This principle can be applied bankwide. Over time, the mind-set of the bank shifts from booking assets to booking risks where the risk-return relationships are highly attractive. Unless you find a woolly mammoth, you don't want the risk. Getting a bank to think like this requires real leadership because the classic banker mentality assumes that the bank retains all the risks it originates. Transforming a bank's mind-set, not to mention building the capabilities to manage the risk/ reward tradeoffs, is a multiyear effort.

From this global commercial bank example, you can see just how critical leadership really is. Corporations with leaders who view the world as a set of options and choices, who think and act like global capitalists, and who have the capacity to lead, will win.

—11—

Buy Stocks, Shun Bonds

It usually takes a while, but whenever we discuss our research with friends, colleagues, and clients, everyone inevitably asks the same question: "So, where should I invest my money?"

It is a good question.

Anyone with any savings is a capitalist. We all want more returns for less risk.

It is also a hard question to answer generically because all of us have different amounts of capital, different personal investment skills, different access to information, different time available to put into personal investment management, different time horizons, different appetites for risk, and different investment objectives.

Despite these differences, and although neither of us are investment advisers, in this chapter we will do our best to outline some thoughts that we believe make sense for most people as they are driven by the global integration of the markets to become, personally, global capitalists. As you read this chapter, however, remember that the financial markets are inherently unpredictable and neither we, nor anyone else, can know what will happen. If you take our advice, it is your money you are risking, not ours.

We will, though, describe how we think about investing in this market ourselves. Acting as a global capitalist is hard for all of us because our minds are generally tied to where we sit and we all think from the perspective of our home country. To become a global capitalist, you need to shift your mind-set. There is no escaping the transformation in the world's economy that is coming, so you might as well embrace it and benefit from it. Governments are losing their ability to protect citizens from risk. Many of the opportunities and risks become apparent only with a global perspective.

How should an individual investor regard this market? Returning to the world of the woolly mammoths, stay out of the way of the big-time hunters. The global foreign exchange markets, bond markets, and derivative markets they prowl are filled with professionals, some of the smartest people in the world, with far better tools, and far better information. Right or wrong, they are powerful enough to move the market in the short term simply through the financial resources at their disposal. And, they are very focused and spend all their time trying to make money from the market. The nonprofessional is not going to outthink them.

The opportunities are in equities. The next 20 years have the potential to be a golden age for equity investment. The trends we have described are likely to lead to real productivity increases, which will translate to real earnings increases and thus to higher values to equities. If the annual rate of return from investing in equities increases by 2 percent above the historic average real return earned on equities of 7 percent over the past 70 years, the magic of compound interest could make a huge difference to your ability to accumulate wealth. For example, $100,000 invested in 1994 at the historical real rate of return to 3-month U.S. Treasuries of 0.5 percent (over the past 70 years) would be worth only $108,000 in 2010 (in 1992 dollars); $100,000 invested in equities at the historical real rate of return of 7 percent would be worth $276,000 in 2010. And $100,000 invested in equities at a 2 percent rate above the historic real rate of return, or 9 percent, would be worth $364,000 in 2010.

BUY STOCKS

As in the past, we expect that the best returns to be earned will be in the equity markets rather than in the bond markets or in the money markets or in bank deposits. This has been generally true, as many academics have demonstrated, for as long as reliable, comparable records are available. Over the past 70 years, U.S. equities have earned a real rate of return of 6.9 percent versus long-term Treasury bonds, which have earned a real rate of return of 1.7 percent (versus 0.5 percent on 3-month Treasuries). By 1994, one U.S. dollar invested in 1925 would have yielded $3.10 in real dollars (or $26 nominal) if it had been invested in long-term U.S. bonds versus $97 in real dollars (or $810 nominal) if it had been invested in stocks (see Exhibit 11.1). And, both bonds and equities have outperformed money in the bank for at least the past 50 years. As described in Chapter 6, the real returns on bank deposits have been at best, break-even, if not actually negative, in the United States, and likely worse in other countries.

Exhibit 11.1.   Return to a Dollar Invested from 1925 to 1994

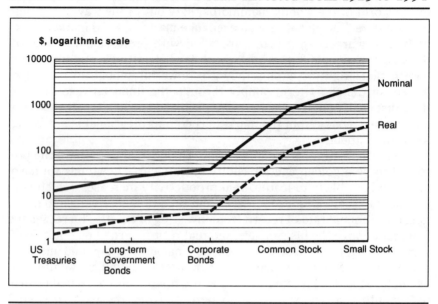

* Return to $1 dollar or remaining invested in financial asset from 1925 to 1994: $1 invested in U.S. Treasuries in 1925 was worth $12 nominal, $1.5 real by 1994; $1 invested in small stocks in 1925 was worth $810 nominal, or $97 real by 1994.
Source: Ibbotson Associates.

We also believe that equities will be even more attractive than bonds and bank deposits over the next two decades than they have been historically because investing in bonds, in particular, is going to be less attractive given the trends described throughout this book.

The primary reason for this probable pattern is straightforward. Equities will capture most of the returns from the transplants of techniques of production from foreign direct investment described in Chapter 7. In particular, companies with the best production techniques, who are the first movers in their industry to globalize, will be able to capture extraordinary returns through either direct expansion, acquisitions, or licensing their technologies. Even equities in companies in countries with little historic competition, who are operating with poor techniques of production, can do well if they have a unique valuable asset, such as a customer base, a distribution system, or employee skills. These companies can benefit either by capitalizing on that unique asset, or by licensing it out or selling it to someone who can make better use of it.

Because the equity markets are not yet fully integrated, they are more accessible to ordinary businesspeople than to professional traders. Investing capital to transfer superior techniques of production globally, which involves disaggregating not just foreign exchange risk and interest rate risks, but also operating risks such as labor risks, production risks, regulatory risks, or legal risks, is currently best undertaken by knowledgeable line business managers rather than traders—and extraordinary returns are possible. Simply investing in the equity of a company with good line management, superior techniques of production, and a global outlook can capture a rich flow of global anomalies in markets for goods and services. In contrast, market anomalies in the foreign exchange, bond, and financial derivatives markets are most easily captured by financial traders.

There is also much juice left in equities simply from getting businesses to perform better. With the significant exception of the United States, many companies in many countries have not experienced much performance pressure. As global investors increase the performance pressure on these companies, they will develop the potential to deliver large returns to shareholders. Much embedded value can come from restructuring, spinning off assets, or eliminating cross-subsidization of weak businesses by strong businesses. Simply bringing in management skills and performing better can make a big difference. This process was a significant component of the strong returns earned in the U.S. equity market over the past decade, but it has been much less significant outside the United States. Over the next decade, this process will probably play a major role in increasing the value of owning non-U.S. equities.

Yet another reason why equities are becoming more attractive is the expected surge in household savings for retirement, described in Chapter 6. Despite overwhelming evidence to the contrary, households have an "irrational" preference for "safe" bonds and bank deposits and for money market funds versus "risky" equities. This is particularly true of retirement savings and is even more true outside the United States. This preference for deposits, among market funds and bonds, provides "cheap" debt, which can be leveraged by equity to increase returns. This effect has been in operation for decades (it is the source of the higher returns for equity over debt for 70 years) but should be even more true because of the surge in savings. As the developed world populations age, their relative preference for bonds and bank deposits will increase as they near retirement; and year after year, as a larger share of the population become retirees, this effect should increase.

Because the global equity markets are still integrating, diversification across countries still pays off in accordance to modern portfolio theory. Diversification in equities across national markets allows you to earn high returns while lowering your risk due to the relative lack of correlations of prices across equity markets. While this benefit to equities will erode over time as the pricing of equities integrates, it will remain an important investment consideration for at least the next decade (and probably far longer). In contrast, since bond prices are now significantly aligned, geographic diversification in bond portfolios does little to mitigate against risk.

Moreover, corporations that compete globally provide better returns than companies that are competing in a single national market because they can seek out national markets where they are competitively advantaged and avoid those where they are disadvantaged. This not only increases returns, it also provides more diversification against the political and other risks in any one country, particularly their home country. While political risk is not a big issue in the United States, it is a significant factor for companies based in heavily indebted nations and in emerging markets. Many corporations have overwhelming exposure to the political and other risks in their home country, and by becoming global, they can mitigate these risks through diversification. We expect a dramatic increase in the number of companies that compete globally. As this happens, risk-adjusted returns to equities should improve overall.

Finally, equities are attractive because of the high impact of active management. In a rapidly changing, turbulent, open global system, management can respond to changing conditions. In contrast, once a bond is issued, the only thing that can adjust to a change in circumstances is the price. Thus, equities have "self-hedging" characteristics that bonds do not have.

Of course, you don't necessarily have to invest in equities as a class. While investing in equities as a class through different country index funds can be a successful strategy, you may want to look for specific stocks instead. Because the equity markets are not yet integrated and perfect, there are opportunities to seek out individual stocks particularly in countries where information is less readily available than in the United States or the United Kingdom. Even in relatively perfect markets like the United States, investors such as Warren Buffet have long demonstrated that you can successfully pick stocks.

Moreover, throughout the world including the United States and the United Kingdom, there are many companies with attractive franchises who are not exploiting their global opportunities either because they are not aware of them, because of the fear of expanding due to the lack of historic performance pressure from stockholders, or because of the lack of willingness to consider opportunities outside the country.

With a little work, it should be possible to identify such companies with advantages in production techniques that can be exploited globally. This is particularly true in nascent emerging global industries such as retailing, fast food, health services, automobile repair, and formerly local industries such as building materials, retail banking, or utilities. Even in industries where a number of global companies are operating (e.g., consumer packaged goods, with giants such as Unilever and Nestlé) or energy companies (with giants such as Shell and Exxon), there are still abundant opportunities.

In this environment, U.S. equities should probably be the backbone of a portfolio. While this is certainly true of dollar-based investors, it is also true of non-dollar-based investors. Since the United States generally has experienced the most competitive markets, it has a proportionately larger percentage of companies with world-class productivity advantages to be exploited and it has the largest, deepest equity market with the best protection for the investor. For a dollar-based investor, investment in U.S. companies that are expanding globally combines the opportunity to capture global productivity advantages without having to take foreign exchange risk directly. Rather, the investor can let the company with the resources to do so manage the risks of global expansion (including foreign exchange risk) directly. Investing in non-U.S. equities, by a dollar-based investor, requires either the investor to manage foreign exchange risk, personally, or to take those risks.

On the other hand, most investors should be very wary of investing in the equities of companies in emerging nations directly. These markets are still very much insider markets, and unless you are an insider, you are at a major disadvantage. Remember also, that many of the local companies have inferior techniques of production and are unlikely to be competitive unless they can acquire outside techniques of production. Most investors will find it more rewarding to invest in developed world companies that have proven technologies and are making significant foreign direct investment in developing countries than to acquire stakes personally in these countries. Moreover, unless you have professional management, investing in emerging market equities, even through a mutual fund, can be very risky since these markets are very thin and are subject to spectacular booms and busts.

Despite all the potentially attractive characteristics, equities, even U.S. equities, are not without risk. When we first wrote the manuscript for this book, the Dow Jones Index was under 4000. Now, as we are making our last edits at the end of 1995, the Dow is well over 5000. Part of this growth could be the market's increasing recognition of the powerful forces described in this book. Or it could be that the market is becoming overvalued temporarily. Only time will tell. We are taking a long-term perspective: We believe over the next decade or two, equities will be unusually attractive relative to their risks. We fully realize that, even before this book is published (or at any other time), we could have a major market correction (such as 20 percent or more) in the world's equity markets. And, in the worst-case scenario, as described in Chapter 6, there is the potential to experience stock market crashes as severe as the crashes of the 1920s and 1930s.

Nevertheless, in the world we see emerging over the next 20 years, we believe equities are relatively attractive.

SHUN BONDS

Our base case points to an extraordinarily turbulent, global bond market.

Price volatility in bond markets will be high because national governments, in at least some countries, will likely experience severe market crises as a result of sustained fiscal imbalances. Particularly in democracies, entitlements such as state-funded pensions and health care are particularly hard to cut as populations age. Over the next 35 years, there will be a 30 percent increase in the percentage of the voting age population in the United States and Germany that will be retired. Retired people in both countries will grow to be 25 percent of the voting age population. In Italy, the share of retirees of the voting age population will increase over 60 percent reaching 34 percent.

Similarly, cutting unemployment and welfare benefits will also be very difficult. Entrenched labor will make these hard to cut. The inevitable conflict between the power of the market to control pricing and the power of the nation state to issue debt will be resolved in the global bond markets. Cutting the state-funded subsidies of businesses will be resisted strongly by the corporations benefiting from them.

As the global bond market becomes progressively larger, more integrated, and simultaneously, as more and more long-term fixed rate paper is issued by governments, the probabilities of the global market experiencing a series of major bond crises becomes more and more likely.

This price volatility will be compounded by the high probability of future, unexpected shocks. We should expect significant social, labor, and political turbulence as nations grapple with cutting entitlements and liberalizing product and markets restrictions. Sudden collapses of governments, national strikes, and civil unrest will be likely. These are likely to be particularly severe in the most indebted countries with the most generous entitlement benefits. This turmoil is likely to explode into the market suddenly. And as the market gains size and integrates, such unexpected shocks are likely to lead to extreme price volatility in the pricing of bonds.

By the year 2000, when the stock of global financial assets is some $80 trillion, any external, negative shock will instantaneously lead to worldwide simultaneous decisions to sell as soon as the new information becomes available. When new, negative information causes even a small fraction of an $80 trillion, integrated global market suddenly to change its mind about the relative attractiveness of any particular security, that security will become illiquid immediately until the price adjusts and the new information is fully processed. And, if the evidence of Mexico in 1995 is any guide, this price adjustment could be on the order of 30 percent or more practically overnight.

While such extreme volatility is true of individual equities as well, the equities of companies with globally diversified cash flows are far less exposed to specific country risk than are national bonds. Indeed, national government bonds are a pure play on the country, whether you want that play or not. And now that the bond markets are substantially integrated, as described in Chapter 5, much of the volatility that used to be absorbed by the foreign exchange markets has been transferred to the bond markets.

External shocks are bound to catch even the saviest market participants by surprise and anyone who is not active in the market has no hope of being able to react fast enough to avoid massive price adjustment.

Professional traders are skilled at taking aggregated risks, disaggregating those risks, and keeping only the risks where they have comparative advantage. They will leave the nonprofessionals with only the poorer risk-return relationships wherever they operate. If you want to participate in the markets they dominate, that is, the globally integrated foreign exchange markets, the bond markets, and the related derivatives markets, you had better hire one of them to act as your agent, through a mutual fund, hedge fund, or an investment market advisor rather than participate directly.

This advice is particularly germane where the risk premiums are large. If a country's government is paying a significant real risk premium over the rates paid by the United States, Germany, or Japan, you probably do not want to take the risk. Many private U.S. investors who were attracted by the high apparent returns on Canadian and Mexican country bonds in the fall of 1993 found themselves experiencing huge losses by early 1994.

In an integrated global bond market, there are typically very good reasons for huge risk premiums. These risk premiums are not woolly mammoths. Unless you have the skills, information, and tools to disaggregate these risk premiums, and take only those risks where you have a comparative advantage, you should stay away from them.

If you are truly risk averse, and can't stomach the equity markets and want only to earn the global risk-free rate of return, stick to U.S. Treasury instruments—particularly the short-term instruments, which have relatively little interest rate risk. We like U.S. Treasury bonds, particularly for dollar-based investors who want to avoid currency risk. The United States, as described in Chapter 6, has the youngest population in the developed world and the least generous entitlement programs, and has begun to demonstrate the will to get its budget in balance. Moreover, the United States is a major beneficiary of most of the economic trends described in this book, because its private sector is the most globally competitive in the world. It should therefore grow more rapidly than the economies of most other developed countries, which would make its debt burden less onerous.

And, remember, in a globally integrated bond market, you increasingly get the real risk-free return in whichever country's bonds you invest. (Everything else is either inflation premium or a risk premium.) Therefore, if you gravitate to bonds because you do not want to take risk, and you are a dollar-based investor, stick to U.S. Treasury bonds.

WHAT ABOUT CASH?

With all of this turbulence, shouldn't you just leave all of your funds in the bank?

The answer to that question is no.

The real returns earned on bank deposits have been break-even, if not negative, after adjusting for inflation, for the past 50 years. While losses on bank deposits are gradual, the slow erosion of the relative spending power of your money in the bank is real nonetheless. The risk-free rate of return, estimated as the U.S. Treasury bond rate less the holding period premium is already low (under 2 percent), and could go still lower with the surge of savings coming our way. Bank deposits are likely to earn even less than this risk-free rate of return due to the costs of bank intermediation. In particular, interest rates on consumer bank deposits are likely to be relatively low in major countries without serious debt problems (yet) such as Germany, Japan, and the United States because of low demand for loans in these countries. Because of an aging population, there are proportionately fewer people in the age groups in these countries who borrow. This is already true and will become more true as the population continues to age. In other words, banks will be awash in bank deposits because of demographic effects and will be short of loans. This will leave banks with little incentive to pay much interest to attract depositors. Money market mutual funds will continue to offer slightly higher interest rates than banks, partially by taking some interest rate risks, but net of fund management expenses, these money market funds are unlikely to earn more than the global risk-free rate of return (2 percent or less).

It is hard to finance a comfortable retirement when you are earning less than 2 percent compounded on your savings unless you save an awful lot of money.

Should you, therefore, as a global capitalist, keep *all* of your savings invested in equities?

Again, the answer is no. We have painted a picture of a market filled with turmoil. Extreme price volatility is likely in the bond market and major market corrections, even market crashes, are possible in the stock markets.

In such a market, liquidity is critical. You don't want to have to sell assets when prices are artificially depressed by overcorrections in the market. Rather, you want to have cash to buy assets at depressed levels. Moreover, you need some liquidity to protect yourself from the worst-case scenario outlined in Chapter 6. If the world's economy falls apart, you want some money to fall back on.

How much liquidity you need depends on your personal circumstances. If you have well diversified, secure cash flows, or if you have the skills and time to start over, you need less liquidity than someone who has already retired. You also have to understand your own tolerance for risk. For some investors, keeping 10 percent of their assets in cash instruments, may be all the liquidity they need. For others, it may be 50 percent. No one but you can make this judgment.

ACTIVE MANAGEMENT

While we believe equities will be more rewarding than investing in bonds or bank deposits over the mid-to-long term (10 to 20 years) this is only a directional strategy. Because real social, political, and labor turmoil will likely manifest itself as financial turmoil, some equity markets in some countries and some companies could also experience extreme volatility such as losses of 20 percent or more in a week or two. Unless you are an unusual person, this probably bothers you. While it is true that in the long-term equities will outperform bonds, as Keynes said, in the long term it is also true we are all dead.

Most readers will therefore find it more comfortable and rewarding to manage their portfolios actively by adjusting their portfolios continuously along the risk-return spectrum. This does not mean active trading to capitalize on short-term price movements. Rather, it means continually adjusting your mix of investment assets as conditions change (e.g., the proportion of cash, the mix between U.S. and non-U.S. equities). For some readers, their confidence to raise the percentage of their portfolios invested in equities will increase when they have already made large gains, and are "playing with their winnings." Others will feel more confident right after a sell-off; these include "contrarians" who believe the market always overshoots and the time to buy is on weakness. Others will feel more confident when the price-value relationships are approaching new lows, otherwise known as "bottom fishing." Others will have a bias to "buy and hold" to avoid "churning" their portfolio and lowering returns due to large transaction costs. Whichever of these or other investing strategies fit your personality and skill, you will get better performance if you actively manage your portfolio. This will mean that as you gain confidence in your understanding of the market, and this understanding is borne out by market price movements, you will become more aggressive in your portfolio mix. On the other hand, if the market keeps surprising you, a more defensive posture will be appropriate. In some ways it is like playing poker. If you continue to lose money, it's probably not just bad luck. It's probably that you are playing against better poker players and that your judgment is not as good as theirs. If so, you had better rely on a professional manager.

However, even if your only decisions are which professionals to trust and which categories of assets to invest in, you still need to determine continually whom to work with and what portfolio mix you want. To pick individual securities yourself, will require more time.

At the heart of active management is gathering information, getting feedback from the market, and thinking. Make sure you understand the risks you are taking. Experiment with small amounts of money, not the bulk of your savings. With this in the background, we will describe some of the actions you should take to be a global capitalist.

Keep on Top of the Market

Active management starts with awareness of what is going on in the market. By this, we do not mean you need to watch computer screens all day. It doesn't mean trading your portfolio continually since transaction costs can quickly erode your returns. Rather, it means you need to follow, on a regular basis, the market prices of your key investments as well as other key prices so that you are prepared to move. If your investments are not doing as expected, try to find out why. A wealth of information is available simply by reading.

Probably the most important information to track is the relative value of the equities as a class (not just those equities you own). You need to be able to continually make judgments of whether equities, as an investment category, are fundamentally under-valued or overvalued. Track, in particular, the stock prices of indexes against the earnings and the cash flows of the underlying indexed companies. Track also the dividend yields on stocks versus the yields on bonds.

However, some of the key prices you need to know are not just the relative prices of equities. Using statistics regularly available in the back pages of the *Economist,* you can calculate the real (inflation-adjusted returns) on government bonds in each nation (simply take the 12-month rate of consumer price increase and subtract it from the economic indicators page from the government bond rates). If the real rates of a country go suddenly up or down, either the market is changing its risk assessment or central banks are intervening. Either way you should be alerted. Similarly, watch the yield curves. Are they steepening or flattening? How closely are the real yield curves aligned?

If they are steepening, without upward movements in short-term rates, the market is demanding more premium to take holding period risk. If they are steepening because of downward movements in short-term rates, it is probably because central banks are deliberately trying, through coordinated action, to lower rates.

The purpose of gathering and thinking about such information is, for example, to decide when to make mix adjustments in your portfolio. If you are heavily invested in equities with significant exposure to a particular country, you may want to watch the bond markets in that country, not so you can invest in that country's bonds but to get warning signs that trouble is coming. If government bond yields shoot up and pass corporate bond yields, it is probably a sign that some professionals in the market have become worried about the risks in that country. Or, if dividend yields are falling, while bond yields are rising, watch out because a "bubble" may be forming. You may want to consider getting out of any equity investments you may have with significant exposure to that country.

Watch What Governments Do, Not Say

As described throughout this book, while national governments are losing power, their actions over the next few years will be critical to whether we have global prosperity or devastation. Watch what national governments do, not what they say. Are they cutting entitlements and controlling their deficit spending or not? Are they liberalizing product-market restrictions or not? The more governments move in the direction of cutting deficits and liberalizing restrictions, the more likely will be the case for prosperity and the more attractive it will be to invest in those countries.

Plan on Volatility in Equity Markets

If you follow our advice and invest disproportionately in equities, you need to be prepared for stock market panics, manias, and crashes. Watch out for "bubbles." Given our expectations of the savings surge, there is the real potential for stock market euphoria that leads to a mania, if not an outright bubble in some of the individual national stock markets. These are particularly likely in the smaller, thinner stock markets (in both the developed world and in the developing world). We hope we won't see a bubble develop in major equity markets but even a market such as the United States is susceptible to becoming overvalued. If you believe any stock market is becoming overvalued, take a more defensive approach such as increasing your mix of assets in cash equivalents.

Even if we do not have major market crashes, you should expect high volatility. Equity values are notoriously volatile, which is why diversification of risk in equities is so important. Because the equity markets are not yet fully integrated, diversification really does reduce risk. This has usually meant owning stocks in multiple national equity markets. Going forward, we believe that in addition, you will want to diversify across industries. As national bond markets become more integrated, they will naturally increase the cross-national integration of equity markets since the bond markets in each country are linked to their respective equity markets. In some markets, such as the United States, these linkages between the bond and equity markets are already quite close. In the future, you may want to get diversification by spreading your equities among industries or individual companies for which stock price movements show little global correlation, such as pharmaceuticals, construction materials, and oil and gas producers.

Another advantage of diversification is that it reduces the need to spend all your time following our first principle: "Keep on top of the market." The more you store all your eggs in one basket, the more time you have to spend making sure the basket is safe. If you are a dollar-based investor and want to invest in equities, but have low confidence in your personal abilities or lack the time to manage your portfolio actively, you probably should just invest in a U.S. index fund.

Have a Contingency Plan for the Worst Case

While we think it is unlikely, the worst-case scenario laid out in Chapter 6 is possible. If it starts to unfold, you need to be prepared by having thought through in advance the safest haven you can find. One of the points of watching both market prices and government action is to be able to make your own assessment of the likelihood of a major global economic dislocation. Although you cannot totally avoid being hurt by a devastating market and economic dislocation, you can protect yourself by deciding in advance what your trigger points will be for taking defensive action. Establish some "stop losses" for yourself that will trigger defensive action, such as shifting your investments out of equities and into short-term U.S. Treasuries.

A global economic disaster would be devastating to everyone. But it is all relative. If much of the world's wealth is destroyed, having preserved some of yours will give you an advantage as the economy is rebuilt. In the valley of the blind, the one-eyed man is king.

—12—

Stop Worrying and Learn to Love the Market

In the mid-1960s, shortly after the Cuban missile crisis, Stanley Kubrick directed a disturbingly funny satire on the Cold War called "Dr. Strangelove or How I Stopped Worrying and Learned to Love the Bomb." The movie, starring Peter Sellers and George C. Scott, was about how the combination of an insane Air Force colonel, accidents, blunders, miscommunication, and bureaucratic policies led the United States to drop a nuclear bomb on a Siberian city, unintentionally, despite all of the "fail-safe" procedures in place. This, in turn, triggered a Soviet "Doomsday" bomb that ended the world.

At the time, given the reality of living under the perpetual threat of a nuclear holocaust, most of us had no alternative to having absolute faith in the U.S. government and the reliability of its safeguards. But the movie was sufficiently plausible, given the nature of the human condition and our commonsense understanding that things often go astray at the worst possible time, to force the viewer to confront that unquestioning faith. The title of the movie was incongruous. The movie gave no sane person any reason to stop worrying and love the bomb.

Fortunately for all of us, history has shown so far that faith in the "fail-safe" procedures of the United States is not misplaced. Given the existence of nuclear weapons, there is no alternative to "fail-safe" design solutions to protect society from their destructive potential. We do not want terrorists to have nuclear options.

In contrast, economists, social scientists, and politicians have long debated whether open or closed economic systems are best. With Marxists at one extreme and "laissez-faire" capitalists at the

250

other extreme, there has been endless, passionate debate on the virtues of central government versus market decision making for over 200 years.

Wherever along the spectrum between Marxism and "laissez-faire" capitalism the debate is centered at any given moment, it seems that there is always one camp that tends to trust government economic decision making and to distrust market decision making, while the other camp tends to trust market decision making and to distrust government economic decision making.

Friedrich Von Hayek, a contemporary of Keynes, was a pivotal figure in helping to crystallize the debate. Throughout the 1930s and 1940s, Hayek analyzed the problems of rational economic planning under socialism and compellingly argued that the rationality of such a system could not hold given the problems of knowledge. It would be impossible for a single central authority to acquire all of the dispersed knowledge that it would require to make the best economic decisions.

However, it is hard to deny that during the Bretton Woods era from the late 1940s to the early 1970s, social democracy and centrally planned market economies worked pretty well in Europe and Japan. On the other hand, the U.S. economy also did very well with little central planning and with far less generous social programs. As we described in Chapter 2, it was a prosperous era for the developed world, although the developing world tended to take one step backward for every two steps forward.

In Europe and in Japan, the nations were small enough and the populations and business interests were sufficiently homogeneous that the knowledge problems described by Hayek were manageable. Moreover, the national economies were sufficiently under the control of national governments through financial regulations and product, market, and labor regulations that market forces could be used, in combination with monetary and fiscal policy, to manage the economy.

But, as we've described throughout this book, the financial markets have been unbound. The increasing power of the global capital market and the increasing mobility of capital are accelerating the globalization of the real economy. We are well along our way to transitioning from local, closed national economies to an open, global economy. The more open and global the economy becomes, the greater are the information difficulties of central planning described by Hayek and the less control a national central planner has over the national economy through financial market regulation and product/market regulation.

In fact, it is increasingly less meaningful to talk about managing national economies. We are headed toward a world, like it or not, where no one is at the controls.

We must realize that the debate of the last 200 years is over. Decision making is going to continue to migrate away from central authorities and toward markets. The fall of Communism was only the start, not the end, of the increasing role of markets and global capitalism. The market pressure will be relentless and will work to curtail unsustainable policies and regulations designed to restrict open, fair competition. And, increasingly these market pressures will be brought to bear on entitlement spending and central planning structures.

The time has come to stop worrying and learn to love the market. The time has come to shift the public debate away from whether to entrust economic decisions with governments or with markets. Decision power is going to move toward the markets whether anyone wants it to or not. There is no path back to the conditions of Bretton Woods.

Therefore, the real debate needs to move toward how to get markets to work better, how to use the economic power of the government to achieve legitimate government objectives, such as better education, better health care, social cohesion, and public safety through market incentives, how to get through the transition to a fully global economy without experiencing destructive financial or social turmoil.

Again, we have not been arguing that national governments are powerless. Indeed, they will remain the most powerful agents on the planet through their power to borrow, to tax, to regulate, to print money, to exercise military options, and so forth.

We are arguing that their power to control, or even to manage, their national economies is diminishing. The would be central planner increasingly has the problem similar to a nation with a stockpile of nuclear weapons. Such a planner has vast potential power, but in an open, global system, has declining ability to use that power to achieve policy objectives. And, careless use of that power, as we described in the last pages of Chapter 6, has the potential to trigger the economic equivalent of a nuclear war. We truly believe, however, that governments, once they adopt a different mindset, will be better able to achieve their objectives by the more productive use of the financial resources at their disposal. This will require that they use financial resources not to create unsustainable entitlement policies but rather to make sustainable investments in infrastructure, or put private agents in competition with one another to provide better services (including education, health care, and pensions) at lower prices.

The specifics of what to do are beyond the boundaries of this book. Our objectives have been to help the reader make a mind shift transition away from thinking about the world as a series of closed, national systems under the control of governments. We hope the reader begins to think about the world as one open, global system under no one's control but with a global capital market as its center which will have increasing power to motivate businesses to become more productive and to motivate governments to dismantle restrictive regulation, cut unsustainable deficits, and pursue sound fiscal and monetary policy.

Instead of worrying about the market, and trying to restrain its evolution, we must start taking responsibility for shaping the outcomes associated with the relentless maturing of the global capital market and the resulting acceleration of the global economy. Taking responsibility will be increasingly critical at all levels—the national, corporate and the individual.

Earlier we described how true national leaders, those who are willing to take responsibility and forge new directions, tend to emerge only in times of crisis. Today, there is an opportunity for leadership to come forth before a crisis occurs. Indeed, there is an opportunity for national leadership to act in order to avoid many crises altogether. Our challenge is to encourage these leaders and support them, especially when they point in the better, if difficult, direction.

And the need for leadership and responsibility is not limited to the national arena. It is just as necessary at the corporate level, whether the corporation is local and small or global and enormous. The overwhelming strategic challenges and the unprecedented opportunities facing corporations make true corporate leadership throughout organizations more and more imperative, even as they make it more and more difficult.

Finally, these developments place the greatest responsibility on the individual decision maker. Individuals will have the responsibility of backing effective leaders, and the responsibility of addressing and alleviating the social outcomes which are largely inevitable. It is telling that the developed world's most advanced market economy, the United States, is also the economy where private individuals contribute the most as a share of GDP and in number of volunteer hours to charities that build communities and provide social safety nets. In a world of deteriorating safety nets, where the array of choices is multiplying, foresight and planning, decision and direction, compassion and commitment gain importance rapidly. Going forward, the responsibility and leadership for economic decisions will increasingly be exercised by millions, indeed billions, of individuals around the world.

About the Authors

Lowell Bryan is a director (senior partner) of McKinsey & Company and leads the firm's North American Financial Institutions practice out of its New York office. Mr. Bryan has worked almost exclusively with financial institutions since he joined McKinsey in 1975. In addition to leading the practice, Mr. Bryan consults with the top management of several major financial institution clients on a wide range of issues including business strategy, corporate strategy, revenue improvement, cost redesign, and organization design.

In addition to this book, Mr. Bryan is the author of *Breaking Up the Bank: Rethinking an Industry Under Siege* (1988), which described the breakdown of the U.S. credit system and the importance of securitization of credit to the banking system. He is also the author of *Bankrupt: Restoring the Health and Profitability of Our Banking System* (1991), which proposed a new blueprint for reforming the regulation of banks.

Mr. Bryan earned a BA from Davidson College in 1968 and an MBA from the Harvard Business School in 1970. Prior to joining McKinsey & Company, he worked for the State Street Bank of Boston.

He lives with his wife Deborah, a real estate professional, and has three children, Russell, Amanda, and Nathaniel. He likes to play basketball and tennis. They share their home in New Canaan, Connecticut, with four Labrador retrievers, one Cocker Spaniel, and five very independent cats.

Diana Farrell is a senior engagement manager at McKinsey & Company and a member of the firm's Financial Institutions Group. She has worked in the New York office as well as at the McKinsey Global Institute, and is currently a consultant in the Washington, DC, office. She serves leading financial institutions on a broad range of issues.

During her stay at the McKinsey Global Institute (1993–1994), Ms. Farrell led the research which is the foundation for much of this book. She has presented and discussed the findings and conclusions of the research with a wide array of leading financial institutions, think tanks, journalists, and other private and public organizations.

Ms. Farrell earned a BA in economics and in the College of Social Studies from Wesleyan University in 1987, as well as an MBA from the Harvard Business School in 1991. She previously worked at Goldman, Sachs & Company in New York.

She currently lives in Washington, DC, with her husband, Scott Pearson. She enjoys hiking, reading, and running.

Index